Panzer Killers

Panzer Killers

Anti-tank Warfare on the Eastern Front

By
Artem Drabkin

Translated by
Stuart Britton

Pen & Sword
MILITARY

First published in Great Britain in 2013 by
Pen & Sword Military
an imprint of
Pen & Sword Books Ltd
47 Church Street
Barnsley
South Yorkshire
S70 2AS

ISBN 978-1-78159-050-8

A CIP catalogue record for this book is available from the British Library.

Typeset in 11/13 Ehrhardt by Concept, Huddersfield, West Yorkshire
Printed by MPG Printgroup, UK

Pen & Sword Books Ltd incorporates the Imprints of Pen & Sword Aviation, Pen & Sword Family History, Pen & Sword Maritime, Pen & Sword Military, Pen & Sword Discovery, Wharncliffe Local History, Wharncliffe True Crime, Wharncliffe Transport, Pen & Sword Select, Pen & Sword Military Classics, Leo Cooper, The Praetorian Press, Remember When, Seaforth Publishing and Frontline Publishing.

For a complete list of Pen & Sword titles please contact
PEN & SWORD BOOKS LIMITED
47 Church Street, Barnsley, South Yorkshire, S70 2AS, England
E-mail: enquiries@pen-and-sword.co.uk
Website: www.pen-and-sword.co.uk

Contents

Translator's Note

The material in this book results from face-to-face interviews conducted between 2001 and 2006 with surviving Red Army veterans who served in the anti-tank artillery. The interviews with Moses Dorman and Mikhail Chernomordik were recorded by Grigory Koifman, who lives in Israel. As expected, the anti-tank artillerymen's roles and paths varied. Some served strictly in the anti-tank artillery, while others began their service in the infantry, or wound up as a self-propelled gun crew member. There are a few notable contributions to this book. Mikhail Borisov became a living legend in the Soviet Union for his actions in front of Prokhorovka on 11 July 1943, where he continued to man and fire a gun alone while helping to repel the attempt by the 1st SS Panzer Regiment to seize Prokhorovka the day before the 5th Guards Tank Army's dramatic counterattack on 12 July. Borisov's actions were witnessed by the commander of the Soviet 2nd Tank Corps, Lieutenant General A.F. Popov. Eager for a heroic role model [particularly one who was a Komsomol member and Russian] to help rebuild the morale after the 2nd Tank Corps' battering in the Battle of Kursk, Popov helped secure the title Hero of the Soviet Union for Borisov, then wined and dined him and used him to give pep talks to survivors and new recruits. Two of the contributors, Aleksandr Rogachev and Nikolai Shishkin, are rare representatives of the very few that served from 1941 (or in the latter case, from the Winter War with Finland) right up until the end of the war. The actions span the entire sweep of warfare on the Eastern Front, from Finland's Hanko Peninsula to Stalingrad, and from the gates of Moscow in 1941 to Germany and Czechoslovakia in the war's final days.

The interview process was similar. Each veteran was asked to provide a basic narrative of his service and experiences. At times, the questioner would ask questions to help flesh out the story or to solicit additional information. At the end of the narrative, the questioner would ask follow-up questions, again seeking the veteran's thoughts on a variety of topics related to morale, superstitions, equipment, the treatment of captured German soldiers and German civilians, etc. For this English translation, an editorial decision was made to remove the questions and to note new topics of conversation prompted by the question by a line break from the preceding material. This explains some of the choppiness in the text, particularly toward the end of each chapter.

Naturally, over the passage of time since the war ended, the veterans' memories began to fade. Some stories remained firmly planted in their recollections, but other details might be lost. The personalities of the veterans also contributed to a diversity in the responses – some were simply more taciturn than others, so while their contributions are no less valuable in helping build this mosaic portrait of the Red Army anti-tank artilleryman in the Second World War, they are correspondingly briefer.

When a veteran mentions something that I think may be unknown to the typical Western reader, as the translator I have added brief bracketed comments to the text, or for longer explanations, used end notes to clarify what the veteran is saying.

I want to thank Rupert Harding, chief editor of Pen & Sword, for commissioning this translation and for helping edit the Russian interview material. I also want to thank Pamela Covey for her usual superb proofreading effort that caught any errors missed by a tired translator's eye. Of course, any remaining mistakes in translation are mine.

Chapter 1

The Burning Snow of the 'Pakfront'

Aleksei Isaev

Anti-tank artillery appeared soon after tanks arrived on the modern battlefield. At first these were field artillery pieces, allocated for firing at tanks. Grapeshot, through its shock effect, served as the first armour-piercing shell. The time for specially-developed anti-tank guns came after the First World War. The fledgling Workers' and Peasants' Red Army didn't remain on the sidelines during this process. The 'System of Artillery and Infantry Arming of the Red Army' was adopted as a protocol at a session of the Revolutionary Military Council of the USSR Soviet on 22 May 1929. According to this document, each artillery battalion would be equipped with 37-mm infantry anti-tank cannon 'for the struggle with enemy armoured vehicles'. Since no suitable gun for this purpose was then in domestic production, it was purchased abroad from the Rheinmetall AG firm. The gun was put into service under the designation '37-mm anti-tank gun model 1930 [M1930]'. The evolution of this weapon in the 1930s led to the appearance of the 45-mm anti-tank gun with the factory designation 53-K, which became known as the '45-mm anti-tank gun M1937'. Thus appeared the gun that became so well known to many as the '*sorokopiatka*' [literally, the 'forty-five-er']. Production of this gun was assigned to Kalinin Factory No. 8 in the Moscow suburb of Podlipky.

One characteristic of the anti-tank gun is the necessity of a high rate of fire. Small-calibre anti-tank guns were effective only out to a range of several hundred metres, so the anti-tank gunners had very little time to knock-out the tanks before they reached their own positions. Therefore the 45-mm anti-tank gun had a semi-automatic, sliding block breech mechanism. After firing a shot, the gun would roll backwards, and the recoil mechanism would return it to its former position. At the end of the counter-recoil cycle, the automatic mechanism would open the breech and eject the empty shell casing. The breech would remain open and the loader could, without wasting time to open it, reload the gun. The quick-firing round forced home by the loader would knock the breech from the toes of the shell-casing ejector, it would close, and the gunner could then send another shell toward the target. Extendable split trails were vital for the anti-tank gun. Such a design in place of the block trail gun mount permitted wide angles of traverse for shifting fire toward various targets. Since tanks could use folds in the ground in order to bypass the anti-tank gunners' positions or break through in the sector of a neighbouring unit, the guns had to be ready to change the direction of fire. Light, small-calibre guns didn't present any difficulties in laying the gun on a new target. For heavy anti-tank guns (57-mm, 76-mm and greater), a gun-crew member stood by each trail, ready to turn the gun.

The *sorokopiatki* were highly respected by the Japanese that encountered them at Khalkin-Gol – the only conflict in which the Red Army participated prior to the start of the Great Patriotic War involving the use of large numbers of tanks on both sides. Japanese prisoners testified to the 45-mm anti-tank gun's great accuracy and effectiveness.

The *sorokopiatka* was simple and inexpensive (approximately 10,000 rubles for each gun) to produce. This led to the rapid equipping of units and formations of the Red Army with 45-mm guns. By 1941 the troops were fully equipped with 45-mm guns according to the requirements of the MP-41 mobilization plan, and production of them even temporarily ceased. The resumption of production was contemplated only with the start of the war in order to replace the losses in the quantities foreseen by MP-41. It should be noted that anti-tank guns were not the only means of combating tanks. Armour-piercing shells were part of the standard ammunition loads of the divisional 76-mm guns, anti-aircraft guns, and the regimental artillery.

The organization of the Red Army's anti-artillery units before the war was not marked by diversity. Prior to the autumn of 1940, anti-tank guns were on the tables of organization and equipment of rifle, mountain rifle, motorized rifle, motorized, and cavalry battalions, regiments and divisions. Anti-tank batteries, platoons and battalions were in this manner imbedded in the organizational structure of units and formations and became inseparably part of them. The rifle battalion of a rifle regiment of the pre-war table of organization No. 04/41 had a platoon (two guns) of 45-mm anti-tank artillery. The rifle regiment of the No. 04/41 table of organization and the motorized rifle regiment of the No. 05/86 table had a battery of 45-mm anti-tank guns (6 guns). The former used horses to tow the guns, whereas the motorized rifle regiment had specialized tracked, armoured Komsomolets prime movers. The rifle division of the No. 04/400 table of organization and the motorized division of the No. 05/70 table each had a separate anti-tank battalion of eighteen 45-mm guns. Interestingly, the anti-tank unit subordinate to the division had a mechanized tow for both the rifle division and the motorized division. Again, the Komsomolets prime mover was the workhorse to tow the guns. The motorized anti-tank unit was to give the division commander the possibility to deploy anti-tank weapons quickly to a threatened axis. The anti-tank battalion was added to the Soviet rifle division's TO&E (table of organization and equipment) for the first time in 1938.

However, at that time the manoeuvring of anti-tank guns was possible only within the division, and not on the scale of the corps or the army. The command thus had very limited possibilities to strengthen the anti-tank defences on directions vulnerable to tanks. A division defending a sector in terrain inaccessible to tanks had just as many anti-tank guns as a division occupying a sector where an enemy tank attack was likely. In both cases, the division commander had only fifty-four authorized 45-mm guns. In inaccessible terrain, this number was excessive, but in a threated sector, it was inadequate. The strengthening of the anti-tank defence could be achieved at the expense of artillery that was not formally anti-tank artillery – anti-aircraft and corps guns. Another characteristic of the Red Army's pre-war anti-tank artillery was the absence of anti-tank guns in the tank division.

The first attempt to place the means for a qualitative strengthening of anti-tank defence in the hands of the command followed in 1940. Studying the experience of Germany's combat use of its panzer forces in 1939 and 1940, Soviet military theoreticians came to the conclusion that it was necessary to strengthen anti-tank defences both qualitatively and quantitatively. The decision was made to create the 'cannon artillery regiment' of the Reserve of the Supreme Command as a test organizational form, armed with the 76-mm F-22 divisional guns and 85-mm anti-aircraft guns. On 14 October 1940, the USSR People's Commissariat of Defence proposed new organizational measures to the USSR Council of People's Commissars and the Party Central Committee, to be implemented within the Red Army in the first half of 1941. Among other items, it proposed:

> The formation of 20 machine-gun artillery motorized brigades, powerfully armed with cannons and machine guns, intended for countering and fighting the enemy's tank and mechanized forces. The brigades will be allocated as follows:
>
> (a) Leningrad Military District – 5 brigades;
> (b) Baltic Special Military District – 4 brigades;
> (c) Western Special Military District – 3 brigades;
> (d) Kiev Special Military District – 5 brigades;
> (e) Trans-Baikal Special Military District – 1 brigade;
> (f) Far Eastern Front – 2 brigades ...

The proposal regarding the formation of these brigades was received on 4 November 1940. It was planned to complete their formation by 1 January 1941. The 'machine-gun artillery' designation was dropped as the units were being organized and the brigades became motorized brigades. Altogether, each brigade was to have 6,199 men, 17 T-26 tanks, 19 armoured cars, 30 45-mm anti-tank guns, 42 76-mm F-22 guns, 12 37-mm automatic anti-aircraft guns, and 36 76-mm or 85-mm anti-aircraft guns. The idea of inserting the seventeen T-26s in the brigade's TO&E was in a certain sense ahead of its time: the growing role of tanks as a means of combatting other tanks took its place by the end of the Second World War.

However, the initial experiment of creating anti-tank formations of the Reserve of the Supreme Command [RGK] was acknowledged to be unsuccessful. In February–March 1941, the twenty brigades were disbanded. The final measure before the war to form anti-tank brigades was the joint Party Central Committee and Council of People's Commissar's Decree No. 1112-459ss of 23 April 1941, 'On New Formations within the Red Army'. According to this decree, by1June 1941 it was proposed to form ten anti-tank artillery brigades of the RGK. By its TO&E, each brigade was to have forty-eight 76-mm guns, forty-eight 85-mm anti-aircraft guns, twenty-four 107-mm guns, and sixteen 37-mm anti-aircraft guns. The authorized strength of the brigade was 5,322 officers and troops. The formation of these brigades was not completed by the start of the war. The majority of them did not have the authorized number of vehicles, artillery tractors and other equipment. Most of the brigades never received the 107-mm divisional gun M-60 and replaced them with 85-mm anti-aircraft guns. In May 1941, the mechanized corps lacking their authorized tank component acquired the de facto status of the anti-tank formation. Instead of tanks they received 76-mm divisional guns and were supposed to become the mobile means of combating enemy armour.

With the start of the Great Patriotic War, the anti-tank potential of the Soviet forces was tested through rigorous trials. In the first place, most often the rifle divisions had to defend wide sectors that exceeded established military doctrine. Secondly, the Soviet forces had to contend with the German tactic of the 'panzer wedge'. The panzer regiment of a Wehrmacht panzer division would attack a very narrow sector of the defence, overwhelming it with a density of up to fifty to sixty tanks per kilometre of front. The task of overwhelming the Soviet anti-tank defences was made significantly easier because of the evenly-spaced deployment of anti-tank guns across the rifle division's entire sector of defence. Technical problems also played a role: a number of lots of 45-mm armour-piercing shells were overheated during production. The flaws in the heat-treating process produced shells that could not penetrate German tank armour even at those ranges where the shells were supposed to be capable of doing so. Salvation in these crisis conditions lay in the 76-mm divisional and regimental guns. The short-barrelled 76-mm M1927 regimental guns were closest of all in weight and dimensions to the 45-mm anti-tank guns. At the same time, their armour-piercing and even their shrapnel rounds were sufficiently effective against the German tanks in 1941.

The organizational problems and the general, dissatisfactory course of combat operations prevented the first anti-tank brigades from realizing their potential. However, already in the first battles the brigades demonstrated their sweeping possibilities as an independent anti-tank formation. As early as the end of June, the decision was taken to form separate anti-tank artillery regiments within the RGK. These regiments were equipped with twenty 85-mm anti-aircraft guns. In July and August 1941, thirty-five such regiments were organized. In the period August to October 1941, there followed a second wave of forming anti-tank regiments of the RGK. These regiments were equipped with eight 37-mm and eight 85-mm anti-aircraft guns. The 37-mm anti-aircraft gun M1939 even before the war had been created as both an anti-tank and anti-aircraft weapon and fired a proven armour-piercing shell. An important advantage of the anti-aircraft guns was their 360° gun mounts. In order to safeguard the crews that had been retrained for the anti-tank role, the anti-aircraft guns were equipped with a shield to protect them from small-arms fire and shell fragments.

The heavy losses of anti-tank guns in the first weeks of the war led to a reduction in the number of anti-tank guns in the rifle division. According to the TO&E No. 4/600 from 29 July 1941, the rifle division had only eighteen 45-mm anti-tank guns in place of the fifty-four they'd been given under the pre-war TO&E. According to the July table, the rifle battalion's platoon of 45-mm guns and the separate anti-tank battalion were both fully eliminated. The latter was re-established in the rifle division's TO&E in December 1941. The cavalry division of the 1941 table had only six 45-mm guns instead of the sixteen they'd been given under the pre-war table. The shortage of anti-tank guns was to a certain extent offset by anti-tank rifles, which had recently been approved as a replacement. A platoon of anti-tank rifles was introduced at the regimental level in the rifle division's TO&E No. 04/750 in December 1941. Altogether, the rifle division had an authorized number of eighty-nine anti-tank rifles.

The armoured, tracked Komsomolets artillery tractors were for the most part lost in the summer of 1941, and their production was ceased in favour of tanks. Horses and vehicles became the means for towing the 45-mm anti-tank guns. The situation regarding the movement of anti-tank artillery significantly improved with the arrival through Lend-Lease of vehicles with better off-road capabilities. The famous Willys jeeps not only served as command vehicles; they were also used to tow the 45-mm anti-tank gun.

The overall tendency at the end of 1941 in the area of organizing the artillery was to increase the number of independent anti-tank units. On 1 January 1942 the acting army and the Supreme Command reserve had one artillery brigade (on the Leningrad front), fifty-seven anti-tank artillery regiments and two separate anti-tank artillery battalions. In the autumn battles of 1941, five anti-tank artillery regiments were awarded the Guards title. Two of them earned it in the fighting at Volokolamsk, where they supported I.V. Panfilov's 316th Rifle Division. The anti-aircraft guns were gradually withdrawn from the anti-tank regiments and returned to the system of anti-aircraft defences. The ZIS-3 76-mm divisional gun began to play an ever greater role in the Soviet anti-tank artillery. The Germans called the 76-mm guns '*ratsch-boom*': a shell would strike the target (*ratsch!*) before the sound of the gun's firing (*boom!*).

The year 1942 marked the period of the growth in the number and strength of independent anti-tank units. On 3 April 1942, the State Defence Committee issued a decree on forming the anti-tank destroyer brigade. According to its table strength, the anti-tank brigade would have 1,795 officers and men, 12 45-mm guns, 16 76-mm guns, 4 37-mm anti-aircraft guns and 144 anti-tank rifles. Following a decree from 8 June 1942, the twelve anti-tank destroyer brigades that had been formed thus far were merged into anti-tank destroyer divisions, with three brigades in each. It was proposed to deploy the destroyer divisions in the following manner: the 1st to the Southwestern Front, the 2nd to the Briansk Front, the 3rd to the Western Front, and the 4th to the Kalinin Front. Soon the 1st Anti-tank Destroyer Artillery Division received its combat baptism, defending against the attacks of Operation Blau.

Even the anti-tank rifle elements were strengthened. In April 1942, four separate anti-tank rifle battalions were formed. Each consisted of three to four companies, with twenty-seven anti-tank rifles in each company. On the whole, 1942 became the heyday of the anti-tank rifle in the Red Army as a means to combat enemy armour. According to the March 1942 TO&E No. 04/200 for the rifle division, each regiment was assigned an anti-tank rifle company. Each battalion of the rifle regiment was also given an anti-tank rifle company (in place of the pre-war 45-mm anti-tank guns). One more anti-tank rifle company was assigned to the anti-tank battalion. Thus, according to the table, each rifle division would have 279 anti-tank rifles. The effectiveness of these weapons, of course, left something to be desired; however, their massed application did yield certain results. Moreover, the torrent of heavy-calibre bullets forced the German tank commanders to keep their hatches closed and forced them to view the battlefield only through the shatterproof glass of the vision slits. The restricting of the tank crews' field of vision eased the task of the anti-tank gunners, who used the more effective 45-mm and 76-mm anti-tank guns.

Order No. 0528 of the USSR People's Council of Defence became the next step for the Red Army's anti-tank artillery. Signed by Stalin, it stated:

> With the aim of improving the quality of combating enemy tanks, of creating and increasing the cadres of artillery-destroyers of tanks,

of raising their qualifications and distinguishing anti-tank artillery units from other types of artillery, I hereby order:

1. The light and anti-tank artillery regiments of the RGK, the anti-tank battalions of the rifle divisions, and the rifle regiments' 45-mm gun batteries to be relabelled as destroyer anti-tank artillery regiments, battalions and batteries [respectively].

2. To raise the pay rate for the command staff of these units and elements by one and a half times, and to double that for the junior command staff and the rank and file.

3. To take all the command staff of the destroyer anti-tank artillery units and elements, up to the battalion commander inclusively, under special tracking and that they be used only in the indicated units.

4. For the gun commanders and the deputy gun commanders (the gun layers) of these units to acquire the military rank 'senior sergeant' and 'sergeant' (respectively), and to introduce the position of deputy gun layer with the military rank 'junior sergeant'.

5. To return the command and deputy command staff and the rank and file of the destroyer anti-tank artillery units receiving medical treatment at hospitals to their assigned units upon their recovery.

6. To create a special sleeve insignia of the proposed description for all the personnel of the destroyer anti-tank artillery units and elements, to be worn on the left sleeve of the uniform jacket and shirt.

7. To establish an award for each knocked-out tank in the sum of 500 rubles each for the gun commander and gun layer, and 200 rubles each for the rest of the gun crew.

8. The number of tanks destroyed by the gun to be noted on the figure of a tank, painted on the upper right corner of the inside of the gun shield. The tank figure is to be drawn in black, while the number indicating the quantity of knocked-out tanks is to be in white.

9. With the aim of using destroyer anti-tank artillery units for resolving tasks of direct support to the infantry, the personnel of these units are to be trained not only to fire at tanks over open sights, but also to fire at other targets from open and defiladed firing positions.

10. Point 2 of the given order will not apply to the anti-tank artillery units of the Far Eastern, Trans-Baikal and Trans-Caucasus Fronts.[1]

An arm patch in the form of a black diamond with red edging, bearing crossed gun barrels, became the insignia of the anti-tank gunners. The formation of new destroyer anti-tank artillery units paralleled the increase in the anti-tank gunners' status. Already on 16 July 1942, by State Defence Council Decree No. 2055ss, ten light artillery (each with twenty 76-mm guns) and five anti-tank artillery regiments (each with twenty 45-mm guns) began their formation at training artillery centres, with the order to be ready by 30 July. On 26 July 1942, there followed a decree to form thirty-five additional regiments – twenty equipped with twenty 76-mm guns and fifteen equipped with twenty 45-mm guns. The regiments were quickly organized and immediately thrown into the fighting on threatened sectors of the front. In September 1942, by a decree of the State Defence Council No. 2259ss, another ten destroyer anti-tank artillery units were created, each with twenty 45-mm guns. Also in September 1942, the most distinguished regiments were given a supplementary battery of four 76-mm guns. In November 1942, a portion of the destroyer anti-tank artillery regiments were combined into destroyer divisions. As of 1 January 1943, the Red Army's destroyer anti-tank artillery establishment numbered 2 destroyer divisions, 15 destroyer brigades, 2 heavy destroyer anti-tank regiments, 168 destroyer anti-tank regiments, and 1 destroyer anti-tank artillery battalion.

The development of the Soviet system of anti-tank defence was noted by the enemy. Commenting on the results of the winter 1942–1943 campaign, on 24 April 1943 the commander of the 17th Panzer Division wrote:

1. The Panzer tactics that led to the great successes in the years 1939, 1940 and 1941 must be viewed as outdated. Even if today it is still possible to breach an anti-tank defensive front through concentrated Panzer forces employed in several waves behind each other, we must still consider past experience that this always leads to significant losses that can no longer be endured by our production situation. This action, often employed in succession, leads to a very rapid reduction in the Panzer strength.[2]

The Germans called the Red Army's elaborated system of anti-tank defence the *Pakfront* (derived from the German abbreviation for *Panzerabwehrkannone* [anti-tank gun], 'Pak'. In place of the linear and evenly-spaced deployment of the anti-tank guns across the entire defensive sector as was the practice at the start of the war, the anti-tank guns were now assembled into groups under unitary command. This allowed the fire of several anti-tank guns to be concentrated against a single target. The 'anti-tank region' was the new basis of anti-tank defence. Each anti-tank region consisted of separate, mutually supporting anti-tank strong points. A single target could thus come under fire from several neighbouring strong points simultaneously.

These anti-tank strong points were filled with all sorts of weapons. The basic system of fire of the anti-tank strong points came primarily from 45-mm and 76-mm anti-tank guns, which were supplemented by deployed batteries of the divisional artillery and destroyer anti-tank artillery units. Each anti-tank strong point was commanded by a commandant, appointed from among the commanders of the artillery units that comprised the strong point. As a rule, the commander of a destroyer anti-tank regiment or the commander of the divisional artillery regiment (or of the artillery battalion) was placed in charge of the anti-tank strong point.

The next stage in the development of Soviet anti-tank artillery was the introduction of new types of shells. The first novelty was the armour-piercing discarding sabot (APDS) shell. It consisted of a high-density core with a penetrating cap, set within a rifled sabot made of a lightweight alloy. In order to improve the aerodynamics of this design, the tip of the sabot is covered by a ballistic cap. Its principle of action consists of increasing the initial velocity of the projectile (due to the light rifled casing), vastly reducing the aerodynamic drag on the sub-projectile and thus resulting in a high terminal velocity at impact. The high-density core of the 45-mm APDS shell was 20mm; that of the 57-mm shell was 25mm; and that of the 76-mm shell was 28mm. When the shell struck the target, the high-density core would penetrate the armour, while the steel sheath surrounding the core would peel away. Due to their small dimensions, the core could not carry an explosive charge. However, the enormous stress on the core while penetrating the armour often led to its fragmentation into white-hot splinters, which once through the armour would spray the interior of the tank, striking the crew and internal equipment.

The first APDS shell to be designed was the 45-mm shell. It was created in February–March 1942 by a group of engineers under the direction of I. Burmistrov. The new ammunition was approved by a decree of the State Defence Council on 2 April 1942. While the 45-mm APDS shell was going through its design and testing, the *sorokopiatka* 45-mm anti-tank gun was quickly updated. In January–March 1942 the OKB Factory No. 172 designed a 45-mm anti-tank gun with a longer barrel. A prototype model went through testing in August–September 1942, and in April 1943 the new gun went into mass production. At ranges of fire of 300 and 500 metres and a 90° angle of impact with the armour, the 45-mm APDS shell fired by the updated anti-tank gun would penetrate 95-mm and 80-mm of armour respectively. The main shortcoming of the new shells was their costliness to produce, due to their use of domestically scarce tungsten to make the cores. In connection with this, it was even necessary to purchase tungsten from abroad – approximately 4,000 metric tons were imported from China in 1942.

The design and production of 76-mm and 57-mm APDS shells quickly followed the creation of the 45-mm APDS shell. They were also designed by Burmistrov's group and approved for use by State Defence Council Decrees No. 3187 on 15 April and No. 3429s from 26 May 1943 respectively. The 57-mm APDS shell with its initial velocity of 1,270 metres/second would penetrate 165mm of armour at a range of 300 metres, and 145mm of armour at the range of 500 metres. This enabled the 57-mm anti-tank gun to fight effectively even against those heavy German tanks that were appearing toward the end of the war. The 76-mm APDS shell could penetrate 105mm of armour at a range of 300 metres, and 90mm of armour at a range of 500 metres. These capabilities enabled the anti-tank units to fight effectively against the German Tiger tanks, which began appearing on the Eastern Front battlefields in greater numbers in July 1943. It was the destroyer anti-tank units that received priority in receiving the new APDS shells.

One of the unpleasant surprises of 1941 was the German use of shaped charge projectiles. Shell holes with melted edges were found on knocked-out Soviet tanks, so the shells that obviously created them were called 'armour incendiary' ammunition. Theoretically, such an effect could be achieved by high-temperature thermite mixtures. They were already being used at this time, for example, for welding rails in field conditions. However, an attempt in the summer of 1941 to produce an 'armour incendiary' shell based on the description of its effects failed. Thermite slags burned through armour too slowly and didn't achieve the required effect.

The situation changed when German shaped charge shells were seized. In itself the cumulative effect had long been known. It had been discovered that a hollow or void on the surface of the explosive charge, when placed against a barrier, focused the blast energy and facilitated the penetration of a barrier. However, the practical application of this effect in order to penetrate armour initially ran into a number of obstacles that were difficult to surmount. The explosive effect was on the surface of the cavity and in the instantaneous detonator. On 23 May 1942, a number of tests of a high-explosive anti-tank [HEAT] shell for the 76-mm regimental gun, designed on the basis of a captured German shell, were conducted on the Sofrinsky proving ground. Based on the results of the tests, on 27 May 1942 the new shell was put into service. Also in 1942, a 122-mm HEAT shell was created, which passed into service on 15 May 1943. Such HEAT warheads were a means to raise the possibility of using artillery that had never been intended to combat tanks. Due to the short barrel of the 76-mm regimental gun, it was difficult to accelerate an armour-piercing shell to a sufficiently high velocity in order to penetrate armour. The salvation in this case was the shaped charge warhead, which didn't depend upon its initial velocity to be effective against armour. The 122-mm HEAT shells gave the divisional howitzers a means to protect themselves. The HEAT shell for the 76-mm regimental gun had wider applications. The regimental guns supplied with these shells became especially effective in urban combat. The shaped charge warheads made them the tactical analogue of the postwar rocket-propelled grenades.

The Battle of Kursk in the summer of 1943 became the high point for the destroyer anti-tank artillery. By this time the 76-mm *ratsch-booms* were the primary weapon of the destroyer anti-tank artillery units and formations. The *sorokopiatka* comprised only about a third of the total number of anti-tank guns at Kursk. The lengthy pause in combat operations that preceded Kursk provided the opportunity to improve the condition of the units and formations through the arrival of weapons and equipment from industry and bringing the anti-tank regiments back up to strength with replacement personnel. By the time of the Kursk battle, the destroyer anti-tank regiments had almost been fully brought back up to strength (up to 93 per cent of their authorized amount of equipment and up to 92 per cent of their table strength in officers and personnel). The means to tow the guns was still inadequate (instead of the authorized indicator of 3.5 motors per gun, the destroyer anti-tank regiments had only between 1.9 and 2.6 motors per gun); the TO&E envisioned that trucks with a load capacity of 1.5 to 5 metric tons would serve as the primary means to tow the guns, but artillery tractors and vehicles with better off-road performance like the Willys jeep, Dodge truck and GAZ-64 were still in short supply. In his report on the results of the Kursk battle, Marshal of Artillery N.N. Voronov even asserted that from 30 to 40 per cent of the destroyer anti-tank regiments and brigades still relied upon the horse to move the guns.

The massed attacks of enemy armour, artillery and the Luftwaffe fell upon the Soviet anti-tank defence at Kursk. By stripping other sectors of the front, the Germans were able to gather major air strength on the northern and southern faces of the Kursk bulge. One of the most important means of struggle, by which the Germans hoped to achieve success, was the massed application of new types of tanks. Approximately 200 Panthers and 100 Tigers operated on the southern face of the bulge, while 90 Ferdinands and 40 Tigers were deployed against the Soviet defences on the northern shoulder. The Soviet anti-tank positions within the Central Front were even subjected to attacks by radio-controlled Borgwardtankettes.

Marshal Voronov wrote:

> In the course of the fighting, the German tank units adopted new tactics in a number of cases ... Their tanks supported the infantry, taking advantage of their superiority in long-range direct fire, and often acted like self-propelled artillery, shooting up the positions

of our firing points that they had detected from a range of 500 to 600 metres while remaining beyond the effective range of our anti-tank artillery. It is practically impossible to penetrate the frontal armour of all the new German tanks with the existing 45-mm and 76-mm guns of the battalion, regimental and divisional anti-tank artillery from a typical range of fire. The heavy Tiger tanks were invulnerable to the guns of the specified calibres. The available 76-mm and 45-mm APDS shells could be effective only against the side armour of the Tiger tank and the frontal armour of the new German Pz-III and Pz-IV medium tanks only from short ranges (not more than 200 metres).[3]

It should be said that N.N. Voronov somewhat blackened the picture in his report. The 1st Tank Army's artillery commander I.F. Frolov wrote the following on the results of the battle for the Kursk bulge: 'The 45-mm gun in the combat with enemy tanks was a sufficiently effective weapon – thanks to [its] high rate of fire, manoeuverability and the presence of APDS shells. There is a full number of cases, when these systems successfully battled and destroyed Pz-VI tanks (35th and 538th Destroyer Anti-tank Artillery Regiments).'[4]

It can be said that other new equipment was not in time for the Battle of Kursk. The production of the ZIS-2 57-mm anti-tank gun, which had begun in May 1941, had been halted in November 1941 due to its costliness and super-fluous armour-penetrating capabilities for the conditions of the initial period of the war. However, the arrival of heavy tanks on the German side forced a resumption of the production of the ZIS-2 gun. It was again put into service by a decree of the State Defence Council on 15 June 1943 under the designation '57-mm anti-tank gun Model 1943 ZIS-2'. By the start of the Kursk battle, the Voronezh Front had not a single unit equipped with the ZIS-2, while the Central Front had only four destroyer anti-tank regiments that were equipped with the new anti-tank gun. It had been thought that the Germans would launch their main attack against the northern shoulder of the bulge, so there-fore it was the Central Front under the command of K.K. Rokossovsky that received the regiments with the new ZIS-2. Given the lack of new anti-tank guns, the task of combating enemy tanks was placed upon new self-propelled guns. For example, the SU-152, which had been designed to support infantry, became the 'zveroboi' ['Beastkiller'] and was used against the new German tanks.

The final stage in the evolution of the Red Army's anti-tank artillery was the consolidation of its units and the appearance of self-propelled guns as part of the anti-tank artillery. By the start of 1944, all the destroyer divisions and regular separate destroyer brigades had been reformed into destroyer anti-tank brigades.

On 1 January 1944, the Red Army's destroyer anti-tank artillery numbered 50 destroyer anti-tank brigades and 141 destroyer anti-tank artillery regiments. By People's Commissar Order No. 0032 from 2 August 1944, one SU-85 regiment (twenty-one self-propelled guns) was added to the roster of fifteen destroyer anti-tank brigades. In reality, only eight of the brigades eventually received their SU-85 regiment. At the beginning of 1944, a TO&E for the self-propelled artillery battalion for a rifle division was adopted, which consisted of three batteries of four SU-76 self-propelled guns in each. In addition, T-70 tanks often served as the command vehicle in these battalions. Battalions of self-propelled guns replaced the separate destroyer anti-tank battalions with towed guns in several dozen rifle and airborne divisions. The self-propelled gun battalions even inherited the numerical designation of the destroyer anti-tank battalion that they replaced in the division.

In the final year of the war, the Red Army's anti-tank artillery arm continued to be consolidated. By 1 January 1945, it numbered fifty-six destroyer anti-tank brigades and ninety-seven destroyer anti-tank regiments.

One of the final surviving reports from German panzer units is a summary by the I.Abteilung/Panzer-Regiment 24, dated January 1945. In it, there is particular discussion of the Soviet use of anti-tank guns:

> The anti-tank guns are the main opponent of the Panzers in the Eastern Theatre of War. The Russians use anti-tank guns *en masse* for defence or by cleverly towing them along behind an attack to bring them into action swiftly. The meaning of **'Pakfront'** does not totally describe the actual situations experienced in combat by the **Abteilung** because the opponent employs this weapon more concentrated in so called **'Paknests'** in an attempt to achieve a long range flanking effect. Sometimes the **Paknest** consist of 6 to 7 anti-tank guns in a circle of only 40 to 50 metres. Because of the excellent camouflage and use of terrain – sometimes the wheels are taken off to reduce the height – the Russians easily manage to open surprise fire at medium and close range. By allowing the lead vehicles to pass by, they attempt to open fire at our formation in the deep flank.[5]

German panzers became one of the main symbols of Germany's victories in Poland 1939, France 1940, and the USSR in 1941–1942. The anti-tank artillery bore the main burden of struggle with tanks. Almost three-quarters of the tanks losses in the Second World War on the Eastern Front were due to anti-tank artillery fire. Air forces, hand-held anti-tank weapons and mines were responsible for only single-digit percentages of armour losses. The Soviet anti-tank gunners broke the back of Germany's panzer forces, which had swallowed up half of Europe.

Notes

1. *Russkiiarkhiv: Velikaia Otechestvennaia: Prikazynarodnogokommissaraoborony SSSR 22 iiun' 1941–1942* [*Russian archive: The Great Patriotic War: Orders of the USS People's Commissar of Defence 22 June 1941–1942*], Vol. 13 (2-2) (Moscow: TERRA, 1997), pp. 263–264.
2. T. Jentz, *Panzertruppen: The Complete Guide to the Creation and Combat Employment of Germany's Tank Force, 1943–1945* (Atglen: Schiffer Military History, 1996), p. 43.
3. M. Makarov and A. Pronin, *Protivotankovaiaartilleriia Krasnoi Armii, 1941–1945* [*The Red Army's Anti-tank Artillery, 1941–1945*] (Moscow: Strategiia KM, 2003), p. 67.
4. TsAMO [Central Archive of the Ministry of Defence], F.1TA, op. 3070, d. 164, l.22.
5. Jentz, *Panzertruppen, 1943–1945*, p. 223.

Chapter 2

The First Battle is the Hardest
Vitaly Andreevich Ulianov

Before the war, having finished six years of schooling in Kiev, I was working in the Arsenal factory, which was producing 45-mm guns. They were being installed in the turrets of T-70 tanks, on submarines, as well as being mounted on gun-carriages for use as anti-tank guns. In the summer of 1941, the factory was evacuated to Votkinsk, and I left for there along with it. In 1942, an idea was born within the factory to raise a military unit, equip it with 45-mm guns and volunteer it for the front. The factory leadership sent a letter to Stalin, and quickly received a telegram in his name, which is still preserved in the factory museum today, which permitted the formation of a battalion, but only if the 45-mm guns for it were above and beyond the planned production target. Within a certain amount of time, twelve such guns appeared, though I am deeply convinced that it was impossible to produce anything above the plan targets. The plan was very ruthless, and we were all forced to work to the limits of our strength in order to carry it out, striving to follow the slogan 'Everything for the front! Everything for victory!'.

However it happened, the 174th 'Komsomol' Separate Destroyer Anti-tank Artillery Battalion was created. Enlistment in this battalion was on a voluntary basis. I and my twin brother Vil were among the volunteers. Since there were many who wanted to join the battalion, a selection process was set up via the Komsomol's city committee.

On the appointed day, Vil came out of the room in which the selection commission was working. I asked him, 'Vil, how did it go?' He replied, 'Go on in, you'll find out.' I entered the door and found myself in a large room, in the middle of which was a stool. Members of the district committee bureau were sitting on similar stools along the walls. There was a solitary stool in the corner of the room, where the chairman was sitting. I took a seat on the stool in the middle of the room, and the questioning began: 'What's your name? What's your year of birth?' That's when I told a lie, adding a year to my age, and told them I'd been born in 1924, whereas I'd actually been born in 1925. The questioning continued, 'Who are your parents? Where are they now?'

I had to spin around on the stool, because the questions were coming at me from around the room. Then suddenly someone behind me asked, 'But will you be calling for your Mama at the front?' Only a coward, who was afraid to show his own face, could have asked such a question behind my back. I turned in the direction from which the question had come; everyone was wearing a concentrated expression on their faces, and some even had a sign of intelligence. I said, 'I will not call! What about you?' This response decided matters in my favour, and they signed me up for the battalion.

However, the chairman of the Komsomol's factory committee, who knew both me and my grandmother well (my mother was no longer with us, while my father was at the front), coincidentally found out from her that I was still only 17 years old. Literally the next day after their conversation, I couldn't find my name on the battalion's roster. I headed to the Komsomol committee to find out why. Despite the accusations of lying that came raining down on me, I began to try to prove that my presence at the front was necessary for victory, that there was no way they could get by without me there. When I realized that I was getting nowhere with them, I played my final card and told them that I would run away to the front regardless, though I'd rather go together with my twin brother than have to go alone. It worked! They decided to have nothing to do with me and let me go together with my brother. That's how I wound up in the battalion, where I soon became a gun layer.

The battalion had three batteries, with each battery consisting of two platoons of two anti-tank guns each. In addition to the crews, each battery had twenty-four horses and twelve drivers, as well as a single 1½ ton truck that carried our provisions. We underwent our training in Votkinsk, for which purpose they recruited some reserve soldiers. We were quartered in school buildings and marched in formation to the mess hall. People would gather to watch us, because after all their sons, friends and acquaintances were marching in the column, but our senior sergeant thought that they had come to watch him command us, and he would showboat over us as much as he could ...

Our training was brief; I was given the rank of junior sergeant and I became one crew's gunner. I recall that on the artillery practice range in Kubinka, we were given an opportunity for the first time to fire an armour-piercing shell at a dug-in tank. I hit it, and then with difficulty I gained permission to fire one more round.

Soon we were travelling by train, which took us to the Voronezh Front. At the time it was trying to force a crossing of the Don River, and together with tankers we fought for possession of Kantimorovka [a German-held town on the Rostov–Voronezh railroad].

As the song goes, '*The last battle is the hardest ...*' That isn't so! The first battle is the hardest, because you still don't know anything. Do you know what the thinking was at the front? If you remained alive after your first battle – good fellow! After the second battle – a frontline soldier! And after the third battle, you were a veteran! Now you knew everything, where to crouch, where to fall prone, where to run, what to eat, and what to discard. The last battle is the most frightening; after all, no one wants to die in his last battle, he wants to return home ...

Thus, my first battle; as I learned after the war, they'd thrown us in to seal a gap torn in the line by Manstein's group, which was striving to bail out Paulus. We were withdrawn from the positions that we were occupying, and having conducted a march, by evening we were approaching a settlement (I no longer recall its name), which was located on a low rise. On its outskirts, an exchange of fire was going on, but it was dark and quiet in the depression into which the main road leading into the settlement descended. One could hear only the squeaks of the sledges and some snorts from the horses that were pulling our guns up the slope. Their crews were marching alongside them. The scene became somewhat eerie. Atop the gentle rise, the platoon commander Junior Lieutenant Kurbatov met us. He indicated a thatch-covered hut at the end of the street as it left the village, and said that a sniper and a submachine gunner were firing from it.

We unhitched the gun from the limber and having manhandled it off the road, set it up next to a well. This was a big mistake, because the area around the well was covered by an icy layer, created by splashes of water from the bucket. I set the sight on 'anti-personnel', took aim, and fired. The shell struck the roof timbers (if it had hit the thatch, it would have simply passed cleanly through) and smashed the roof. No one fired any further shots from it.

We then spent some time crouched behind the gun shield, not seeing any other targets, when suddenly a burst of fire rang out in front of us. I took a peek out over the gun shield. Several buildings were on fire, casting a yellowish glare on the road. In the light of the flames, I saw a German in a white camouflage cape about 25 metres in front of me, who was holding a machine gun braced on the top edge of a trench. He had plainly risen to take a look around. While I struggled to line him up in my gun sight, he dropped out of sight. Why did I take so long aiming the gun? Because we had done careless work when switching to winter lubrication and remnants of the summer-formula grease had become frozen. Nevertheless, I went ahead and gave the place where he'd been two or three rounds.

At that moment platoon commander Kurbatov issued the order to fall back. Huh?! We still hadn't had enough of the fighting and had only begun to fire, and now we were falling back!? Crouching we grabbed the trails, but we slipped onto our butts and couldn't move the gun – we could find no traction underfoot because of the ice. So then I leaped around the gun shield to the side facing the Germans and gave the gun a shove, budging it from the built-up ice onto the trampled-down snow of the road. A burst of machine-gun fire rattled against the shield and shattered the canister in which I kept the gun sight when it was not in use (I uttered an oath, because the key from the gun sight was still inside it), but somehow missed me. Without waiting for the Germans to open fire once again, I dived behind the gun shield, and together, crouching and digging our feet into the snow, we were able to drag the gun away.

When we sensed that it had become quiet, we swung the gun around and began to roll it down the street. Behind us we were hearing the sounds of a tank – the rumble of an engine and a clattering of treads. Someone shouted, 'I hear a motor!' To our right about 10 metres away there was a barn, but we had to move through wet snow that was above our knees in order to reach it. I suddenly recalled the film *Aleksandr Nevsky* and a famous line from it: 'Die where you stand.' So I spoke it aloud. Thank God, no one paid any attention to me. The crew grabbed hold of the gun and began to haul it toward the barn. However, the lower shield situated between the wheels began accumulating snow, and after just 1½ metres it had become impossible even to nudge the gun forward – it had become stuck in front of the wall of snow that it had thrown up. I knew the weapon superbly; there had been a reason why I'd been working in the factory's technical control department. I had the personal identification stamp No. 183, and it was present on many parts of this gun. I said, 'Stop!' I bent over, freed the latch and raised the shield. The gun started moving again, and I'd redeemed myself with my action.

We rolled it into the barn and turned it in the direction of the tank, which hadn't tarried in appearing. Just out in front of us was a building where the wounded were being gathered. Passing them, we could hear them laughing and joking – they'd done their share of the fighting and they knew that soon they'd be sent to the rear. The panzer drew even with the building, pivoted to face it, and began to shoot it up from a machine gun. I took aim and fired. The shell flew about 15 centimetres above the turret. Later, when analyzing why I'd missed, I realized that when I'd been firing at the hut and the Fritz who had the machine gun, I had set the sight on 'anti-personnel', but when firing at the tank, I was using armour-piercing shells, which had an initial velocity twice as great as the high-explosive shell and a different flight trajectory. It hadn't occurred to me to change the setting! After the shot, because the spades at the end of the split trail hadn't been dug in, the gun leaped backwards. A second shot! Another miss!

The panzer pivoted and started moving toward us. It was firing its machine guns and the bullets were striking the shield. It fired a round from its cannon, but missed – we were in a slight hollow and the shell flew overhead. After my second shot, because the spades hadn't been dug in, the gun's left wheel had pressed me against the wall of the barn. I had to step over the trail and aim the gun by its barrel.

I fired a total of five rounds before I finally hit the tank at a distance of just 10 metres and it burst into flames. I leaped up, waving my arms, and shouted, 'The tank is burning!' At this moment, Germans in white ponchos came running out from behind the tank, dashed behind a building directly across the road from us, and from there they began to spray our position with submachine-gun fire. Since I had raised the lower shield, I was wounded in the right foot, while the loader Tolia Shumilov took a round in the knee. The gun commander Dydychkin, who I hadn't seen before this, issued the order to fall back into the yard. We ran into the yard, spotted a shed, and ran into it. It had no door and I took a seat on a bench opposite the entrance. Shumilov came running into the shed behind me, while Golitsyn who was following him was killed by a burst of automatic weapons fire at the entrance.

Through the doorway I could see a round henhouse made from a woven lattice of poplar branches about 30 metres away. A German stuck his head out of it and began to shout something. I grabbed Tolia Shumilov's carbine, since I'd left mine behind on the gun limber. Even though I knew that I shouldn't fire, lest I give our position away, the Fritz was shouting so brazenly that I couldn't stand it, so I took aim and fired. The German dropped face first. A second German, not realizing what had happened, sprang over to him, exposing his back to my second shot. They began to return fire from behind the henhouse. I ducked behind the door jamb. In the exchange of fire I dropped two more.

I began to reload the carbine, and a cartridge became jammed; rather than extracting it, I tried to force it into the barrel, thereby rendering the carbine inoperable. When I realized that I'd screwed up the carbine, I raised my head and saw two Germans running toward me. Suddenly our gun commander Dydychkin jumped out from the right, stopped in front of the shed, and fumbled a bit before grabbing an RGD grenade. He gave it a shake like it was a thermometer before tossing it at the Germans' feet. One of the Fritzes stooped to pick up the grenade and throw it back, but it blew up in his hands and the Germans were blown apart. Meanwhile Dydyshkin had darted past the door and taken cover.

We decided to hide in the shed behind a steel barrel. Tolia somehow managed to find a place behind it, but there wasn't room for me. Germans were in the yard, shouting something. Suddenly a stout German gripping a submachine gun appeared in the doorway. He queried, 'Rus, you in here?' I thought that now Shumilov would begin to moan – he'd been moaning before this – the German would finish us off, and my life would end in this damned shed. But then there was an order and the German disappeared.

A short time later the Germans brought their wounded into the yard, which were soon transported away. The fighting began to subside. I said, 'Tolia, we need to get out of here.'

'Yes, Vitya, we must. Shall we go?'

'Let's move.'

We kept laying there for a few minutes. I spoke up, 'Are we going?' I heard his reply, 'Let's go.'

We lay there for a while longer, before I spoke up for the third time: 'Well, let's go.' He asked me in reply, 'Vitia, are you wounded somewhere?'

'In the foot.'

'In one?'

'In one.'

'I'm wounded in both. So you go first.'

'OK.'

I crawled out of the shed, and since I was wearing my greatcoat (the camouflage white poncho was horribly uncomfortable, so we didn't wear it), I decided to cover myself with snow for camouflage. I rolled around in the snow – it was useless. The greatcoats were good quality – no snow would stick to them. Realizing the entire senselessness of the endeavour, I got up on my hands and knees and started crawling. I reached the henhouse and tried not to look in the direction of the dead – it was ghastly. I turned to the left in the direction of a brick building, next to which was a pile of hay. Near this haystack, in the light of the village's burning buildings I saw a seated old man. A woman was on her knees in front of him, while a second was walking back and forth like a pendulum not far away and moaning. I asked what had happened.

It turned out that this family had been hiding in a cellar. Some German, having raised the access door, had asked, 'Rus, are you there?' From down below they answered him, 'Yes, there are civilians here.' The Fritz grabbed a grenade and tossed it down. An old woman was killed. The old man had been badly wounded, while the woman who was walking had taken a fragment in the chest. Only the other woman had been left unharmed, but she was in a state of shock and was simply insensate. I asked them, 'Are there Germans up ahead?'

'Yes.'

'To the left?'

'Yes.'

'Behind us?'

'Yes. They're everywhere.'

I then asked them to give me some civilian clothes and to hide me until our guys would arrive. To which I received the reply, 'What business do we have with you?' Well, I thought, I had to get out of there; otherwise they'd turn me in. Incidentally, Tolia, who I later met in the hospital, told me that having waited for 30 minutes, he set out after me in a crawl, and these same people redressed him and hid him for 48 hours. Apparently their conscience had been stirred.

Meanwhile, I slithered down the slope of the hill into the valley, rose to my knees and took several 'steps'. Suddenly quite nearby a shot rang out. I felt a bullet pass right next to my head. I instantly dropped onto my right side and kept still. The snow was deep and damp. I heard the sound of footsteps: 'Khryp, khryp . . .' Silence. I had a Finnish knife with a wooden handle on my belt, but I was lying on my right arm, so I could only draw the knife with my left hand. But what could I do with it? I decided to act dead and to strike the foe in the face with the knife when he bent over to check me, well understanding that in my position, I wouldn't be able to penetrate a greatcoat or any other outerwear. I held my breath so as not to emit any steam, but all the while it seemed to me that my heart was pounding so loudly that it would be audible several steps away. Again there was the squeak of snow underfoot and then . . . silence. I thought, 'You have to approach and bend over. Then I'll have one single chance . . .' Again the sound of a footstep in the snow. From the sound I realized that the man was standing and was shifting from the right to the left, trying to get a good look at me. Suddenly the footsteps began to recede.

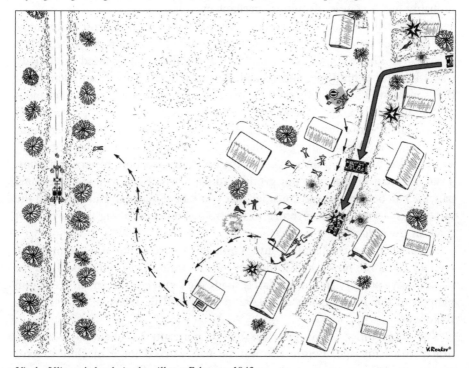

Vitaly Ulianov's battle in the village, February 1943.

Who was it? I still don't know, but I think that it wasn't a German. It was one of ours, and when he saw that he had killed one of his own soldiers, he didn't want to come any closer and had left. Meanwhile, I continued to lie there. I was now feeling warm and comfortable, and I realized that I was freezing to death. Then I rose abruptly to my knees. I was thinking, 'Let them fire!' However, no shot ensued, but I was afraid to look around. On all fours through a small patch of scrub brush I climbed up the opposite slope of the hollow, where a road was running along the crest.

I heard something squeaking and took a look; there was a horse team towing one of our 45-mm guns. The drivers were leading the horses by the bridles. Two men were marching on either side of the gun and one was marching behind it. Very disciplined and by-the-book. They were all our guys, but soldiers wearing helmets, while we hotshots refused to wear them: 'We're not infantry!' That's the sort of foolish courage we had. Indeed, there was no commander that would force us to wear them.

They were moving past me. When I realized that they were passing me by and would soon leave me behind, with all my remaining strength I shouted, 'Comrades!!!' and attempted to hurry to my right. Well, make a dash – how? Where could I, bleeding as I was, rush through deep snow?! I crawled a bit, probably just a couple of metres, perhaps even less.

I then heard a shout: 'Who's there?' Then when I heard him and understood 'OURS!' the rest of my strength left me. I couldn't shout a reply – I couldn't even move. They stopped, came running in my direction, spotted the bloody trail I had left behind me, and picked me up. It was a crew from Lieutenant Bou's platoon. They laid me on the closed gun trails and took me to a hospital.

For this battle I, the first in the battalion, was awarded the 'For courage' medal. After recovering in the hospital, they sent me into a reserve regiment.

En route, a comrade and I decided we had nothing to do in this regiment, so we took a seat on a train moving in the opposite direction, toward the front. True, the man in charge of our group told us, 'I won't give you your personal papers. You better stop and consider that you'll be deserting.' But it was all the same to us – we wanted to return to the front. Somehow along the way, I lost track of my sidekick.

Well, when the train pulled into Voronezh where a unit was forming up, nobody asked me how I had wound up on the train. They only asked me for my military specialty and immediately made me a gun layer in an anti-tank gun platoon of the 1st Battalion of the 92nd Guards Rifle Division's 280th Rifle Regiment.

The commander of my gun was Senior Sergeant Korobeinikov – a man nearly twice my age. Before the war he had worked for a machine-tractor station, and he'd passed through the fires of Stalingrad. Our ammunition carrier was Maksim Strogov – a Muscovite who lived on Stromynka Street. Before the war he'd been a taxi driver, and as far as I can remember, he'd spent some time in prison for 'hooliganism'. Our loader was Iura Vorob'ev, a guy my own age, who had the same amount of combat experience as I had.

In April 1943 we were sent to the Korocha area. We were placed in a small forest. We selected and set up firing positions on the forest fringe. Within several days an order arrived – to get crow-bars, pickaxes and shovels ready and to wash out and refill our canteens with fresh water. The following evening, our platoon under the command of Lieutenant Serdiuk, leaving behind four sentries to guard our position, set off toward the place where we would be working. We marched in darkness. We had been warned not to smoke and to keep our voices down. After some time (none of us had watches), an officer met us and directed us to follow him.

When we had arrived at the spot, he pointed at some stakes that had been driven into the soil and an outline marked on the ground, and told us: 'This will be the covered firing position for a 45-mm gun. You must finish your work before sunrise. Camouflage the position and wait. They'll come for you.'

How are positions set up for the *sorokopiatka*? We dug out a pit with a diameter of approximately 3 metres and a depth of 40–50 centimetres, around which a low breastwork was thrown up using the excavated earth. In the forward part of the pit, we created a recess for the gun, covered with logs, in which the gun could roll in case of a barrage or bombing. To the left of the gun we dug a slit trench for the gun commander and a bit behind it a pit for the boxes of shells. To the right of the gun we dug another pit to shelter the gun crew.

The work was hard. We broke up the earth with pickaxes (of which we had two) and removed the rubble with shovels. We didn't take any breaks: we only took turns, giving each other a chance to take a short rest. We finished our work by dawn and when the officer arrived, we were having a smoke beneath the cover of our shelter halves. He looked over our work, told us, 'Good job!' and indicated the place where we were to go next. At the indicated assembly point, a roll call was conducted and then we moved out on our return path.

We returned to our current position just after sunrise. We received our breakfasts and then slept until dinner. With the onset of darkness, we moved up into our new positions. That's how we advanced repeatedly: we prepared firing positions for the anti-tank artillery and dug entrenchments. As we familiarized ourselves with our new positions, we could see columns of men, one or two wide, moving back and forth along parallel courses. Their shouldered shovels would flash in the moonlight. It seemed that we had enough 'excavators' like us and more to spare. They were constructing a second belt of defences.

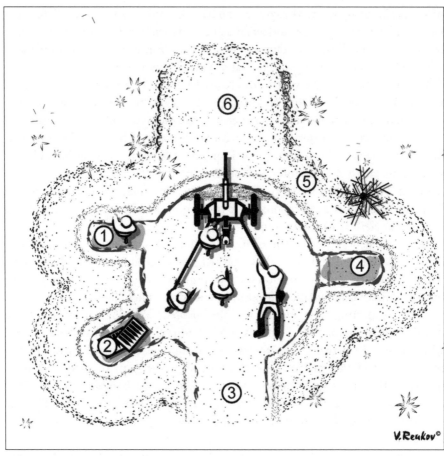

A 45-mm gun position: 1. Gun commander, 2. Ammunition storage, 3. Ramp, 4. Crew shelter, 5. Breastwork, 6. Rampart.

Upon finishing our work we would make ourselves ready: rehearse the actions for bringing the gun into the battle and calibrate the guns. We pulled back far to the rear into deep balkas [gulches in the landscape caused by erosion] in order to conduct gunnery exercises. Our targets were mock-ups of German tanks and self-propelled guns. In addition we studied the vulnerable spots of German armour in coloured 'fold out' instruction booklets. We prepared well.

On the night of 4 July, flashes of lightning began to play in the sky in the direction of Korocha and Belgorod, and we began to hear a rumble, whether of thunder or artillery firing we couldn't tell. The next morning we were ordered to prepare for a march and soon we were standing in a column, nestled in the forest fringe. Vehicles drove up, out of which stepped a group of men. Two generals in handsome uniforms walked up to us, as well as several other military men. They told us that a battle had begun, in which we were also to take part. Then they asked us:

'Do you know that the Germans now have Tigers, Panthers and Ferdinands?'

'We know!' we replied.

'And the vulnerable places where you need to hit them?'

'We know that too!'

The army commander and the member of the Military Council (we determined their status from the discussion of the generals and officers among themselves) gave speeches and expressed their confidence that we wouldn't waver in front of the tanks, and assured us that we wouldn't be alone on the battlefield.

Then gun commander Korobeinikov declared, 'When the tanks come, I'll take position behind the gun sight myself.'

I parried with the words, 'I will shoot anyone who tries to come and take the sight when in action!'

One of the generals stopped us: 'Well, why all this? You must trust each other. In the battle, there will be enough tanks for everyone.'

Having wished us success, the generals drove off; 30 to 40 minutes later we moved out and by dawn we were already settling into our positions, perhaps even one of those that we ourselves had dug the night before.

We were positioned on the northern slope of a wide valley, facing the Germans. No one was visible in the valley below us or on the lower, southern slope opposite us. The opposite slope of the valley smoothly levelled out into a steppe that was as flat as a table; the view extended for many kilometres. On our left flank, in the distance down in the valley was the dark smudge of a forest. In front of it, in the fringe of the woods, a battery of 76-mm guns was deployed. To the right and behind us was vegetation, in which our rear services were situated.

As far as our position went, I'd have to say it wasn't a good one. Of course it was difficult to spot us, because our positions were well camouflaged, but after opening fire we would have no way to manoeuvre, because to roll the gun along the slope in full sight of the enemy was equivalent to death. Preparing for combat, we took our positions around our gun. We opened the boxes of ammunition, wiped and stacked the shells, including the APDS [armour-piercing discarding sabot] shells that had arrived just recently. Having finished our preparations, we took a look around.

That's when I saw for the first time a battle, as they say, from the sidelines. Approximately 20 German panzers were heading toward the battery of 76-mm guns. My attention was caught by the following detail: when a shell would strike one of the moving tanks, it would stop. However, the tank moving behind it would also stop, making no attempt to go around the obstacle. Both tanks stood as if they'd been dug-in! One more observation: when a tank in the second wave erupted in flames, it would continue to advance for a short time, but then would suddenly disintegrate in front of your eyes. Then we realized that in an effort to intimidate us, the Germans had come up with a clever ploy. They were creating the appearance of a large number of armoured vehicles, hooking up wooden dummy tanks to a real ones! We had no other way to explain the strange spectacle we'd seen. The combat ended when the German tanks withdrew.

That night a battle flared up in the valley below us, involving our infantry. We couldn't see anything, because the slope upon which we were positioned blocked sight of part of the valley that was closest to us. When it became light, Strogov and Vorob'ev crept down into the valley to check things out and later told us that there were several German vehicles down there. Apparently the Germans had been moving without scouting ahead and they had unexpectedly run smack into our guys, who, incidentally, also hadn't distinguished themselves with any special vigilance. The fellows brought back an automobile seat, which gun commander Korobeinikov placed in his own entrenchment.

At dawn the field kitchen arrived with our breakfast. Pea soup with American sausage was in the Thermos. We ate while seated in the covered position of our gun, leaving Maksim Strogov up above to keep watch. Suddenly he said:

'Tanks have shown up!'

'Well, how many?'

He began to count, 'One, two, three ...'

We realized that he was counting them as each new armoured vehicle appeared on the horizon. When Maksim reached thirty, he swore and exclaimed, 'There's so many of them!'

We stuck our heads up out of the shelter. The panzers were visible as if spread out on a palm. It seemed as if the entire horizon was filled with them. The morning was sunny and there was a shimmering heat haze over the steppe. The Tigers and Panthers seemingly were swimming silently in this haze: their gun barrels and antennae clearly stood out.[1] Among the large tanks that looked like battleships scurried little (in comparison with them) light tanks. This entire armada was rolling toward us. We didn't begin to try to count them all – it was useless.

We didn't speak; we understood that it was going to be a hot one and hardly any of us would survive it intact. The tanks were now about 800 metres away from us. Korobeinikov gave the order, 'Fire!' I replied, 'It's too early!'

'Fire!'

'Too soon!'

I knew that at this range, there was nothing we could do to them. The gun had been loaded with an APDS shell, which wasn't effective at such a range.

Korobeinikov reached for his submachine gun, as if reminding me that he could take certain measures against me. There followed another order, 'Sight 5!'

This meant that he had determined the range to be 500 metres. I understood that if we hastened to open fire, then we'd only reveal our position prematurely. Yet one more thought flashed through my mind at that moment: 'Why is no one else firing? What, is no one else around? When will they start?'

I had to submit to orders: I took aim and fired. The shell struck my target. A puff of dust appeared where I hit the tank. Korobeinikov ordered, 'Another!'

I fired another shell, which also hit the target; 500 metres is fairly close range. Another cloud of dust appeared. As I later found out, the Germans had covered their tanks with an anti-magnetic paste. At the time, I was only surprised.

The panzers didn't open fire. It was still quiet. Having drawn up to the crest on the opposite side of the valley, they stopped moving toward us. Some of the tanks turned to the right, while the rest pivoted and moved to the left, where there was a road. Possibly, the German tankers had assessed the abruptness of the ascent leading to our position and realized that they wouldn't be able to climb it. Even if they could, they knew that they'd be exposing their bellies to us as they clambered over the military crest. They weren't stupid. Thus they began to spread out in different directions like an opening fan.

... Then it started. The artillery began to work. Aircraft appeared, both ours and German. They were flying over the battlefield at an unbelievably low altitude. Our aeroplanes swept low over the German tanks, launching rockets at them and releasing bomblets over them. Meanwhile the Germans were keeping us pressed to the earth with cannon and machine-gun fire. Everywhere there was firing and explosions, and the constant din of battle. It is said correctly, 'The earth turned upside down.' Panzers, firing, were outflanking us on the right and left. They had crossed the valley and some were now disappearing into the woods – there, where our field kitchens had been parked that morning. Emerging from the woods, they deployed and came at us from the right, apparently having decided to take us from the flank unnoticed at short range. If they had managed to do so, then I'm not confident that we could have quickly redeployed and met them with fire. But they had missed the mark somewhat. In training, all the crews operate smoothly, and everything is worked out to the tiniest details. Battle is different.

I don't recall who, but someone shouted, 'Tanks on the right!' I turned and saw three Panthers [*sic*] moving below us and from the right, with their gun barrels pointed straight ahead. They hadn't seen us; otherwise they would have turned their turret toward us to fire. They were moving as if in a staggered formation, with one tank leading. The range to them was about 40 to 50 metres, and I could see each bolt on their hulls, every weld. I was completely calm, just as I am now as we're sitting and speaking.

The turret of the lead tank entered the sight's field of view, and as soon as the crosshairs centred on it, I fired. The shell struck the turret. This I saw plainly. The tank didn't stop. It continued moving to the left along the slope at the same speed. I realized that I hadn't penetrated the armour. I glanced to the right. Two more tanks were moving, one a little closer, the second trailing behind and a bit lower down the slope. I hunkered down behind the gun, knowing that I had to fire at the side. As soon as this part of the tank entered the sight, I fired. The tank didn't stop immediately. It rolled past us to the left and then burst into flames. A puff of smoke rose from the flames within it. The second tank drew a little nearer. There was the scent of burning from it. I fired at its turret. It rocked and stopped opposite our gun. I realized that the shell hadn't penetrated. Its turret slowly began to turn in our direction. I shouted, 'Iura, give me another!' The breech clanked shut. I had to lower the barrel of the gun, but I couldn't do it! Again I fired at the turret. Why had I done so? I don't know ... Probably because it was occupying the entire field of the gun sight.

I managed to fire several rounds: I aimed and fired at the turret automatically. I couldn't force myself to lower the barrel in order to strike the side of the hull. Once again I repeat that I wasn't sensing any fear at this moment. I was totally consumed by the task of destroying this tank. The tank fired. The shell missed high. It was firing armour-piercing shells. Behind us we'd laid the Thermoses and greatcoats: they all went flying into the air.

After the first shot by the German tank, we all scrambled into the pit for the gun crew. But the German tank remained in place. After some time we crawled over to the gun and loaded it. In the gun sight I could see the side of its gun barrel: 'Since I see the barrel, the shell will miss.' I fired again at the turret before taking cover in the pit. The tank fired – and missed. In that fashion I managed to fire three shots. When I crawled out again and took a look in the sight, the side of the gun barrel was no longer visible. A black aperture was gazing directly at me. I placed the crosshairs of the gun sight on this aperture – and fired. Then – I blacked out.

When I came to and stood up (I'd been lying on my back), my gun was tipped over on one side and the left wheel was missing. At that place where I'd been standing, my submachine gun, anti-tank and anti-personnel grenade were scattered about and a shell crater yawned. To my right, Strogov and Vorob'ev were lying in the strangest poses. To the left, face down, gun commander Korobeinikov was silent. His head was turned and he was seemingly looking at me. When the cobwebs cleared from my head, I realized that I was only seeing out of my right eye. I wiped my left eye with my hand. When I pulled it away, I saw a grey material on the fingers – brains. I felt no pain and couldn't figure out what had happened. I again wiped my eye. It began to see. I told Korobeinikov:

'The tanks have been knocked out.' He was silent. I slid over to him and grabbed him by the shoulder. His head flopped and detached from the body. The trench in which he was positioned, from which he surveyed the battlefield and gave the commands 'Take cover!', 'To the gun!', was exactly opposite the wheel of the anti-tank gun and less than a metre away from it. The projectile that the German tank had fired had struck the wheel spring casing and had blown it and the left wheel off the gun, and had swept away everything located nearby. These parts of the anti-tank gun, my submachine gun and two grenades might have been what had split Korobeinikov's skull and decapitated him.

I peered out of the trench warily. The first tank, having advanced a bit to the left along the slope, was now motionless. I don't know who finished it off. The second tank was burning fiercely, while the third stood with a lowered and mangled barrel. The crew of this tank was gone. The turret hatch was open. There were also no other German tanks, and the fighting was now going on behind us.

Strogov and Vorob'ev started to regain consciousness. Iura had been wounded in the neck, under the left armpit and in the left leg. I felt myself all over and didn't find any sort of wound. Maksim Strogov was also uninjured.

We had to leave. Iura couldn't walk. I told him, 'I'll carry you.'

Even though it was hot, I donned my coat – I didn't want to abandon my government-issued equipment. We also gingerly put Iura's greatcoat on him. Strogov said, 'I'll head to the right. There, I know, I might find our medics. I'll find them and then send them back to you.'

I got on all fours, having placed the strap of my submachine gun around my neck. With Strogov's help, Iura clambered on to me, and on all fours I began to move with him. We were making slow progress; the greatcoat kept getting trapped under my knees and was interfering. We crawled directly across the field, over the crest. Yura helped me with his good right arm.

Suddenly a vehicle carrying Germans appeared to our left, which was going in the same direction we were. The Germans noticed us. They began to fire, but they didn't hit either Iura or me. A bullet only punched through the strap of my submachine gun. The vehicle stopped and several Germans leaped out of it and came running in our direction. We kept our heads down and tried not to move. Then there was an explosion and I heard cries. Next there was some sort of commotion. Apparently the Germans were collecting their wounded. Soon the vehicle drove away.

When I dared to look around, I saw a sign: 'Mines'. It turns out that the Germans had run into our minefield. Whether the entire field had been mined or just the road, I don't know. We were lucky that the Germans seemingly wanted nothing to do with us after the mine went off.

Now we began to crawl cautiously, vigilantly checking for signs of mines or the enemy. We finally made it over the crest of the hill and started down the opposite side, where we found shelter in some sort of bunker. Iura, since he couldn't walk, requested that he be left in the bunker. I left the bunker and found a road running not far away from it. Having gone a little bit further down the road, I came across the battalion headquarters.

The chief of staff asked, 'Where's the gun?'

'The gun has been destroyed, and I left Vorob'ev over there. Strogov went to find you.'

They told me that Strogov was already here. I wanted to explain to them how to find Vorob'ev and to show them the place. But I was told that there was no need to go there, because a group had already left to get him. Later my parents, who were residing in Votkinsk, received a letter from Vorob'ev, which unfortunately has since been lost.

We began to fall back together as a group. As we moved, we watched a team of horses harnessed to a 76-mm gun attempting to escape a German tank in the ravine to our left, but it was crushed together with the crew. Artillery fire blanketed us and shells began to explode quite nearby. The battalion's chief of staff was wounded, and from our walk we went into a run, darting from cover to cover. We sheltered behind buildings and trees, and in the ditches on either side of the road.

I won't begin to recount everything that I witnessed. But having experienced more battles later, I will say that a retreat is a depressing and awful matter. People seem to become inhuman, they run, ready to trample anyone in their way, even ready to kill one another. It is better to attack for a month than to run for just several hours. But we ran for 15–20 kilometres. Then we stopped, turned around, and went back.

Our 45-mm anti-tank gun was gone. Gun commander Korobeinikov had been killed. The wounded Iura Vorob'ev had been sent to the *medsanbat* [medical and sanitary battalion]. For a time, I and loader Maksim Strogov attached ourselves to some mortar crews. For the entire following day, I brought mortar shells up to the firing positions. But a day later I found myself commanding a squad in a reconnaissance platoon. The platoon leader was Junior Lieutenant Lavrentii Semenovich Beliaev, born in 1911. He was a Communist, a brave man and a most experienced scout, who subsequently became a Hero of the Soviet Union. There was much to learn from him.

Once I was on a reconnaissance probe with him. At night we stealthily reached a German observation post. We were able to get documents, three machine guns, and submachine guns. We took everything back to headquarters. We didn't have a single loss.

Soon I found myself commanding, it seems to me, the remnants of a regiment. It happened that after one battle, we stopped for the night in a ravine. There were around sixty to seventy of us. At twilight Germans reached this ravine and opened fire on us from above. There were around fifteen or twenty of them. Firing back, we clambered out of the ravine. With the cry, 'For the Motherland! For Stalin!' – and with swearing – we rushed at the Germans. They hadn't expected there to be so many Russians in the ravine, and they started running. We chased them, firing, shouting things and cursing. There was everything in these shouts: fear, which still hadn't passed, insult, malice and guilt, because some of our comrades had been killed, while we by some miracle had remained alive.

I also was running with a rifle, but I wasn't firing. I wanted to run down at least one German and stick my bayonet into him. It seemed to me that if I killed him cleanly with a gunshot, it would be too little repayment for everything I'd gone through, for my comrades who'd been killed in the ravine. What came over me, I don't know. We didn't pursue them long. They made it back to their trenches, from where the Germans in them began to fire back at us.

We stopped and hit the dirt. We had no shovels, nothing with which to dig. I had found an old tank track and tried to hide at least my head in it. This was an instinctive desire. I recall that I wasn't afraid of death. It was frightening that I'd cease to be a soldier, a fighter. I also remember that I feared being taken prisoner ...

So, I had dived into this tank track and I was keeping my head down. I pulled a can of American sausages out of my kit bag. I opened it, pried out the weenies and wrapped them in something, and I began to pick at the ground with the empty can. The ground didn't yield. For some reason at the time it didn't occur to me that the ground had been compacted by the tank. Others had also found whatever they had handy that they could use to deepen their 'foxholes'.

In this fashion we were digging ourselves in until it became dark. Once night had fallen, someone reported that several sapper's shovels were available. I ordered foxholes to be dug for firing from the prone position, and then passed the shovel to a neighbour. I was cheering up inside: we're digging in – we'll hold. Realizing this, the Germans went on the attack. They were seen coming against the backdrop of the slightly brighter western sky. One of the soldiers started to shout, 'The Germans are coming!'

Gunfire erupted. Everyone fired without any sort of command. From the direction of the attackers, shouts and curses were audible in both the Russian and German tongue. The enemy was almost in our line. That's when it became frightening, moreover because frequent cries were ringing out on our side: 'Commander! My rifle is jammed!' Many of our soldiers, located in freshly dug foxholes, had tossed their cartridge clips on the ground, and then were trying to force the dirty cartridges into the chamber. Nevertheless, though with enormous difficulty, we repulsed this attack.

Now what should be done? After the fighting ended I found a soldier with a can of grease and an individual first-aid dressing packet, and I went around all the positions. I gave each soldier a piece of bandage and cotton wadding. Then each soldier in my presence wiped clean and greased their rifle's cartridge chamber. As they did so, I told them to prepare a place for their cartridge clips and grenades – to dig a little pit for them and to cover the ground with their tent halves. We had a total of twenty-two men. We were armed with our rifles, both German and our submachine guns, an anti-tank rifle with several rounds of ammunition and a Degtiarev light machine gun.

The Germans repeatedly attacked as if according to schedule – twice a day, in the morning and the evening. Moreover, as they advanced, it was clear that they were making these attacks without any particular enthusiasm, plainly with no hope for success. When the German lines of infantry appeared again, we all fired at them with our rifles. We shot poorly and ineffectively. When the Germans approached more closely, I would give the order, 'Submachine gunners, fire!'

The difference between single-shot rifles and automatic fire was enormous. The Germans would immediately falter and go rolling back, and we would then cease fire to conserve ammunition. In addition, we were running low on rations, so I as the commander had to make some difficult decisions: 'Who will go for grub? Whom should I send?' The time when the field kitchens would arrive and the Germans attacked almost coincided. So you had to give some thought about who to send for the Thermoses and who to keep on hand for the fighting. It was necessary for the soldiers both to return with the food in time and to take his position in his foxhole, if a battle was underway.

Sometimes one or two soldiers couldn't withstand the pressure of the German attacks and abandoned their positions. I had to fire in the air over their heads to get them to stop. One soldier disobeyed and left, but he was stopped in the ravine behind us and forced to return to our position. That in fact is when we first learned that we still had someone backing us up.

On the second day we received a few replacements. They sent up nine men, drivers and cooks from the administrative platoon, who were green and had never seen fire. They brought with them cans of sausage and everyone topped themselves up with food. However, the most important thing was that they brought shovels. I ordered full, deep trenches to be dug for standing fire, and for the shovels to be passed down the line like relay batons.

Having completed the entrenchments, we linked them with communication trenches. We obtained a fully equipped position according to all the rules of the infantry manual. I, however, kept my foxhole for firing from a prone position, to which communication trenches linked up from two different directions. It never dawned upon anyone to help me, and I didn't even entertain the notion of forcing someone to help.

Soon a German light tank appeared and began to move along in front of our trenches, trying to entice fire in order to reveal the positions of our machine guns. One of our new replacements leaped out of the trench. The tank fired its main gun and the small-calibre shell struck him in the left arm, nearly severing it. He grabbed a knife, walked up to a comrade, and requested, 'Take hold.' The other guy extended the dangling part and the wounded soldier cut the few remaining tendons. They placed a tourniquet on the stump. Clutching the amputated part of his limb to his chest, he said his farewells to everyone and headed for the rear, happy, beaming and content – he was still alive! I don't know whether he made it back to the aid station or not – he was bleeding profusely from his stump – but he set off in a joyful mood.

I recall how in the evenings, just as the exchange of fire started up, I could see arms and legs sticking out above the trenches. Many were hoping in this way to get out of the war. Of course, not everyone did this, but neither would everyone rush to a firing slit or advance in a head-on attack either. People are people. Take the example of my 45-mm anti-tank gun platoon commander Junior Lieutenant Serdiuk. I don't know where he was while we were engaging those three Panthers [*sic*] back at Kursk, but I know he survived. At some point we had moved into the front line together with him as ordinary riflemen, but he ran away. We were moving through a cornfield. There was a terrible stench of corpses. He said to me: 'Wait a minute here.' I replied, 'I'll wait.'

I shouldered my submachine gun and waited, but the sun was scorching. I stood there for several hours, but I couldn't wait for him forever. Later, after the fighting had already subsided, some men started asking me, 'You're still alive? Your platoon leader Serdiuk said that a shell had exploded between the two of you; he received concussion while you fell. He doesn't know whether you're alive or not.'

'And where have you seen him?'

'He showed up, totally shaken and concussed. They took him away to the rear, to a hospital.'

When the war ended, I was a battery commander. Once we gathered at the divisional headquarters for a meeting. When it began, an officer stepped into the room and said something to the division commander. The commander rose and said, 'Comrades, the chief of the Political Department and I have been invited to the Party city committee regarding a serious matter. The commander of the division's artillery Colonel Serdiuk will continue the meeting.'

A tall colonel rose and started to speak. As soon as he began to talk, I realized, 'My God, that's my Serdiuk, my platoon commander!' I was flabbergasted. It was a horror! After the meeting ended I returned to my unit and went to see the regiment commander, where I told him what kind of bird this Serdiuk was, how he kept running away, and now he's healthy, sleek and well groomed, wearing a pile of metal on his chest and issuing orders. I requested an investigation, a check into his personal records to see where he'd fought later.

A few days passed and I asked, 'Well?'

'They're looking into it.'

Another ten days passed. I asked, 'Well, what's with Serdiuk, have they investigated?'

'But he's left for Germany.'

They were hiding him. That's the whole morality tale for you … and the whole notion of honour.

We held our line for several days. Once after repulsing an attack, that night I fell asleep in my foxhole without eating dinner. I don't know what woke me up, but when I saw several unknown men standing over me, I was gripped with terror. I was sure they were Germans or Vlasovites![2] I began to grope around in the darkness, trying to find a weapon, but there wasn't one handy. However, thank God the commander showed up. It turned out that a unit had arrived to replace us – men from the 89th Rifle Division. He asked me to give him a detailed briefing on the situation. I told him everything and showed him the line that we were holding. I was told: 'Tell your men to fall in and lead them down into the ravine. There you'll be told where to go.'

I was asked to leave behind the anti-tank rifle and a machine gun. I said that the ammunition for them had almost run out. That didn't matter to them; they had their own weapons, but not enough support weapons. At first I wanted to know whether or not I'd have to account for the weapons. They reassured me, and we set off to the rear for rest and refitting.

After the summer battles of 1943, the 1st Battalion of the 92nd Guards Rifle Division's 280th Guards Rifle Regiment, in which I served, received replacements. Several guys from the Barnaul' Infantry School arrived in my platoon, which because of my insubordinate nature was known in the battalion as the 'feral PTO [anti-tank defence]'. They brought with them a new song: 'I've done a lot of strolling around the world …', which we liked a lot. When the regiment in September was conducting the march from Khar'kov to the Dnepr, we started singing it the very first night. We marched and sang, or more accurately bellowed. What of it? – we were young. Moreover we felt that nothing would go wrong for us. Whenever the song ended, we started it up again, and literally within 20 minutes a crowd of soldiers would encircle our platoon. The column would bunch up around us, the men keeping in step with us as they listened to us sing, until the commanders intervened and sent everyone back to their places in the column, having first established how many men and at what time they might march with us and sing. Soon the entire regiment took up the song.

Why was I commanding a platoon when I wasn't an officer? Because I kept refusing promotions; I didn't want to be an officer. Once I was lying in the hospital and witnessed the following scene. They would send home a wounded soldier or sergeant for six months' leave and re-registration. They'd go home, and six months later they were to go to the commission, which would reassign them and send them back into the army. First, all this time he'd get to live at home. Secondly, he could go to work and receive an exemption from active duty. Meanwhile, an officer was sent to the military commission or into a separate regiment of reserve officers, or even somewhere else into a 'hot command'. Officers weren't allowed to go home. Was it because I was braver than others? No, I simply also wanted the chance to go home in case of a wound.

The march to the Dnepr was a hard one. It would begin each evening as soon as it got dark and continue until dawn, or even until the middle of the day. Each night, we in our boots and foot wrappings would march 40 kilometres. We marched along a road that had been ground by our boots and horse-drawn wagons into the finest dust powder, which coated our uniforms and made it hard to breathe. Every few days rain would fall, which turned this dust into impassable muck, making every step enormously difficult. The soaked, exhausted men and horses were a pathetic sight. Soon we not only stopped singing, we were prohibited from smoking or speaking loudly. So we marched silently; only the mess kits and gun would softly clank and rattle. Someone smoked a cigarette on the sly; the others hissed at him and swore at him for possibly unmasking the column. The mud adhered to the wagons, forming enormous clods around the hubs of the wheels. The soldiers hunched over under the weight of their wet greatcoats and ammunition. I can't even imagine how the crews of the heavy machine guns or the 82-mm mortars could carry not only their own personal weapon and gear, but also the heavy base plates and tubes of the mortars or the mounts and the machine guns through this mud! Incidentally, we artillerymen didn't even think of lightening our load by placing our carbines or rucksacks on the limber or gun trails – we felt sorry for the horses. I remember walking behind the gun, having clasped my hands around a bevel of the gun barrel, and having rested my chin on them, I'd sleep while on the move. Some men, having fallen asleep, would wander off the road and fall into the roadside ditches. Such a soldier would spring to his feet and begin to rush around in fear, unable to figure out what had happened or where he was.

We were fed in the evening and at dawn. It was unlikely that anyone monitored the cook or the slop he was preparing. It happened that they'd pass out lentil soup, but in your mess kit you'd find one solitary lentil – no meat, nothing other than broth. At the gun we'd receive a loaf of bread, and with a piece of string we'd strive to cut it into equal-sized portions according to the number of men. One of the men would turn his back, while another would cover a portion with the palm of his hand and ask, 'Whose?' The man with his back turned would give a name, and that man would receive that piece of bread. Meanwhile, you're swallowing your saliva and dreaming that you'll get the ends – there's a bit more bread in them. True, once they cooked some rice kasha with milk for us. If you tell this to another veteran, he won't believe you. I never ate a whiter, tastier kasha in my life. What an aroma it had!

In the daylight hours they'd arrange for halts in villages or in patches of woods. Everyone slept like the dead. There were no Germans nearby, and their airplanes weren't making an appearance. Only once, in the morning, as we were marching past some orchards, a twin-engine aircraft, flashing in the sunlight, came roaring low overhead and passed along our column. I made out a dragon painted on its nose and could see the pilot, who was shaking his fist at us.

My soldiers asked, 'Commander, why is your face pale?'

'It's nothing. If he takes a crack at us, we'll all immediately hit the dirt.'

We were lucky. He pulled into a climbing turn and departed, without firing a single shot. Perhaps he was out of ammunition, or maybe he was carrying out a more important mission. Some men began firing their rifles at him only after he was already climbing away. See, I wasn't the only one who'd been given a scare . . .

The closer we approached the Dnepr, the more frequently we encountered devastated villages and fallen trees. The Germans were trying to lay the left [eastern] bank of the river bare, so that the troops closing on the river couldn't find any cover.

I recall when we reached the river. I'm from Kiev, and there is no river dearer to me than the Dnepr. In my childhood I swam across it, but only in certain places, where I knew the current might sweep you to a shoal of the opposite bank. This time, however, I had to swim across it three times – neither out of bravery nor of my own volition. Somewhere around 10 or 12 September, the regiment was called to form up on a hillside. It was cloudy, raw and damp. A thin, wearisome rain was falling. Everyone walked towards the place of formation quietly and dejectedly; there was no sound of conversation or jokes. Hardly anyone snuck a smoke. The soldiers in their heavy, thoroughly saturated greatcoats kept slipping on the mud, and their foot wrappings were becoming unwound. Recently, the number of formation assemblies had perceptibly increased, as well as the number of speakers at them. Some sort of new orators, which I'd never seen before, appeared.

However, this time it turned out that the new regiment commander Plutakhin, who had replaced the previous commander after he'd been killed in the summer fighting, had arrived in order to hand out medals to the personnel. He said something; I could hardly hear him. Suddenly someone jostled me: 'Go on, they're calling for you.' All I could say was 'Huh?' But then I heard, 'Junior Sergeant Ulianov for the Order of the Patriotic War First Degree.' In my wet greatcoat, I made my way down the slope. I walked up and reported that I was there to receive a medal, but the regiment commander stretched out his hand in front of himself and was twirling the medal. Gazing at it, he said, 'What a beauty!' I took hold of his hand and declared, 'I serve the Soviet Union!' Then I spun around and returned to my place in the formation. Guys were clapping me on the shoulder and asking to see the medal. Gleefully, of course! Our mood brightened considerably. All was well.

That night we set off on another march. I allowed the guys to move along the dry roadside, while I, as I've already mentioned, slogged along behind the gun. Understand, I was just 18 years of age. I was the youngest platoon commander, and I had to command men even twice my age. Everything that happens in the platoon depends on the platoon commander – everything. You had to make the soldiers know that you'd praise them for the good, bawl them out for the bad and that you didn't encourage snitching and didn't like slackers. You had to take care of the platoon, keep watch over it, to make sure the men always had full bellies, and always had shells and fodder for the horses. You had to know how to take up proper firing positions. At each halt, I made certain each gun was calibrated, so therefore we always fired accurately. Everything depends on the platoon commander!

Just before crossing the Dnepr, I happened to shoot my friend Vania Frolov through the leg. The incident occurred after I was summoned by the battalion commander. I must say that the battalion commander Ivan Anikeevich Zvezdin was a very smart man. Rumours went around that he was a former colonel who'd been demoted for an *affaire d'amour*, because in our opinion, only a colonel could command in the way he did, take charge in his fashion, and have such an air of authority. In reality, his education consisted of just eight grades and courses for junior lieutenants, but he had combat experience from Khasan and the Winter War with Finland, which apparently enabled him to handle the battalion competently. So anyway, I departed as the fellows were beginning to prepare dinner. I returned from it when the battalion was already turning out for the next march.

I walked up to our tent. My soldiers were sitting inside, and in front of them an enamelled pot was hanging on forked branches, in which some borsch was cooking, which was emanating an intoxicating aroma. I shouted at them, 'Why haven't you gotten your butts in gear?'

'Commander, what are you fussing about? Sit, have a bite. Just take a look at the borsch we've prepared!'

That's when I lost it. I grabbed my pistol and fired into this borsch, thinking I would shoot a hole through the pot and show them that discipline was more important. However, the bullet ricocheted and struck Ivan in the calf muscle. Thank God, the bone wasn't hit and the guys agreed to hush up the incident, but for several days I had him ride on the gun, because he couldn't walk.

Once in the middle of the night, word passed along the column, 'The regiment commander, the regiment commander.' I turned around, and on the right behind some trees I saw two riders on horses. Then they disappeared somewhere. We marched on to the next halt. There the road made a sharp turn to the left, creating a dry salient, upon which we set up the gun. I requested pearl-barley kasha for dinner, something I never ate in civilian life. After eating, I told the men, 'That's all! I'm getting some shut-eye.' I threw a tent half down on the ground, laid down on it, and immediately fell asleep. Suddenly I heard, 'Get up, the regiment commander!' I heard and understood that I needed to get up, but I couldn't. I had no strength to rise to my feet. Then I heard, 'I'm the regiment commander.' I said, 'You can go to hell . . .' – and with these words I opened my eyes. I saw the commander's orderly and the regiment commander himself were actually standing there; the commander was trying to throw back a flap of the tent half he was wearing in order to draw his pistol. When I saw this, I stretched and grabbed my submachine gun, which was lying nearby. He understood everything, turned, and they galloped away.

My men said, 'What have you done?'

'What? I didn't know that it was the regiment commander; I thought you were fooling around.'

The march resumed. The next morning we stopped in some village. The day turned out to be sunny, and we hung out all our stuff to dry it a bit. In the middle of the day, two well-groomed sergeants showed up:

'Are you Ulianov?'

'That's me.'

'Give your name.'

'Sergeant Ulianov.'

'Grab your things, let's go.'

'What should I take?'

'Whatever you'd like; you don't have to bring anything.'

'Where are we going?'

'To regiment headquarters.'

I could see everyone's faces were sour. I said, 'Let me say goodbye to the men, just in case.'

They escorted me to the headquarters, the chief of which knew me back from Stalingrad. He asked me, 'What are you doing here?'

'They've escorted me.'

'So it was you that acted strangely last night?'

'I wasn't acting strangely. I was groggy; it was simply a case of mistaken identity.'

'OK, let's go.'

We entered a courtyard, in the middle of which were a table, two chairs and a stool. A combat blouse and shoulder belt were draped over one chair; the regiment commander himself in his undershirt, suspenders and polished boots was sitting on the other one, drinking tea from a cup with a cup holder.

'Comrade Lieutenant Colonel, Sergeant Ulianov has arrived at your order.'

He asked me a question: 'Were you the one who sent me to hell last night?'

What could I say? I acknowledged that I was the one.

'I presented you with a handsome Order, and you're sending me to hell?'

'I earned the Order before you arrived in the regiment.'

Then he turned to the chief of staff and said, 'Take him away.'

They took me into the next courtyard, where 114 men like me had gathered. Someone said, 'We're a penal company.' There'd been no trial, and they didn't take away my documents and Order. After the war I found a document, in which we were referred to as 'volunteers'. They passed out grenades and cartridges to us, and said, 'You will cross over to the opposite bank of the stream in front of us and seize a bridgehead. As soon as you make a landing, the main forces will push off. With this, your task will be fulfilled.'

We swam across that night. There was no firing. We clambered out of the water on the opposite bank. But what could we do there? In front of us was the wall of the right bank, which rose about 40 metres above the water. That was our entire lodgement. The Germans up above began to rain fire down on us, and by evening, when the order arrived to return to the left bank, there was not more than ten of us left. The survivors were released back to their own units. The regiment moved further downstream and began a crossing there.

We approached the Dnepr in the evening. A church and belfry were visible on the opposite bank. The battalion commander ordered me to open fire at this church, suspecting the likely presence of an observer there. We rolled the gun up to the water. I understood quite well that if I fired a shot, I'd immediately come under fire from machine guns at least. In order to conceal the gun, I ordered for some of the shoreline brush to be cut down and to stick the cut branches into the sand around the gun. Once the gun was concealed, I ordered a tent half to be stretched over the barrel, in order to hide the flash of the shot from observers.

We determined that the range to the belfry exceeded 700 metres, for which the sight of the 45-mm gun had been set. Knowing that one turn of the elevation mechanism would increase the range of the shot by 300 metres, I set it for 1,400 metres. I fired and for the first time heard the rustle of the outgoing shell. I missed the belfry. The shell exploded short of it, throwing up a white cloud of dust. We saw this cloud first, and then the sound of the explosion and the yelling and screaming of Germans carried to our ears. On the next day I was informed by some scouts that had been over there that the Germans had dug some trenches in front of this church and a machine gun had been positioned there. My shell had precisely blanketed this machine-gun nest.

We rolled the gun back to the road, and down a dirt road that was edged by planted willows we moved to the crossing place. Soon we saw the raft that had been designated for us. In general, one had to have quite an imagination to call what we saw a 'raft', which simply consisted of several logs that had been bound together, a total of about 3 to 3.5 metres wide and covered with plank boards. We were separated from the water by a strip of wet sand, patterned by the waves washing up against it. As soon as the limber, upon which we always had fourteen to sixteen boxes filled with shells, drove out onto the sand, its wheels sank almost up to the hubs. The drivers lashed the horses so hard that the metallic rings attached to the ends of the whips scattered sparks that fell on the hides of the unfortunate animals. The loading process was accompanied by choice swearing and the shouts of those leading it: 'Faster! Forward!', and by the explosions of German shells and mines. With enormous effort we managed to roll the limber and gun onto the raft and to position the horses.

We pushed off and floated ... that was, for those who weren't there and haven't been able to picture it, the 'forced crossing of the Dnepr River'. This had to be seen and experienced. One had to feel the flimsy flooring of the raft that was rocking on the waves raised by the explosions of shells; to see the geysers of water erupting with the fragments of human bodies, ferries and boats, before crashing back down to the water's surface. One had to hear the frantic whinnying of the horses, which the drivers were holding by the bridle, after each explosion. One had to experience the maddening tension and fear of waiting for the shell that's meant for you, which you never hear, because those shells you do hear whistling and shrieking are flying past you, while 'yours' arrives silently. So you stand there and size up what to grip onto for balance and which way to float, backward or forwards, and whether you'll flounder or sink straight to the bottom in the greatcoat, quilted jacket and cotton trousers, which you didn't remove because they offered protection against the autumn cold.

Yet somehow they missed us ... the raft nosed into the opposite bank and the horses carried the drivers onto the sand. We rolled the gun and limber off the raft and hurried to harness the team. We were being fired upon from above, but no one paid any particular attention to the bullets. With difficulty we made our way up the washed out road that climbed up the steep bank of the Dnepr from the river. By some miracles, in the chaos that reigned on the opposite bank, we found our battalion. The battalion commander embraced me and said, 'Well, sonny, now we'll all live!' We were the battalion's main assault force!

The fighting continued now on the right bank of the Dnepr. Having driven the defending Germans from the riverbank, the battalion went in pursuit. I recall one battle; we were attacking. In the heat of battle, I leaped into a railroad hut with my Parabellum pistol. In front of me was a German. I didn't lose my head, fired, and the German dropped. Through a window I saw another German run out of a different hut. I rushed after him. He ran, limping; plainly he'd been wounded. On the move he threw away a satchel, and then discarded a jacket. Suddenly there were shouts and shots behind me. I stopped. I saw two soldiers pointing their rifles at me, who were shouting 'Where are you going, snake?' When they came up, and once I had managed to convince them that I'd been chasing a German, one said, 'Senior Sergeant, we thought you were running off to their side.' All I could say in response was 'Eh, you let the German get away.'

In one of the battles I knocked out a German self-propelled Sturmgeschütz. True, this time I in fact selected the position not very well. The road was running along the edge of a sand pit, which seemingly had formed a ledge in it before dropping away to the bottom. I set both guns up on this ledge. This way the flash of our shot would be camouflaged by the bright sandy wall behind our backs, but at the same time our ability to manoeuvre was extremely limited. In the valley below us there were the remnants of an orchard, and a bit to our left stood a T-34 tank, next to which a German sniper had deployed. At the order of the battalion commander, I fired several rounds at this tank and the sniper fell silent.

But after I had silenced the sniper, two self-propelled guns moved out toward us from the opposite side of the valley. I don't know if they spotted us, but nevertheless each self-propelled gun fired a round, and a fragment of one exploding shell wounded ammo carrier Vasia Lebedochkin in the butt. Here I must say that although I was now commanding the platoon, I hadn't turned over command of the No. 1 gun to anyone else. Vania Frolov commanded the No. 2 gun. He shouted at me, 'Vitia, fire!', but I was in no hurry. I was confident that as they were descending into the valley, they wouldn't be able to fire at us, while we, having lowered the barrels of our guns, would be firing at their exposed tops.

That's exactly what happened. I clearly saw the top of the leading self-propelled gun's rear compartment in my gun sight and fired. The assault gun stopped. The second gun approached it from behind. We didn't see it, but plainly the Germans hooked up a cable, and reversing away, towed the damaged Sturmgeschütz back to the jumping-off positions. I didn't attempt another shot at them; after all, my task had been carried out, because the Germans didn't pass us.

After the fighting ended, I walked over to check out this T-34 – it had a full load of ammunition on board and the interior was as neat as a pin. Why had it stopped there? Why had its crew abandoned it? I don't know.

Having limbered up the gun and taken our place in the battalion column, we moved on. Toward evening, we took up a defensive position near a knoll. The terrain was heavily convoluted – to the right and left of us there were similar knolls, a small ravine ran across our front, and beyond it was another rise. We were standing on our knoll, next to which ran the road, when suddenly we saw a German amphibious vehicle approaching our position. It came practically right up to us and turned. A German, sitting next to the driver, shouted: '*Russische schwein!*' The chief of staff grabbed an anti-tank grenade and wanted to hurl it, but we stopped him. Where was he going to throw it? If he didn't reach the vehicle with his toss, he might have only wounded his own men. Thus the German vehicle in fact got away.

That night the Germans were launching flares, giving me the impression that we'd been encircled. The battalion commander summoned me: 'Well, what do you think?'

'Comrade Captain, the flares are all around.'

'What did you expect? We're in the German rear. I don't know what will happen here tomorrow, but prepare your platoon for battle.'

That night we dug positions on the reverse slope of the knoll, and the next morning a panzer emerged from the behind the rise that was facing us and headed toward us. It was alone; apparently the Germans had sent it out to probe our positions. The battalion commander ordered me to roll a gun out into the open, to the left of the knoll behind the line of trenches, and to destroy this tank. This was stupidity, of course; this tank would smash my gun before it even had a chance to go into action. I ordered Ivan to roll out his gun to the right of the knoll and to fire several shots at the tank, in order to divert its attention from us. He even asked, 'What if I hit it?'

'That's just what you're supposed to do. You hit it.'

While Ivan fired a couple of shots, we managed to roll out and deploy our gun. I fired, but it was a defective shell. I still don't know why, but the shell's tracer flew off into the bushes, while its rotating band detached and flew downward into a trench where some infantrymen were crouched. One soldier started running away from the trench beside the gun. I fired at him from my pistol, but missed. A few minutes later I looked, and he was back in this trench again, hoisting his rifle over the parapet and firing. I said, 'Why have you come back? You ran off, so why did you return?' He replied, 'There are *osobisty* [officers of the Special Department] over there. They offered me a choice of returning or being shot.' So he came back, and after this no one else ran off. The panzer, however, didn't particularly meditate over this. It fired once and then made itself scarce.

At this time, we noticed about a half-kilometre to our right that the Germans were preparing for a counterattack. Several armoured personnel carriers and vehicles had driven up to there, and German troops began to leap from them like grasshoppers. I shouted, 'Ivan, fire at the far side of their concentration and chase them toward the centre, while I'll fire at the near side.'

After each round they packed in toward the middle. Then we shifted fire onto the mass. The Germans would scatter and then we'd repeat the pattern. At some moment, a German vehicle appeared that was towing a gun. They managed to unhook it, but then I interrupted their work. My shell exploded next to the gun. I'm not saying that I damaged the gun, but after my shot they abandoned it and the vehicle drove away. I hit a vehicle that had driven up behind the first one. It plainly had been loaded with shells, because it produced secondary explosions.

Later, an assault gun came rolling toward me. It wasn't an ordinary Sturmgeschütz, but a heavy self-propelled gun. I was firing at it, but I couldn't hit it – my hands were trembling and the shells passed harmlessly overhead. It kept advancing, and squeaking like a door on rusty hinges. Then this pest stopped and fired in the direction of the No. 2 gun. Shell fragments wounded Ivan. Then at last, if not with my eighth round, then with my ninth round I hit my target. It didn't start burning; it simply stopped, while I continued to batter the Germans. The gun barrel grew hot, and practically speaking it was by now simply spitting out the shells. I was afraid that it would jam, because over a short interval of time I had fired more than 120 shells! It was then that I began running back and forth between the two guns, alternately firing my own gun and then Ivan's. That's how two 45-mm guns in effect broke up an enemy counterattack in strength of up to a battalion.

I took part in my final battle on 22 October 1943. The day before, the battalion commander had gathered his company commanders in a small ravine. He had called for me as well. I walked up to him, and he asked, 'Do you have ammunition?' I replied, 'I do' (indeed, the cover of my canteen had been stuffed with automatic cartridges, which were of the same calibre as my TT pistol). The battalion commander loaded the pistol, fired several rounds in the air, and said: 'The 2nd and 3rd Battalions at the regiment commander's order have gone to clean potatoes for our dinner. We'll come back from battle and eat. But now, for the Motherland, for Stalin, we must take that village over there. Well, sonny, lend us a hand.'

The company commanders headed back to their companies at a run, while I returned to my platoon. We climbed up out of this small depression in the ground, and I saw the village. At this moment the horses started to dash, and I just managed to climb onto the lower gun shield and to grab hold of it with my hands. The drivers began to lash the horses, and they bolted away at such speed that it was terrifying. We flew past a large barn standing to the left of the road, and that's when I caught sight of a woman rising up out of some burdock that had grown down the side of it and was covering a cellar. We almost ran right over her. We flew into this village. There were no Germans in it. The infantry entered it in our wake and immediately began to poke around in an abandoned German vehicle parked in the street.

Gradually everything quieted down, and we took positions next to some buildings. Suddenly bursts of automatic weapons fire rang out in our rear. I leaned out of a building and saw Germans coming, sweeping the area in front of them with fire. They passed down the street, overran a mortar battery, wiped out its crews, and then exited the village to link up with their own forces. It turned out that before retreating, the Germans had rounded up all the residents into that barn that we had passed on our way into the village, but they had remained in a few of the village's buildings that we failed to search. When they realized that we had settled down, they decided to break out back to friendly lines, and in this they were fully successful.

The following day proved to be sunny. I was sitting in an arbour and writing letters recommending all my soldiers and sergeants for medals, including one for Frolov that wrote him up for the highest honour, 'Hero of the Soviet Union'. Then suddenly shells began exploding in the village. I rushed pell-mell to my gun, which stood between two buildings. Then once again, like the German infantry the evening before, enemy armoured personnel carriers from our rear started passing us. My field of fire was very narrow, so I decided to move the gun, but I hadn't managed to bring together the split trails when the battalion commander came running up: 'Don't touch the gun! Don't touch the gun! Otherwise they'll start to run!'

I glanced to my right and saw a weak line of prone soldiers who were firing through the gaps between the buildings, and realized that they were lying there and firing only because my guns were here. If I started to move it, they'd think that I was retreating and they'd start to run. So I decided to remain where I was and fire from this unsatisfactory position. However, I did well. I had a 'short conversation' with one halftrack – I struck it in the side and it obligingly blazed up. I left two or three burning. A panzer came rolling by after them and I also knocked it out. Nevertheless, the German main forces broke out and departed without getting involved in combat.

Soon a messenger from the battalion command post came running up to me and told me that I was wanted by the battalion commander. I went to see him at his observation post, which had been set up on the outskirts of the village in some depression in front of the last building. A plowed field stretched beyond this depression, on the far edge of which was a German earth and timbered bunker. The battalion commander said, 'Do you see that bunker?'

'I see it.'

'That's a German observation post. It must be knocked out. Can you hit the embrasure?'

'I can hit it with an armour-piercing round.'

'It isn't important what you use; you must hit it in the embrasure to blind them. We're about to go on the attack, and if they can correct their artillery fire from there, they'll wipe us out.'

I went to get my gun, brought it back, and with my third shot struck the embrasure. I returned to the battalion commander to report that his order had been carried out. At that moment a shell exploded behind the building, followed by another explosion in front of the shell hole in which we were sitting. The battalion commander asked me, 'Well, isn't the artillery the god of war? What's happening?' I told him, 'They've got us bracketed, that's what is happening. The next shells will be right on top of us.'

At this moment, I believe two shells exploded next to our shell hole. At first I didn't even realize I'd been wounded in the left arm and in the left and right legs. I told the battalion commander, 'Now the parasites have shredded my boots.'

'What about your legs?'

'My legs are intact. I'll go to my gun.'

'That's not important, sonny. If your legs were intact, we'd find your boots.'

I rose, crawled out of the shell hole, and felt that I was falling. I grabbed a tree, and then pushed myself off to move on. I heard the battalion commander say, 'There goes my hero.'

The next thing I remember was this trench, in which two drivers of my platoon were sitting. I asked them to help me reach my gun, but they had no desire to climb out of the trench under the unceasing barrage and they refused ... I woke up later in another trench. In front of me a soldier was sitting. I asked him, 'Where are ours?'

'They've all gone forward.'

'The battalion commander?'

'They've all left. You and several other wounded men have remained behind.'

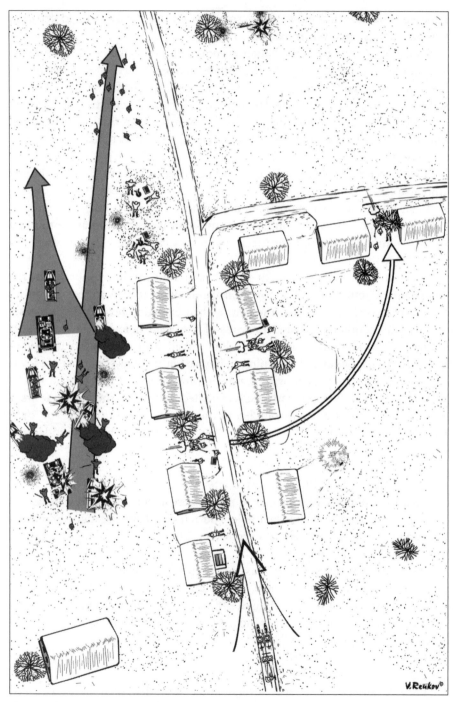

Diagram showing the last battle fought by Vitaly Ulianov.

Later I read that the battalion commander and many of the men were killed in this battle.

When night fell, an ambulance came for us. Where it took us, I don't know, but soon we were hearing German speech. I whispered to the driver, 'Where are you taking us, swine?' We turned around and headed back, and soon we reached the regimental headquarters. They stopped us and asked where we were going. I identified myself and asked who was in charge here. They replied that it was the regimental chief of staff. I asked them to pass the word to him that I wanted to see him. He came up: 'What? Have you been hit?'

'I've been hit.'

'Well, think nothing of it. You'll get better and come back.'

I had a pouch tucked into my belt, from which I pulled out all my medal recommendations for my men, and asked, 'Comrade Major, I request that you recommend my men for medals. Everything has been written down here; all the truth is in these letters.'

'We'll do it. Don't worry.'

Later they took me to some hut and laid me down on the dirt floor. Wounded men were lying on either side of me. I saw how maggots were crawling out from under the bandages on the arm of the guy on my left. I even exclaimed, 'Yuck, maggots!'

'What are you afraid of? They're eating the rotten flesh.'

I fell silent.

The next day, a general and two officers arrived. The general asked, 'Who here is Sergeant Ulianov?'

'I am.'

'Son, I congratulate you on the receipt of the title 'Hero of the Soviet Union'.'

'I serve the Soviet Union!'

Later I found myself on a medical train, which took me to Khar'kov. A captain arrived, took me by the arms and weighed me – I weighed 47 kilograms. He carried me to a bath house. There, a women said, 'Get undressed.' I was embarrassed. The captain spoke up, 'This is our Hero.' One of the women replied, 'Why, he's all skin and bones. What sort of hero is he?!' They washed me and then carried me into a school. There were beds standing in a classroom, and they laid me on one of them. Several fragments had become lodged in the vicinity of the knee joint. The doctors that came and examined my leg said that they could do nothing and assigned me to an evacuation hospital.

I was again loaded onto a medical train. It was clean and freshly painted. I was lying on a lower berth, but I wasn't given a pillow, a blanket, or anything. We went to Zlatoust. My right leg began to swell and be painful. I began to knock for help. A nurse arrived.

'Why are you knocking?'

'My leg hurts.'

'The head doctor on the train is busy; he's conducting an operation.'

'I don't need the head doctor. I need for you to re-bandage my leg.'

She looked at the leg and left. Soon my temperature went up. Then a surgeon arrived, the head doctor. He brought some trays with him. He said, 'What's up? We'll see what kind of hero you are.'

They opened the abscess; the devil knows how both blood and pus gushed out! The surgeon said, 'Well, is it better?'

'It's better.'

'Tough it out a bit more. Now we'll extract the fragments.'

He began to dig around under the knee.

'Is it painful?'

'Yes.'

'Then we won't extract them. You'll be going to a hospital anyway. There they'll wash everything, clean it all out, and give you a new dressing.'

However, in the hospital they made no attempt to extract the fragments. So even today, I walk around with them, with these fragments.

Notes

1. Army Detachment Kempf, which was attacking in the sector defended by the 92nd Guards Rifle Division, had no Panthers. The author is misremembering.
2. 'Vlasovite' was the Russian term for members of the anti-communist Russian Liberation Army, which was commanded by General Andrei Vlasov. However, the term was liberally applied by Red Army soldiers to any Slav found serving with the Wehrmacht.

Chapter 3

There were No Long-term Survivors

Nikolay Dmitrievich Markov

I was born in Moscow on 19 May 1925. We had a large family – there were seven kids in it. In 1941 my older brother was finishing the 10th grade in School No. 605 in Maryina Roshcha. I was an 8th grade student of School No. 241, which was located nearby on Sheremetev Street. My brother's graduation night was to take place on 21 June. Since we were friends with these 10th graders, they also invited us to their celebration. We made merry until 6 o'clock in the morning – it was great! We then went home, went to sleep, but we were soon woken up: 'Kids, get up, war has started.'

When air raids on the city began, the children of the higher grades were made to climb up onto the roofs to toss away incendiaries. Of course I remember the panic of 16 October 1941 as well. All of Moscow stopped working, everything was cast aside and looting of workshops, warehouses and shops began. I also recall piles of German leaflets that had been dropped over the city, which called upon us to surrender.

One still had to survive somehow, and I went to work in the USSR's Prosecutor General's Office as a labourer. I did crap work – carrying all kinds of cargo and so forth. However, I also received a labourer's card, which provided me with 800 grams of bread a day. Office employees received 600 grams, while children were allowed 400 grams. We were all hungry in the winter of 1941/ 1942. Everyone pulled together; we became thin and gaunt, but not rancourous – we understood that a war was going on. At the time, there really was a general patriotic mood among the people.

At the end of October, when the Germans were approaching Moscow, the housing management lined all the adolescents up into a file and sent us off to the Northwestern Front to the vicinity of Dmitrov, in order to build anti-tank barriers. For two months we laboured to chop down trees and built anti-tank obstacles. The front was not far away – German *Ramy* ['Frames', the Russian nickname for the German FW-189 twin-boom reconnaissance aircraft] were flying and calling in fire on us, and we would take cover. The conditions were primitive, of course.

There were thirty of us from the Dzerzhinsky District, and we all were billeted in a school. The snow fell early that winter, and freezing temperatures started in the month of November. Getting up at 5 o'clock in the morning, we would thus head to our place of work 7 kilometres away on skis. The daily norm for a work team of 5 people (with 2 saws and 1 axe per team) was 125 trees, and each tree had to have a diameter of at least 25 centimetres. Only once this was done would you receive your rations. We had no lunches! We were given only black, frozen bread. Then you'd head back to your quarters, returning in the darkness. That's how we lived in this school: no showers, absolutely nothing. We all became lice-ridden. Only when our winter counteroffensive began, around 10 December, did they let us go home.

I was drafted on 23 January 1943. At first there was the intention to send us to a specialist school, but for some reason instead we were assigned to a training company of the 1st Reserve 'Gor'ky' Rifle Brigade. They loaded approximately forty Muscovite men into unheated cattle cars – we were totally out of luck. The train from Moscow to Gor'ky took four days. We'd travel 100 kilometres without any firewood. They'd send work teams into the forests to get lumps of wood for the tender.

In Gor'ky, we and approximately sixty more draftees from Yaroslavl Oblast were billeted in the Red Barracks. I wound up in a training 45-mm gun battery. We trained for 12 hours a day – we receive basic training, and then more specialized artillery training, including learning how to sight and fire the guns.

It was the winter of 1943, the month of January. We would cross the Volga to an artillery range in Bor. Our platoon commander was Lieutenant Prituliak – a combative officer who'd been invalidated out of the acting army after being wounded. Here's how he'd drive us in training: 'Tanks on the right, prepare to fire!' – We'd pivot the gun; 'All clear!' – We'd stand down for a bit; 'Tanks on the right! . . . Tanks behind! . . . Tanks on the left!' Even as we were travelling to the artillery range, we'd be exhausted. But we were fed! We received 600 grams of bread, gruel and a bucket of frozen potatoes per sixteen men. We divided the bread with a piece of string. Everyone wanted an end slice . . . over one month I immediately lost 13 kilograms of weight.

From Gor'ky, in the month of June 1943 we were sent to the Kursk Bulge. I wound up in the infantry, in the 2nd Guards Airborne Division's 5th Guards Airborne Regiment. So I began my service as an infantryman. However, platoon commander Prituliak took my friend Kostia Konakhistov along with him into a battery of 45-mm guns. Kostia and I met during our training in Gorky. He was from the small town of Uglich. We slept on the same double-level plank bed. All the cadets suffered from enuresis and so we switched our positions every night to piss on each other in turns. I'd drop by to see him: 'Kostia, how are things?'

'Okay.'

Then after one battle, I went by to see him, and I asked the guys, 'Where's my brother Kostia?'

'He's been badly wounded in the stomach.'

I returned to my company and said, 'Guys, Kostia has been killed. Let's have a drink in his memory and toss back 100 grams each.' We drank the 100 grams – and then onward, to the West. Later I even forgot about Kostia. The war came to an end and thirty-five years passed – then in September 1978, we met entirely by chance. I looked, and his hair was grey. We embraced and started crying. It turned out that he'd been hospitalized and survived his wound, and in 1944 he was invalidated out of the Red Army.

My first battle was a night combat at Kursk. We went on the attack, and the Germans pinned us down with fire. We hit the dirt; there was darkness all around. The battalion commander was shouting, 'Forward, forward!' The bullets were whistling and tracers were flying. The mood was that no one wanted to advance into that fire. Everyone was prone and digging in. But I didn't have a shovel. Just try to dig into the ground with your nose! I decided that if somehow I survived, I'd find a shovel. Later in one village I found a real Sovok (square-pointed) shovel. The shaft split in two the first time I used it, and that's how I continued to carry the damned thing until I found a regular, small sapper's spade. After this I never discarded a shovel or spade, because it was your life – you'd march and it would be attached to your rucksack, and as soon as you halted, you'd immediately start digging in. That was the law. Just so: you had to have a shovel, your rifle in working order, and you had to know your assignment clearly – all the rest was fate.

Well, returning to my first battle, the platoon commander said, 'Markov, go to the company commander. Tell him that we're pinned down and can't advance, because the German has blanketed us with fire.'

I head out crawling back on my belly, I look, and I see a soldier lying there. In the light of a German flare, I could see that a fragment had ripped apart his chest. He wasn't saying anything, just mumbling. I bandaged him, but he just kept lying there, saying nothing. . . . In general I was afraid of blood as a child. But in the infantry you got used to anything. You'd be sitting in a trench, eating something. A shell would explode nearby and hurl dirt into your cooking tin – you'd just fish it out with a spoon and keep eating. Everything was filthy, and there was nowhere to wash your hands. You bandage a comrade – every-thing's bloody and totally unsanitary. As far as you could, of course, you tried to keep yourself clean, but you weren't always able to do so . . .

Anyway, I carried out my assignment, returned, and we spent the entire night lying under this fire. We hurriedly dug in (someone gave me a shovel).

Then our artillery joined in, pounded the German firing positions, and we moved on ahead.

We liberated Orel, Belgorod, Kursk, and then entered the Ukraine. By 1943 we knew how to fight. Before sending the infantry forward, first we'd work over the German forward zone with all types of weapons. Artillery, aviation and tanks would play. It wasn't like 1941 and 1942, when we plugged holes in the line with infantry! Indeed, the infantry was now seasoned, and the commanders by now had learned how to fight.

If you stood long on the defence, then you did the following: your front lines are here, and the German front line is over there. With the help of aerial photography and scouts, we determined where the German firing positions were, where their minefields were, and so forth. The companies that were to breach the German defences were pulled back into the rear and would rehearse their attacks against recreations of the sector they were to assault – the commanders would *in situ* work out solutions to tactical obstacles. It was no longer simply, 'Come on, charge!', though we still had enough petty tyrants who drove their men: 'Let's go, get moving, charge!'

At first I fought with a rifle, and then later with a PPSh submachine gun and a TT pistol. Once my submachine gun quit working for some reason and I picked a rifle up off the battlefield. I fired, and the bullet plowed into the ground just feet away. Huh? I was confused. I peered down the barrel of the gun, and it was warped like a bow. Of course, I threw this rifle away and found another one. I didn't have a problem with it. We did have grenades, but primarily we stunned fish with them. After all, what's a grenade? It's a burden. At night, when you're making a 30-kilometre march, you kept step. When the column halted, you'd drop where you were and sleep. In order to rouse the soldiers, the commanders would go running down the line of sleeping men, kicking them with their boots: 'Get up!' The men were fighting to the limits of their strength. So grenades were fine on the defence, but you wouldn't lug them around with you on the offensive – we tossed them away. After all, we were also carrying our weapon, extra ammunition, rations, a change of underwear, a mess kit, a shovel. It was all cumbersome . . .

If it comes to the weapon I liked, then of course it would be our Mosin 1890/30 rifle. It was utterly reliable. You could drag it through sand, clean it, and keep firing. Its bullet keeps its stopping power out to 5 kilometres, while the PPSh and PPS are lethal only out to about 400–500 metres, but are only accurate out to 150 metres. Moreover the PPSh and PPS were very touchy and capricious weapons. Even as we were just heading to the front aboard a train, we lost nineteen men because of improper handling of the gun or accidental discharges.

Altogether I took part in thirteen attacks. In this phase of the war, the Germans were retreating, but they'd create a rear guard detachment in the villages. In order to drive it out, they'd send a company or a battalion. We'd attack, and the German rear guard would cut you to pieces. The fire and movement were poorly organized. The soldiers would run and shout 'Ura!' but not fire. That was bad. So many men we lost! Around fifty men would go into an attack, and only 20 would emerge from it. There'd be dead and wounded ... This was war ... By September 1943 there weren't any of the men left in my platoon, with whom I'd started. The platoon was constantly being rebuilt and men were always rotating in and out of it. Indeed I can't say that there was any sort of group of long-term survivors. No, there wasn't. But as for the Germans, I didn't have hatred toward them and I never witnessed German prisoners being shot.

We were 30 kilometres from Kiev, in the vicinity of Brovary, when I went on my thirteenth attack. I was wounded in it. A bullet struck me in the groin from the left. I woke up in a hospital. There they patched me up and sent me to the front again. First we were sent to a replacement depot in the vicinity of Zhitomir, into a convalescent battalion, and there they provided a little more treatment (someone's hand hadn't healed, someone else's leg; this, that and the other) ... We were 140 men in the convalescent battalion. Once we were sitting on a knoll next to a church. The sun was warm ... We see the Mass is ending, all the old men and women have left the church, and the priest comes out: 'In honour of the Russian Army, I'll hold a service for you.' So we went inside, all 147 men of every nationality – even Uzbeks, Georgians and Jews. How the priest preached to us! That was real propaganda! You don't need any sort of political worker – just a priest like that one! I still recall how he spoke: 'You must drive out this foe! He has desecrated our land! ...'

'Shoppers' from the army arrived at this replacement depot one day, saying 'Replacements are needed for a regiment.' I thought: 'Enough. I won't go into the infantry, only into the artillery.' Why? Because I had marched in the ranks of the infantry from Kursk almost all the way to Kiev. In the infantry one had the clear perception that sooner or later, you'd be killed or wounded. And then ... Well, it was simply impossible! Your feet are all bloody. You have to lug everything. You have no tent: rain is falling, it's wet, and you have nowhere to find shelter. You're in the field, you have no escape, and if you do escape, you're a deserter. It was all very hard. However, everybody and his brother relied on the infantry – it is the queen of the battlefield.

In the training regiment, we received good artillery training, so I knew both the types of shells and could calculate firing data. But now two senior lieutenants and a captain were sitting in front of me: 'What is your military specialty?'

'Specialty No. 7. Artilleryman.'

'Reference mark 28, where is the battery?'

'Left front.'

'What types of shells do you know?'

'Armour-piercing, high-explosive fragmentation, armour-piercing discarding sabot.'

'Fine. You will be serving in a destroyer anti-tank artillery regiment as a gun loader.'

Screw it! I thought I'd at least be fighting a little further from the front . . .

They directed me to the 3rd Battery of the 163rd Separate Destroyer Anti-tank Artillery Regiment, where I indeed became a gun loader. The regiment had been destroyed at Vinnitsa, having lost all its equipment and almost 90 per cent of its personnel. The fellows that had survived and had arrived at the re-forming said that very hard fighting had gone on there. The unit reformed in Zhitomir. We received our personnel and equipment (ZIS-3 76-mm guns and Studebaker trucks), and soon set off to the front under our own power.

From January to June 1944, we stood on the defence near Kovel'. This meant a lot of digging! Just as soon as we occupied our firing positions, we immediately had to dig an emplacement for the gun – 6 cubic metres; and then you had to dig a slit trench for yourself, for the gun layer, for the loader, and a communications trench. How much earth we moved! At Kovel' some guys from the western Ukraine joined us. I recall one of these new conscripts – a fine Ukrainian, tall, nice, about 35 years of age. He died in a senseless manner. We were standing around the gun. We heard an incoming shell. We all shouted, 'Hit the dirt!' But he was afraid to make his greatcoat filthy – the mud was awful there. At the last moment he nevertheless began to drop, but a shell fragment struck him in the chest, killing him . . .

One of our replacements was a guy named Petr Alimpovich Peretiat'ko, born in the year 1913, from the village of Dubrovka in Chernigov Oblast. Before the war he had commanded a battery and had participated in the Finnish and Polish campaigns. In 1941, he and his battery had been standing on the Bug River. Their regiment was smashed, and he together with one of his guns and twelve men tried to get out of the encirclement. They were taken prisoner. He was imprisoned in Koshary, Poland. He escaped, but they caught him, tied him to a rack, carved strips out of his skin, and left him there. Military prisoners tended to him. He was successful on his second escape attempt and managed to get back to his own home. When Chernigov was liberated in 1943, he went up to a regiment commander and said, 'I'm a senior lieutenant and battery commander. I was a prisoner, but I escaped.'

'You know that there's not time to look into your case. Grab a rifle and fall in.'

They gave him a rifle; he fell in and immediately went into a battle. After the battle, the regiment commander summoned him and told him, 'Get ready for your rank to be restored.'

'I don't want to be an officer; I want to fight as a private!'

Later he was wounded and after his discharge from the hospital, he wound up with us.

He was a real warrior! A genuine artilleryman! He said to me, 'You *katsap* [goat face[1]]! I'll teach you how you need to fight!' Indeed, he really did teach us kids how we had to fight. When Petia took position at the dial sight, that was it – he wouldn't leave it no matter how much fire we were taking. We'd all pile into a trench, but he'd remain standing.

There was this case once. Petrov, a soldier from Gor'ky and a most dapper guy, had worn out his boots, and there were a lot of dead Germans lying out in front of our position. He went out and took the boots off one of them. He came back and said, 'I found boots!' Petia asked him, 'Where did you get them?'

'Off of a German.'

Then Petia raised his submachine gun and pointed it at Petrov: 'Wherever you got them, put them back. You know what this is called? Plundering! Go around in bare feet, but don't take them!'

There's a man for you! Petia was our unspoken platoon commander. The official platoon commander was a 'six-month' junior lieutenant named Mukhin.[2] Petia would say to him: 'Mukha, where did you deploy your guns? If you don't carry out your assignment, you'll end up getting people killed. You must put one gun here, and the other one there. Understood?'[3]

'Precisely so.'

'Then get going and get it done!'

When we fought with Petia, we didn't have a single non–combat loss, while other batteries did. He and I would sleep side by side – one greatcoat underneath us, one greatcoat over us, so as to keep a bit warmer.

One day we decided to organize a bath for everyone. We occupied a hut and heated up some water. We heated our combat blouses to get rid of the lice. We're washing ourselves, and that's when Messerschmidts appeared overhead and circled briefly before coming in on a strafing pass ... the regiment headquarters was in the building next to our bath house. The Germans were targeting it. Naked, we went scrambling out of the hut in different directions. I dove into another hut. A bomb struck the regiment headquarters, killing the chief of staff, the deputy chief of staff, and a female signaller on the staff.

There, at Kovel, our gun was smashed and we fought as machine gunners – each crew also had a Maksim machine gun. We were standing at the front on the defence, and the Germans were also hunkered down on the defensive. We couldn't fire, lest we revealed our firing positions. In order to give us a bit of practice, one day they pulled us out of the line in order to fire from concealed positions about 6 kilometres behind the front lines. There the battery commander saw a prepared firing position for 122-mm howitzers. Four emplacements, communication trenches – everything had been thoroughly prepared. He decided to deploy the battery in it. He then ordered the scout platoon with portable radios to return to the front: they identified targets and prepared the firing data. All the crews were at their guns, but at first only the No. 1 gun fired. After it zeroed in on the target, we made the necessary corrections to all the guns' settings and then rapidly fired five shells at the target. We hit it or didn't – we didn't really care. We were resting. It was the month of May and the weather was splendid. We were at the rear! We could walk around at full height! No one's shooting at us. It was a real luxury after being at the front, where you were always crawling, under fire ...

So we're sitting in this bunker, covered with straw. Suddenly we hear a 'Pok!' coming from the German lines, then the rustle of a shell, and an explosion in front of our positions. A certain amount of time passed. Then the sound of another incoming round – and an explosion behind our firing positions: 'Guys, they have us bracketed! Scatter!' We went running in every direction. The Germans dropped two more shells right on our firing positions, and then their artillery battalion, how it let loose! We didn't have anyone killed or wounded, but two guns had been knocked out. One shell exploded right between the trails of our gun and smashed the breech end. Another gun's muzzle brake was damaged. We'd just finished taking roll call when another barrage came down on the position. Obviously, we'd selected a position that the Germans had already pre-registered. The day cost us just one gun – ours, which had suffered irreparable damage to its breech. So we removed the muzzle brake from it and put it on the other gun – it returned to service, while we had to fight with our machine guns.

There we were fed boiled cornmeal and American Spam. Each morning and evening, one of the crew would walk to the field kitchen – in the daylight hours you couldn't climb out of the trench without being shot. Three months – cornmeal and Spam!! It was some kind of nightmare. It made us sick to our stomachs and gave us the runs. At night we would creep out onto the battlefield and gather potatoes that hadn't been harvested in the autumn. Since it was springtime, we were saved by the greens we would find.

Once I was chosen to fetch the gruel. It was boring to walk to the field kitchen alone – it was almost 6 kilometres away, so I dropped by the neighbouring gun crew to ask which one of them would come along with me. It had already begun to get light, and I was crouched on my knees, speaking with the senior sergeant. I raised my head a bit and immediately felt like someone had hit me in the back of the head with a log. I saw stars and fell face-first. I could hear the senior sergeant saying, 'Well, I'm finished.' I sat up. It turned out that a sniper's bullet had drilled through the breastwork of the trench, tumbled, and struck the back of my helmet flatwise. The senior sergeant picked up the still warm bullet and handed it to me: 'Here, a souvenir . . .'.

The offensive began in June 1944. Our diet improved – captured German rations and foraged food gave us some variety. True, the local civilian population itself was poor, but they were also tight-fisted. The Poles were always telling us, 'His mother's a bitch. The German has taken everything.' Sometimes we'd drive into some village: 'Lady, give us some water.'

'I don't have any.'

'You don't have water?'

'The German picked us clean; the rest your soldiers have hauled away.'

By now, the soldiers had begun to laugh at them:

'Lady, do you have the clap?'

'What? We had a bit, the German got most of it; the rest your soldiers carried off on self-propelled guns.'

At the railroad station in Okun, three trains were standing, including one with equipment the Germans had captured from us. We looked and saw our ZIS-3 guns on one platform car, only they'd been re-painted in the Germans' yellow colour. On one of the wheels of them, we saw an inscription in Russian made by one of the POWs. We took the gun off the train, test fired and sighted it in, and once again we were artillerymen.

In one of the battles, when we were supporting the attacking infantry, we received an order to advance our guns. We hooked up our ZIS-3 guns to the Studebakers, climbed into the cabs and started rolling. We were driving across open terrain. There was a village in front of us. About 100 metres to our right, two T-34s and a Studebaker were moving. We were sitting in our truck and the bullets started whistling through the air. About 600 metres remained to reach the village, when a 'Ferdinand' [the Russian nickname for any German self-propelled gun] emerged from it. One shot at a T-34 – it blazed up like a torch! A second shot – a second torch! The third shot, and only the Studebaker's wheels were left to go flying in the air. All this took place in front of our eyes. Clearly, the next round would be targeting us. The driver turned the truck around, we leaped out of the cab, quickly unhooked the gun, tossed out two boxes of shells, and the Studebaker roared away. Some of the crew ran away. Gun commander Sergeant Nesterenko ran almost 100 metres away! Only the gun layer, Petia and I remained at the gun. Now we were the target for the 'Ferdinand', and perhaps we only had a minute or two to live. The gun layer was the somewhat cowardly Kuznetsov, 18 years of age, from Sverdlovsk. He took position at the gun sight, but his hands were shaking. I asked him, 'Why are you trembling like that?' He had a psychosis – he felt that the German shell

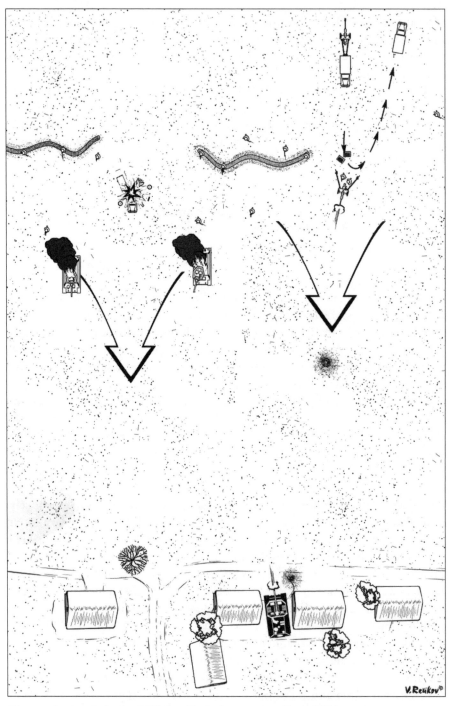

Diagram showing the battle of Nikolay Markov's gun crew with the SPG.

was already on its way toward us. Petia walked over to him, said, 'Get out of here!' and then gave him a cuff that sent him flying over a gun trail. Then he barked at me, 'Kolia, give me an armour-piercing!' A shot! I watched where the tracer went and said, 'Petia, the line was good, but the aim was too high.' Then he said, 'Give me APDS.' I gave him a shell. He fired right away and the 'Ferdinand' burst into flames!

Petia and I sat on a trail, looked at each other, and were silent. After all, we knew that now we were dead meat. Suddenly someone asked, 'Who fired?' I turned my head and saw a major, a deputy regiment commander. It turned out that he'd been crouched nearby in a trench. How he wound up there, I don't know – I didn't know his name. We weren't interested in visiting with the command; we had our own circle. I remained silent, and Petia did too. Then suddenly from behind me I heard: 'Sergeant Nesterenko's crew.'

'Comrade Nesterenko, I'm recommending you for the Order of the Patriotic War.'

When the fighting ended, Nesterenko did in fact receive the Order of the Patriotic War, while the crew was given 1,000 rubles for knocking out an armoured vehicle. However, we never received the money; only a receipt for the funds that showed we'd donated the money to the Defence Fund.

I had no further encounters with tanks for the rest of my service in the destroyer anti-tank artillery regiment. They were always shifting us back and forth across the front of the 47th Army. Over the remaining eight months of the war, I dug ninety-six emplacements, but I never again happened to fire at a tank. Escorting the infantry 'by fire and wheels' wasn't really our experience. We rarely fired at German weapon emplacements. We were the 47th Army's anti-tank reserve, so they deployed us only on avenues of approach that were vulnerable to tanks.

The constant work was perhaps harder to endure than combat with all its nervous stress. First, when changing firing position we had to leave the truck far behind the front line, so that the Germans couldn't shoot it up and so there'd be no losses. This means that the crew at night had to drag the gun, which weighed more than a ton, on slings to the next firing position. Then you had to reposition all the cases of shells, each of which weighed 75 kilograms. Three men were digging the gun emplacement and all the slit trenches for the crew; three were loading and unloading the cases of ammunition; and the driver and an assistant were in the truck. It happened that when you woke up in the morning, you'd see the wall of a brick factory right in front of you! These firing positions were constructed with blood and sweat.

Each gun crew had eight men: the gun commander, the gun layer, the loader, two guys who handled the gun trails, an ammunition carrier, a driver and an assistant driver. We were a friendly family. Once we were digging a trench in

Poland, and we uncovered an iron box. We opened it and found 50,000 zloty in it from the years 1936, 1937 and 1939: 'What shall we do, fellows?' We divided the loot evenly between us and our first thought was to play blackjack. Then someone proposed to spend it all on moonshine. We quickly reached an agreement and with the 50,000 zloty we bought fifty bottles of moonshine. This really helped us whenever we had the opportunity to relax. When I was fighting in the infantry, we received a vodka ration. In the artillery we also got one, but very rarely. So now we had procured our own moonshine.

Some of the gun crew commanders worked with their men more than others. This depended on the individual. Of course, the commander and the gunner didn't make the trips to the field kitchen. But it wasn't like you could say, 'Dig a trench for me, while I stand and watch.' If you behaved incorrectly as a commander, they might simply shoot you. No commander – no problem. There were completely different attitudes. Before a battle, a man is earnest. He works to his utmost and is pure within. The men are straight with each other. It is a completely different psychology.

For example, I was supposed to clean the grease off the shells with a rag, but if they had nothing else to do, the entire crew would help me. Usually the shells were clean – 'From the assembly line directly to the front,' that's what I thought.

The loader had to prepare the shell and load the gun in a timely fashion. He needed to know the different shell types and to take the necessary steps quickly. I recall that the daily combat load was 135 shells, but I don't remember the proportions of the different types of shells. Everything depended on what you were given. There were norms – but who knew them? Our job was to man the guns!

We had to clean the guns after every march, and it was mandatory to do so after every battle. It was the gun layer's job to bore sight the gun and calibrate the optics. In case of some problem or malfunction, there were two armourers in the battery who would repair the guns. However, malfunctions occurred rarely – the gun was reliable.

Depending on the terrain, we would deploy the guns with approximately 50 to 150 metres between each gun. It wasn't like in the movies, where you see them standing wheel to wheel. They might fire that way only at celebratory salutes!

I'm not a superstitious man, but I believe in fate. Before going to the front, my father told me, 'Son, remember – don't plunder from a foe; you'll lose more of your own.' I never plundered. A German is lying there and he's wearing a watch. I'd never take it! I remembered this commandment for my entire life. I also remember once making our way from the front to the rear. We walked back to the truck, and the butt of the driver's assistant was all swollen. We asked him, 'What happened?' He replied, 'A "Ferdinand" socked me in the ass with a projectile.' It turned out that he'd been sitting on a bucket, peeling potatoes. A random projectile, having ricocheted off the ground and lost most of its inertia, caught him right in the ass. It had to have been the 'hand of fate' that brought that projectile and his butt together!

Of course, fear was part and parcel of battle, but the scariest thing was the suspense. For example, you're lugging a case of shells and you don't know where the front line is or even where the Germans are. There was one frightening episode when we stumbled into a minefield. It was night, and having thrown a white sheet on one of our backs to guide the driver, we were walking toward the front lines. The Studebaker with the towed gun was slowly moving about 10 metres behind us. Suddenly there was a muffled explosion; the Studebaker's right wheel had run over an anti-personnel mine. The wheel was smashed. The driver and a hygienist were sitting in the cab of the truck. With the explosion, the latter had barked his shin. He was howling in such a wild voice – but he wasn't even wounded. Then there was another small explosion, and again a cry. We walked over – what had happened? It was one of our soldiers, a new replacement, from the western Ukraine. It is a law of war, you know: you walk in the track left behind by the moving truck. But he had strayed to the right of the track and had stepped on an anti-personnel mine – it removed his leg. We called for sappers. They lifted so many mines; it was a nightmare!

When you know what's in front of you, this you can tolerate; it was who would get the better of whom. But when you don't know the situation, the unknown gets into your head.

As for toilet paper, we had the sort when you don't have any paper at all! There was nothing to write on; we wrote on newspaper! In the summer we used grass, in the winter, snow – that was all. As far as you could, of course, you tried to keep yourself clean, but you weren't always able ...

I do pay my respect to the commissars and political workers. They were engineers of human souls. It is hard for a man in war; someone has to chat with him. These fellows were civilized, mannerly. They did their duty to nurture the human soul. I myself witnessed how before a battle in Poland, the colonel and *zampolit* [deputy political commander] inspired the infantry. We were standing next to the infantry. Rocket shells struck, not at the Germans, but at us. When the order to charge came, he was the first to get up, and by his personal example he led the guys into the attack. It was an example, a conviction – it was what was necessary. So when I served back then, I came across a lot of Party workers in the army. It all depended on the man, but generally speaking, they were ordinary guys. They cultivated a proper attitude among the men toward each other.

I reached Warsaw's suburb of Praga with the 163rd Rifle Regiment. The following incident took place in November 1944. We deployed our gun on the western side of some building, but dug our trenches on its eastern side, so that during a barrage its walls would create a dead space for falling shells. I remember the Germans hit us with a barrage from their '*Vanuishi*' – their six-barrelled *Nebelwerfer* rocket launcher. I was the last to leap into a trench. A shell exploded on the balcony. Fragments and splinters riddled my greatcoat, but didn't even graze me. Then it became somehow quiet. Suddenly I heard shouting: 'Markov to the battalion commander!'

I made my way to him. After reporting, he told me, 'You're going to study to become an officer.'

'I don't want to be an officer. I've already seen all the filth of this war; I don't want to be an officer.'

'Do you understand martial law?'

'I know it precisely.'

'This is a combat order. Go, push off to the rear; report to the sergeant major. He knows what to do.'

I went back to the crew and said, 'Petia, they're sending me away to officer's school.'

'You're lucky. Do you know how much more fighting there'll be before we reach the fascists' lair? How many tribulations? So, take our spoils of war, everything we have, and push off to see the sergeant major. We didn't have much in the way of captured goods. Primarily, all we'd been able to scrounge was lard.

In order to reach the sergeant major, you had to run about 50 metres across some open ground to one of our knocked-out tanks. A trench had been dug beneath it, which we called the 'Stopover'. In this trench you'd wait until the Germans quieted down and stopped shooting, and then you'd scramble out and dash another 30 metres to some low mounds, behind which the Germans couldn't see. I said to the guys, 'Farewell.' I grabbed the lard and took off at a run.[4] I heard the sound of firing and dived beneath the tank. When the shooting stopped, I made another dash – and got away. That's how I ended the war.

Notes

1. *Katsap* is a mocking Ukrainian reference to Russians. It dates back to the 17th Century, when many Russian men wore thin beards below their chins – hence the allusion to goats.
2. 'Six-month' refers to a junior officer who due to the dire need for personnel, didn't go through the full, official period of training before being sent to the front. There, if they survived their first battle, they received their commission as junior lieutenants.
3. Petia's way of addressing the junior lieutenant, *Mukha*, is the Russian word for a fly.
4. Thin slices of lard have always been a common sight on many Russian dinner tables, along with pickles and marinated herring. Lard is considered a food item.

Chapter 4

A Legendary Hero of Prokhorovka

Mikhail Fedorovich Borisov

I was born in the Altai region in a village of the Mikhailovskoe Baevsky District. The village was small – around twenty homes nestled beneath the green crowns of birch trees. Next to our home was a small natural spring, around which nightingales nested. Hemp fields surrounded our village. At the time, nobody knew that you could smoke Cannabis. My grandfather, an old Siberian Cossack, sought to raise me in his own fashion. When I was 2 or 3 years old, he seated me in a saddle. When I had reached the age of 4, my father set up a dressing bureau in the middle of the room, upon which a target had been drawn, and loaded a cartridge with a light powder charge into a Berdan rifle. I fired, and he told me I had hit the target. I don't know, maybe he wasn't telling me the truth. I'm saying all this to show that from my early childhood, I was being prepared for military service. That was the accepted way.

Later we moved to the city of Kamen'-na-Obi. The local school had a fine military instructor, a veteran of the fighting at Lake Khasan who'd been decorated with the medal 'For Combat Services'. Although he wasn't a highly intelligent man, he loved both his job and us, the children. He literally spent days and nights with us, and we followed him around in a throng – he was the first decorated veteran we'd seen. In short, I became quite familiar with rifles, revolvers and machine guns.

On the night of 21/22 June, my father and I were fishing outside the town. We returned home after 4 o'clock in the morning. We had the only radio on our street. When they broadcast that there was going to be a government announcement, Mama opened the window and placed the squawk box on the window sill. Neighbours gathered around and we listened to Molotov's statement. I recall that all the faces were gloomy. We'd just put the Finnish campaign behind us, and now once again ... On the next morning, even before sunrise, I ran to the military enlistment centre. Almost all of my schoolmates who were a little bit older than me were there. Some of them had been called up; others had come of their own volition. The entire yard at the enlistment centre was crowded with people! There, naturally, they sent me on my way – I had just turned 17.

I ran next to the Komsomol's district committee. There they also turned me away – go, they said, study; we'll call you when you're needed. But I couldn't wait! At the time we were thinking that the war would be over in just two or three months. I went back to the enlistment centre. I was received by the military commissioner; he wasn't going to take me under any circumstance. I begged him literally with tears in my eyes! Finally he said, 'Okay, but I'm not going to send you to the front. You're going to the Tomsk Artillery School.' I was upset, of course, but I had no other choice. I had to agree, and already by the end of June or beginning of July, I found myself facing a credentials committee and received my assignment to the artillery school.

I remember the first time I fired a 76-mm anti-tank gun at a moving target. A truck was dragging a wooden mock-up of a tank behind it with a long cable. With my first round, I smashed the target. Captain Epifanov, the battery commander, said: 'That can't be. Let's have another target.' They dragged another one across my field of fire. Again, with my first shot I destroyed it. Epifanov swore: 'Don't give him any more shells, or else we'll be left without targets.' My firing at the 'rifle artillery range' was also successful. This was a target field lying in front of a little 37-mm gun. A pellet rifle barrel was inserted into the barrel of the anti-tank gun, and with the little lead pellets we learned to hit a target. For the sake of justice I should say that we in fact never learned to shoot a pistol or a rifle well. We mastered aiming the anti-tank gun, but although we were instructed in how to fire our personal weapon properly, we were not very successful in this.

Of course, the mood among the cadets was lousy. We couldn't understand why our Red Army was retreating. After all, before the war they had kept blaring, 'Victory with little cost won on someone else's territory!' Some of the cadets said the retreat was some sort of strategy. However, I will say that Stalin and the leadership couldn't be blamed for this. No! God forbid!

That's how we spent four months in training, but when a precarious situation arose at the gates of Moscow, I and another 150 cadets were loaded onto trains and sent to the front. We arrived in Moscow. There, 'shoppers' immediately snapped up twenty to twenty-five of us, including me, either because we were the youngest or the best trained. Again we were loaded into heated freight cars and sent to Krasnodar, to an infantry school that was there. We were en route for a month! We were all ragged and filthy, and those who were a bit older had grown some stubble on their faces. Our appearance was, to put it gently, not presentable. We fell into formation on a parade ground, and the commandant stepped out of the school – an elderly, tall, thin and well-groomed general. He passed down our assembled ranks, looked us over, and abruptly spat out, 'I have no need for such cadets!'

The next day, 'shoppers' snapped us up for various units, and I became the direction layer of a 50-mm company mortar. I must say that our fate was unenviable – a mortar man served in the ranks of the infantry, but if an infantryman could fall prone behind a bit of cover or a fold in the ground, the mortar man had to work on his knees. The 50-mm shell had a range of only 400 metres and was feeble.

We spent a while in reforming and did a bit of gunnery practice, but at the end of December we went to Tiumriuk to load onto a fishing trawler for the Kerch landing. Back in my childhood I very much wanted to serve in the navy. I think it was because of their bell-bottomed trousers and sailor's caps. But how seasick I was as we sailed from Tiumriuk to Kamysh-burun! The sailors told me, 'Son, take a swig of alcohol and a bite of herring; you'll feel better.' I couldn't even think about it! The trawler already reeked of this fish. I crawled up onto the deck and clutched the mast. I 'fed the fish' in a frightful manner. That's when German aircraft appeared. One trawler disappeared beneath the waves, and then a second ... altogether, they sank nine of the boats. I was standing there and imploring that one of the bombs would fall on me, in order to end my torments, because it seemed then that there was nothing in life more terrible than seasickness.

We hit the beach successfully. I jumped into the icy water and clambered up the bank, but we were taking almost no enemy fire. We liberated Kerch literally within a few hours. A couple of days later, only about half of the company's personnel remained. All the rest had been killed or wounded. Our mortars had been destroyed. For around 48 hours we had nothing to do, but then our guys seized three or four German guns. Crews for them were hammered together. We quickly familiarized ourselves with the German guns, turned them around in the direction of the Germans, and for the next several hours fired at their positions. Fortunately, we had no problem finding shells. Piles of ammunition towered next to us. Then they scattered us among different units. I wound up in reconnaissance for one or two weeks, but it was apparent that I, a green youngster just 17 years of age, didn't belong there. I was reassigned to an 82-mm mortar crew. I didn't spend long with it, maybe two months. On 22 March, on the day of my 18th birthday, I was severely wounded and concussed not far from Vladislavovka.

I recovered in a hospital in Essentuki. From there, at the end of summer 1942, I was assigned to the 14th Guards Rifle Division's 36th Guards Rifle Regiment. There I finally began to fight in the role for which I had been trained – I became a 45-mm anti-tank gunner. The infantry, indeed as we did too, called our guns 'Farewell, Motherland' or the 'Crew's death'. Over those four months that I spent at Stalingrad, everyone else on my crew was replaced five times over, while I wasn't even grazed by a fragment or a bullet. That's fate for you. Whatever was written for you at your birth – that's preordained and you can't change it.

What can I say about the fighting for Stalingrad? In the course of it, once we seized part of a village. That night, infantry were passing our position, heading for the rear. We were asking them, 'What, are you retreating?' They would answer, 'No, we're being replaced' – probably they were just lying to us. Soon a group of soldiers appeared. The sentry shouted, 'Stop, who goes there?' Silence. 'Stop, or I'll shoot!' and raised his submachine gun, but it didn't fire! How was the PPSh bad? If just a speck of sand or bit of corrosion got into it, it would refuse to fire. The sentry came running down into the basement where we were resting: 'Get up! Germans!' Another order wasn't necessary.

I got up in my stocking feet – I left my boots behind, but grabbed the dial sight. The Germans were quite close, their submachine guns blazing, crying '*Allez*, Rus, charge!' At the time they were feeling their superiority over us, mocking us, but we ran. They were sending up flares, and it became bright as day ... Then a flare came down onto the road next to me and continued to burn. In its light I became a superb target. I dropped and hugged the earth. The flare burned out. Just as soon as it became dark again, I was on my feet and making a dash for the opposite bank of the Donets across the frozen river.

But I was holding the dial sight! I'd left my boots behind, but brought out the sight. In the morning we were sent to the Special Department. They had no accusations against me – I had the dial sight with me – but they told platoon commander Lieutenant Kuznetsov: 'If you don't bring back the guns, you'll go before a tribunal.'

We went back to get them that night. We tied thick cords to them and hauled them back to the banks of the Donets without a shot being fired. From the top of the high bank, we lowered them down the steep slope onto the ice. That's when the Germans opened fire, but it was too late – we already had the cover of the high bank and so we hauled the guns back into friendly lines.

I remember an incident with armour-piercing discarding sabot shells that took place in the village of Petrovka. These shells first reached us at the end of 1942. We were given two of these shells per gun and warned that they were still classified. But somehow we managed to lose them. The point was that local residents or partisans had offered to lead us that night into the enemy rear, so that with a simultaneous attack from the front and rear we could take this village. So that night the battalion, reinforced with our platoon of 45-mm guns, a mortar platoon and an anti-tank rifle platoon, set off into the German rear through ravines and deep gullies. At sunrise we went on the attack and easily seized half of the village. However, those that were attacking from the front were thrown back, and we wound up in a pocket. True, at the time we didn't realize this. The men scattered into the different huts, some to shave, some to wash up. Meanwhile, I and this guy with the last name of Podkorytov stayed with the gun. We looked, and about 2 kilometres away spotted German vehicles. At that range, they were visible, but you couldn't do anything to them.

They approached to within about 800 metres and infantry spilled out of them, and started to rush in our direction. The whistle of bullets kept growing and growing. We jumped into a little trench. Bullets began to snap along the breastwork. We were sitting there, feeling that if we stayed there, the Germans would come and grab us with their bare hands. We leaped out of the trench and took cover behind the gun shield. The Germans were close. Our soldiers were running out of all the huts, including our platoon commander, who was pale: 'Men, do we have time to hitch up the gun?' We had to try, whether we had the time or not. We brought up the horses, limbered up the gun, hitched it to the horse team and immediately drove them into a ravine that began directly next to our position. The Germans would shoot us in the back! Then there was a burst of machine-gun fire – the horses were falling while we were running, so we continued to run. I had the dial sight clenched in my fist. I never parted with it, day or night. Then a Messerschmidt appeared and went into a strafing run along the length of this ravine. At some moment I realized that I was trying to burrow beneath a dead soldier, even though I knew perfectly well that this body would be no defence. In such situations, very many reflex actions are in no way connected with reality.

We were able to break out into the German rear. From our platoon, there remained around seven men, several mortars and some riflemen; altogether, perhaps seventeen men. We were exhausted and frozen. We came across a haystack and crawled into it to warm up. I lay there and thought, 'The Germans are coming for us. If not now, then they'll be here in a half-hour. They'll take us with their bare hands.' I crawled out. The others also started to clamber out, and then we ran a bit further.

In one village we asked the villagers if they had anything to eat. The response: 'Fellows, we have nothing. So we can only feed you linseed cake.'

'Give us some.'

They gave each of us a piece of the cake. Do you know how tasty it can be, when you're famished?

The group then split up – the infantrymen and mortar men took a direction a little more to the right, while we climbed a low rise, dug a shallow, crescent-shaped trench in order to get some shelter from the wind, and lay down in it. One of the guys said, 'Let's hide our documents.' We began to dig holes to conceal our papers. I also hid mine.

We waited until darkness fell. The platoon commander spoke up: 'What will we do?' We had to get back to our own lines. Down below was a road, along which from time to time small groups of enemy moved. How to cross it? It was frightening; we might suddenly run smack into one. Then to our misfortune or blessing, God only knows, a very long column of wagons appeared. The Germans or Romanians were shifting their position. We waited and waited; there seemed no end to it. We decided we had to go, before it grew light and we remained stuck in the German rear, waiting to be taken prisoner at any moment.

Very stealthily we descended the slope and crept up to the side of the road. Spreading out, we separately waited for a gap to appear in the column before dashing across the road into some sagebrush on the other side. Now alone, I kept moving to put some distance between the road and me. I'd gone about a kilometre and was thinking I needed to stop. I looked around and spotted a comrade. A short time later we saw the rest of the guys and linked up with them.

One soldier said, 'I groped around in one of the wagons and pilfered a flask. Let's take a swig, perhaps there's wine or water in it.' I was thirsty, so I took a swallow. Yuk! Screw it – it was vegetable oil! We all nevertheless took a swig, but in my opinion, it was simply out of hunger. We made our way to the Donets and somehow crawled our way across the thin ice to the opposite bank. Literally within a half-hour, we encountered the remnants of our battery. We asked for something to eat. The guys said, 'We don't have anything but flour.'

'Give us some.'

The sergeant major gave each of us a half of a mess tin of this flour. We mixed it with water, gave it a stir and drank it up. It was our breakfast, lunch and dinner.

The platoon commander Kuznetsov and us were again hauled before officers of the Special Department. They summoned me and asked where my documents were. I told him that I'd buried them. 'Fine, we'll check.' they said, 'Where's your dial sight?' I showed it to them.

'We have no other questions for you. Go.'

There were also no questions for the rest of the men. The other gun layer in the platoon had also returned with his dial sight. But the platoon commander, for the loss of the guns and the armour-piercing discarding sabot shells, as well as the preceding episode, was sent before a tribunal.

Later, in 1945 I was crossing a bridge over the Oder River and a one-and-a-half-ton truck overtook me. In the back of the truck, some captain was pounding on the back of the cab with all his might. The truck came to a stop. The captain leaped out of the back and came running up to me: 'My boy!'

'Greetings, Comrade Captain.'

'You don't recognize me? You don't know your own commander?'

'Oh, Lieutenant Kuznetsov!'

I learned that in the penal battalion, he'd been wounded in the first battle, and thereby had erased his guilt with his blood. By the end of the war, he was now the chief of staff of an artillery regiment. We spoke for about 5 minutes, before the driver started shouting and hurrying him. We didn't even have time to exchange addresses. We embraced upon parting, he climbed back aboard the truck, and I hurried to catch up with my unit.

I recall that at Morozovskaia Station, we seized German army depots. Both us and the local residents stuffed ourselves on the food we found. As we marched down the street, citizens grabbed soldiers out of the column and took them home as guests. An old woman came up to me with tears in her eyes: 'Son, everyone else has guests, but no one is coming to my place. Come with me.' I went with her.

In one room there was a kettle with hot water, in another – a washtub with some clean underwear next to it. She spoke: 'Sonny, you wash up, change your underwear and toss the dirty pair into the corner; I'll wash it later.'

'I don't need the underwear.'

'No, change; this is my son's underwear; perhaps someone is warming him up wherever he is now.'

I washed and redressed. I went into the next room. On the table, there was already a frying pan with potatoes and tinned stew meat. Their potatoes, naturally, were Russian; but the stew meat was German. For the first time during my service at the front to this point, I ate my fill!

'Thank you, thank you,' I said.

'No, thank you, that you came by and could stomach it.'

I departed to search for the rest of my crew. I stopped by a hut, took a look, and found them sitting there inside it. They'd already eaten and were now lounging about. The driver Il'ia Belikov was sitting at a table – a strapping fellow, approximately 180 centimetres [6 feet] tall and 100 kilograms [220 pounds] in weight. If the soldier's rations were inadequate to us 'small-calibre' men, it was even more so for him! He had a large frying pan in front of him. It had also been full of potatoes and tinned stew meat, but no longer – everything had been gobbled up; he was still scraping the pan and had a droplet of sweat on his brow, from the diligence of his effort. Then he stepped outside, and I followed him soon after. I looked, and he was sitting on a gun caisson with a large cask of captured marmalade in front of him, and he was digging at this delicacy with a sapper's spade. We roared with laughter together.

That winter there was nothing to feed the horses. Forage was supplied only rarely. We had to take apart thatch roofs for fodder. But really, if the straw is half-full of clay, can it really be fodder? The horses could barely move themselves, much less a gun. At the foot of one low hill, this Belikov had unharnessed the horses, walked them up it, and then returned for the gun. Having placed the trails of the 45-mm gun on his shoulder, he alone man-handled it up the hill! Later, when I wound up in a mechanized brigade, I sighed with relief. I love horses, but in war a horse is the wrong type of transport.

There is another episode involving Belikov. Once we sent him to the field kitchen. He loaded his ruck sack with little loaves. As he told us later, 'I'm walking and I think that if I don't eat a piece now, I'd drop.' He cut a piece off one loaf and ate it, then another and another. Soon he'd wolfed down the entire loaf. It made him drowsy and he wanted to sleep. He thought he'd doze for just a half-hour, then make up the lost time at a run. He woke up and the sun was already setting. He thought, 'The guys are going to cut my head off. They've been sitting without their bread.' He started off at a run, but felt pain. He checked and saw that the heel of his boot was torn up and bloody. As he was sleeping, a shell had exploded nearby, a fragment had wounded him in the heel, and he hadn't even woken up! We bandaged his foot and he never went to the medical and sanitary battalion. We were young – everything healed quickly.

At the beginning of 1943, the division redeployed to a different sector. I was ill and apparently had a high temperature. We were marching at night as snow fell. I grabbed hold of a wagon and dozed on the march. My hand lost its grip, I fell, and I didn't wake up! The other guys noticed this, shook me awake and picked me up. I again took a tight grip on the wagon, marched a bit further, and again fell. This time nobody noticed, and when I woke up, there was no one around. I was sprawled on the road. I tried to figure out the direction I should take, but then I simply snuggled up on the shoulder of the road and started to fall asleep. At this time a vehicle came by, in which as I later learned Major Shchukin was seated. He was the chief of the 2nd Tank Corps' 58th Mechanized Brigade's Political Department. He spotted me, placed me in the vehicle, and drove on.

A short time later I was back on my feet and learned that I'd been assigned to be the gun layer of a ZIS-3 gun in a separate destroyer anti-tank artillery battalion. Many, many years later, now as a member of the Union of Writers, I decided to write my memoirs. For more than two months I was sitting in the Ministry of Defence's archives in Podolsk, leafing through the documents of the 14th Guards Rifle Division. I came across a report from the Division's Political Department that the very next morning after that night, when I'd fallen behind, the division was standing on the defence. The 45-mm gun battery was in its firing positions. During an enemy air raid, a crew was killed that was under the command of Sergeant Il'chenko. It was my gun crew. Had I not gotten sick and collapsed, I would have been together with them ...

I'd like to say a few words here about the ZIS-3 anti-tank gun. It was light. If I pulled my socks up, I alone could pivot it, while for two men this presented no problem at all. Two men could also roll it to a new position, while five men could manhandle it across sand. It had a large angle of traverse, both horizontally and vertically. It was rare when we had to turn the gun. It had only one shortcoming – its range of direct fire was only 600 metres.

We went on the offensive. In Voroshilovgrad Oblast, for the first and only time in the war I saw a German human wave attack. Not like in the film *Chapaev*, where the infantry is advancing shoulder to shoulder, but here they came at us in three waves, with just about a half-metre of distance between the soldiers. It was wild … They told us back then that this division had just arrived from France and hadn't yet taken part in combat actions. We allowed them to approach to within 400 metres and then we fired at will. It was fearsome – there were a lot of them. Then two more machine-gun crews came running up to our assistance and things became a bit easier. I was firing at the Germans, when platoon commander Lieutenant Volodia Krasnonosov called out to me, 'Misha, look, a truck is moving along that crest with a gun behind it, with soldiers sitting in the back of it.' I gave it one shell – the vehicle flew into the air, the gun went into a somersault, and then I switched back to firing at the lines of attacking infantry. We cut them all down. Later the guys walked across the field, searching for canteens with cognac in them. Since they were from France, shouldn't they be holding cognac?! There were a lot of canteens, but nothing was in them, because not one of them was intact. They were all riddled with shrapnel. That's how devastating our fire had been. When we had been firing from the German guns back in the Crimea, no one had bothered even to thank us, but here for the first time I heard the platoon commander say, 'Thanks, you shot well.'

Two or three days later, around the 11th or 12th of February, we entered the Cheliuskinets State Farm. The platoon now had only one gun, ours; where the second gun was, I don't know, but the platoon commander was with our gun. We deployed the gun next to a hut on the edge of the residential complex, beyond which a ravine began. We had none of our infantry around, and indeed, we didn't know where the enemy was. We spotted a tank moving beyond the ravine. It had a cross on the turret. I gave the command, 'Armour-piercing.' The gun was loaded. I turned the thumb screw until I had it directly in my sights. Just as I was about to fire, a man in a greatcoat with colonel's epaulets on the shoulders and holding a pistol came running out of the ravine toward the farm. He came running up to me: 'Don't fire, it's our tank!'

'What do you mean? I asked. 'It has crosses on it.'

He again shouted, 'Don't fire!'

The platoon issued the order, 'Belay that!'

The colonel ducked around a hut and we didn't see him again. The tank moved behind some bushes as it fired a round at us. The shell flew literally just several centimetres above the shield and collapsed a wall of the hut. But it was too late for us to return fire. We later among ourselves said that the man had been a German scout. I cannot confirm this, but even today I can't forgive myself for obeying him and the platoon commander. We only had to detain him, and then let them find out who he was. The panzer fired only one shot and then gained concealment behind cover.

As we were talking over what had happened, bullets began whistling past us and rattling against the gun shield. I looked and saw a line of German infantry advancing at full height toward us from the right flank across the deep snow. The range to it was only about 100 metres. We pivoted our gun and let them have it! We cut down many of them. I fired fifteen to twenty shells. Those who remained alive were pinned down in the snow. I began to fire at the crowns of solitary trees that were growing nearby the prone Germans. I fired five rounds and they could no longer withstand it – they jumped up and dashed into the ravine. Not more than ten of them were left. We pivoted the gun again, and if any of them had appeared on the opposite slope of the ravine, we would have blasted them. At that moment our scouts came running up with submachine guns. We said to them, 'Guys, there are Germans in the ravine.' They lined up along the ravine and began to pick them off, killing them one by one. Only one made it across to the opposite slope, and with his last remaining strength he was clambering up it. The submachine gun fire could no longer reach him. Volodia Krasnonosov grabbed a carbine, rested it on the gun shield, took aim, and bang! The German dropped face-first to the ground and didn't move.

Then Volodia and I walked across this field. Out of curiosity we began to count the number of dead Germans. I counted up to 140; we spat and stopped counting. Putting it briefly, I had to my credit approximately 100 German dead during their human-wave attack and around 150 for this one, plus an armoured vehicle I had destroyed in one of the battles, so I was recommended for the Order of the Red Banner. Two days prior the commander had expressed his gratitude, and now an Order! For the next several months, I walked around not sensing my feet on the ground! But I never received the decoration. It was like it vanished without a trace. Our 2nd Tank Corps was in the command reserve, and sometimes they reassigned us to a different army two or three times a day. Since only an army commander could bestow such an honour, we might be recommended for an Order in one army, but as the recommendation made its way up the channels of command we would already be reassigned to a different army. Indeed, in general we were always like strangers, so what could they award us? I survived.

Now when our veterans say that we weren't fighting for an Order ... Of course, not for an Order! However, I don't know a single one who would have said, 'No, I don't need one! I'm not fighting for an Order!' Everyone wanted to be noticed, somehow mentioned or distinguished ...

Then there was the campaign to liberate Khar'kov and the inglorious flight from there. On my birthday on 22 March 1943, just as in 1942, I received a severe concussion. I spent days, it seems, in the medical-sanitation battalion, then left it. Back at the battery they gave me a little purgative, I was listless for another week, but attempted to keep working like everyone else. We rolled back to the Northern Donets River. There we had to do a lot of firing. The situation with ammunition wasn't bad, not like it had been at Stalingrad, when we had only two shells a day.

Soon we were withdrawn for rest and refitting to the Staryi Oskol area. Our brigade was re-designated as the 58th Motorized Rifle Brigade. In the month of March I was summoned to the Political Department and was invited to become the Komsomol organizer (Komsorg) of the battalion, even though I was only a senior sergeant. The fact that I had a rather high education apparently made the difference. For example, the battalion's deputy commander for political matters had just a 5th-grade education, but when later he was transferred into the Political Department, he replaced a captain, a Kirghiz by nationality, who had only four years of schooling and in a Kirghiz school at that.

I agreed and threw myself into Komsomol work. I began to write verses. In truth, I was only attempting to do so, because either there was no paper or no pencil available, or then when you did jot down a few lines, some other duties called you away. I'd stick the paper in my pocket, and within several days only a tattered, washed out remnant would remain of it. Thus, I never wrote a single poem in that time. Of course, the battalion's Komsorg was a part-time duty, but in fact I was giving all of my time to it, which neither my battery commander nor the battalion commander liked. However, they couldn't do anything about it – it was an order from the chief of the Political Department that I dedicate myself fully to Komsomol work. Here I should say that 80 per cent of the battalion's personnel were Komsomol members. They in fact bore the war on their shoulders. Older men over the age of 35 comprised not more than 10 per cent of the personnel, and the other 10 per cent were men between the ages of 21 and 35. Much had to be done with the youth, since they were of different backgrounds, different nationalities, different education levels, yet it was necessary to forge a soldierly collective from them, ready to fight through common effort. More than half the replacements had no prior combat experience.

Well, soon the Battle of Kursk began. Although in fact we were positioned about 100 kilometres behind the front lines, you can't fool a soldier; we could sense that something big was about to begin. I remember how one night we could see flashes on the western horizon and a rumble like thunder carried to our ears. I thought, 'It has started.' The alarm was raised. Everyone ran to their places, the tank brigades received an order, and they departed for the front. Soon the motorized riflemen followed them, but for some reason we weren't disturbed until dawn on 11 July. Two batteries received an order to assemble in one place, while ours, the 3rd Battery, was ordered to cover the road running from Iakovlevo to a village that was totally unknown to anyone at the time, Prokhorovka. We moved up in vehicles that were loaded with cases of ammunition. Prokhorovka and the Oktiabr'skii State Farm, which was situated to our right, were burning. Smoke crept across the ground. Suddenly someone began to bawl, 'Tanks in front!', and after it, 'Ready the guns!'

We leaped out of the vehicles. We looked – wide, squat tanks were moving about 1 kilometre away on a tangent to us. We'd never seen such tanks before. Then we counted them – nineteen. We unhitched the guns and deployed them in an open field. We only had time to dig in the trail spades, unload and stack the boxes of ammunition from the vehicle, and drive the vehicles away. We prepared for battle. The Germans didn't notice us – the same smoke from the burning buildings that was drifting across the ground concealed the battery's deployment and saved us. If they had spotted us, not even a damp spot would have remained of us.

The battery commander Senior Lieutenant Pavel Ivanovich Azhippo was running from gun to gun: 'Fellows, don't fire! Fellows, don't fire! Let them approach.' We let them close to within about 500 metres, and when they drew even with the battery, and having exposed their flanks to us, we opened fire. After the first salvo, two of them burst into flames, and we already felt a sense of relief – we had proof that these tanks too would burn. There had been nineteen of them, and now there were seventeen! They detected our position and opened fire. From somewhere to the right, a mortar battery started lobbing shells at us. Two Messerschmidts appeared overhead. That little patch of ground was literally shaking like in an earthquake – explosion followed explosion. Again we were lucky. If just one enemy shell had struck the stack of ammunition, we would have been blown to pieces. Their shells were striking around the guns as they were targeting the firing positions, but they didn't hit the stack of ammunition. What was I doing? At first I was carrying shells to the loaders, but then wounded began to appear. I hastily bandaged them and dragged them off to the side, to what seemed to be a safer location.

Guns began to fall silent. At first the gun on the left flank was knocked-out, and then a neighbouring gun. Within a short time, only Senior Sergeant Ivan Grigor'ev's gun continued to fire. I was assisting the crew. I dragged the wounded loader Private Supoldiiarov a metre or two away and was crudely bandaging him, when suddenly there was something like a clap of thunder. I regained consciousness quickly. The entire gun crew had been killed or wounded. I ran over to the gun and found a shell was in the breech. I grabbed the deflection and elevation knob ... then fired. My target burst into flames. I ran and picked up another shell, carried it back to the gun, loaded it and fired – another hit. I made another run for a shell. Then I heard some sort of commotion, turned my head, and saw the battery commander with two shells running toward me, followed by Krasnonosov with another shell. Two shells were discharged at the third tank. I fired several more times, and three tanks were left burning. A tanker leaped out of the turret of one of them. I can still remember him – a lean man in black overalls, his face angular and gaunt, standing there and shaking his fist in our direction. I immediately roared, 'Fragmentation!' The two men loaded a fragmentation shell. I fired at the turret and hit it. My action was totally needless, but I was in a state of combat frenzy ...

Azhippo cried, 'Tanks on the left!' We rapidly pivoted the gun. Quickly turning the knobs, I caught the lead tank in the cross hairs of my sight and pressed the trigger – nothing! I shouted, 'Shell!' Again I pressed the trigger – no shot! I hollered, 'Shell!' and pressed the trigger a third time – silence!! I turned; a couple of metres away, the severely wounded Azhippo was lying there, still gripping a shell; the badly concussed Krasnonosov was doubled over by the ammunition pile. I grabbed the shell from Azhippo, loaded it and fired – the tank erupted in flames. While I ran for the next shell, one of the panzers broke through to within a distance of just 60–70 metres of the gun. Several more seconds and it would be crushing me beneath its track. Here I had no thoughts whatsoever; I waited until he would expose a vulnerable spot to me. I very roughly pointed the barrel at its front and fired – there was a splash of sparks. Of course, it did no damage to it. But it stopped and fired. I remember seeing a patch of blue sky and a wheel from my gun twirling in it.

This was my eighth tank, but they didn't credit it to me. I receive credit and was compensated monetarily for only seven. Back then, you know, they paid 500 rubles for each knocked-out tank. Altogether in this action, the battery destroyed sixteen of the nineteen tanks. Three got away in the heat of the fight, retreating in the direction of Iakovlevo. The battery had carried out its assignment in a shining fashion. Yes, it cost lives, but had those panzers seized Prokhorovka, even more blood would have been spilled.[1]

I was again lucky. Not far from our position was the command post of General Aleksei Fedorovich Popov, the commander of the 2nd Tank Corps, who witnessed this entire fight. I'm still grateful to him that he, as I later learned from the chief of the Political Department Shchukin, demanded that 'this fellow' be saved. Shchukin hopped into a vehicle and literally extracted me out from under fire. I was sent to a hospital with wounds in my leg, back and head. There they immediately operated on me. As I later found out, General Popov ordered my brigade command to find me, so I could be treated in the 2nd Tank Corps' medical-sanitation battalion. Three groups spent several days searching for me, but there were a lot of hospitals, and to find a Senior Sergeant Borisov in the flood of wounded that was coming from the front was very difficult.

After the operation they transferred to me to a large hall, apparently in some school. There was a layer of straw on the floor, covered by burlap. The wounded were lying side by side. Soon they moved me to the attic. There was the same straw and burlap, but nevertheless the conditions were more comfortable. I was rather quickly back on my feet. About five days later, I began saving the army biscuits that they passed out in the mess hall, and once I had accumulated around ten of them, I hit the road back to my unit. In general, I never once stayed in the hospital until my official discharge; I was always running away to get back to the front lines.

There were a lot of men like that, and their motivations varied. Some wanted to get back to their unit; others wanted without fail to be at the front at that very moment. I, for example, was wounded the last time prior to the assault on Berlin. Indeed, I once again ran away so I could take part in the final offensive.

This time I fled the hospital before dawn, and later that same day the chief of the Special Department from the 2nd Tank Corps' headquarters drove up to the hospital, while I at the time was on the road, walking and hungry. I'd already eaten all of my biscuits. In one village I asked a resident to give me something to eat. She said to me, 'Son, I have nothing but cornmeal mush.' What a delicacy! Especially with milk! I, like a calf, scarfed down everything I was given. I expressed my thanks and went on my way.

A vehicle came my way. I hailed it and it stopped. I told the driver that I was making my way back to my unit.

'Climb into the back!' he replied.

I climbed aboard. The truck was carrying bread; the loaves were laid out in rows and they were covered by a tarp. There were already two soldiers seated on the tarp. The motion of the truck made me drowsy, and as I was falling asleep, I heard the soldiers talking about some sergeant who had 'raked the Tigers over the coals'. Only later did I understand who they were talking about. It turned out that this truck belonged to one of the tank brigades of the 2nd Tank Corps. When we reached their brigade, I approached one of the officers with a request to point me towards the location of the 58th Motorized Rifle Brigade. He was alert and immediately reported my arrival to the chief of the Political Department. The latter phoned the chief of my brigade's Special Department and announced that a certain sergeant was searching for the 58th Brigade. He was told, 'Hold him until my arrival.' The chief of the Political Department followed him to the letter. I glanced, and a submachine gunner suddenly materialized not far from me. At first I couldn't understand why, but then I saw that I couldn't leave – he stayed behind me, but remained at a discrete distance.

The chief of the Special Department drove up on a motorcycle with a sidecar: 'Take a seat.' I did so. We drove about a hundred metres, and then he said, 'Misha, I congratulate you.'

'Why?'

'You don't know anything? They've put you up for the title 'Hero of the Soviet Union'!'

I gave the appearance that I was happy. In my heart I knew that this nomination wasn't even worth mentioning.

He took me back to the 58th Motorized Rifle Brigade's position. They sent me to the rear, to the medical-sanitation battalion, where they kept me for another week and fattened me up.

A month passed. General Popov was taking me around to all of his combat units, compelling me to address the young soldiers. I spoke to the groups about one thing or another.

One day a car pulled up. The General had sent a car for me at the front. The chauffeur reported, 'The General is summoning Borisov.' The battery commander and battalion commander both had dead-pan expressions on their faces. Well, what?! But I had to carry out an order.

We drove to headquarters. I went to see General Popov and reported that I had arrived. Together we walked to the house where he was staying for lunch; he was living there together with his campaign wife, and they'd already had a daughter together, Polina. We sat down to eat. Wine glasses were filled. I said, 'Comrade General, what's the occasion?'

'Are things bad for you here?' he replied.

'No, not bad.'

'Then have a chat with my wife, while I return to work.'

I stayed with the General for two or three days. Then a car pulled up and took me back to the front lines. I couldn't understand what the point of my sojourn there had been. Now I think he just wanted a son. He was around 50 years old, while I looked about 15, probably. Maybe so; or perhaps he simply wanted to pluck me out of the trenches and give me a respite.

A month went by, then another two or three; there was not a rumour or even a hint about my nomination. I was thinking that was all there'd been to the matter. However, Ivan Ivanovich Shchukin sat down at a table and wrote a letter to Shcherbakov, the head of the Red Army's Political Department. Plainly, this letter worked, and on 10 January 1944, the decree came out that awarded me the title Hero of the Soviet Union. The corps commander and I climbed in a car to drive to Front headquarters in order to receive our Orders; I, the Order of Lenin with a star, and he – the Order of Lenin. We drove a little way and the General spoke up, 'It's become a bit chilly.' The chauffeur had been well coached; he immediately stepped on the brake, pulled over, spread a table cloth out on the road's shoulder, and pulled out a flask and a simple snack. We had a drink. We drove another 25 kilometres, and again Popov spoke up: 'Oh, for some reason I'm freezing.' Again, the same scene unfolded. I had a second drink. The third time, I said, 'Comrade General, I can't.'

'What has happened to the young?! They can't even hold their liquor.'

We arrived at Front headquarters. A member of the Military Council handed us the medals, and we drove back.

Those fellows of my battery that survived were also decorated, but not all of them. You understand, it was some sort of joke. When firing over open sights, the gun commander has nothing to do. Two men do all the work – the gun layer and the loader. But when it came to medals, the gun layer and loader were sometimes overlooked, while the gun commander got the medal. Or he and the gunner would be honoured, but not the loader. This was unjust. Well, and then, for example, there was my case; if General Popov hadn't witnessed this stand against the tanks, no one would have nominated me for the title. In the best case, I might have been given some sort of medal. When I was sitting in the archives in Podolsk, I saw the commendation lists: a man would be nominated for the title Hero of the Soviet Union, but someone higher up writes, 'I think an Order of the Patriotic War is sufficient.' That would be that. Or on the contrary, someone would be nominated for the Order of the Red Banner, but someone higher up writes, 'In my opinion, he's worthy of the Hero.' It was a lottery, in general.

It was 22 March 1944. The guys came by to congratulate me on my birthday. In 1942 I had been wounded on this day. In 1943, I had received a concussion. The chemical section's chief came by, as well as someone else: 'Misha, we congratulate you on your birthday!'

'Thanks, guys.'

'You should at least get hold of a little something to drink.'

'Go on! Where am I going to get something?'

I was so naïve back then.

One guy said to me, 'Can't you go to the brigade commander? He can give you something?'

Thinking it over briefly, I went to the commander: 'Comrade Colonel, can I have a bottle of vodka?'

'What, you want something to drink? We'll fix you up right away.'

I explained to him that the fellows had congratulated me on my birthday and would like to have a drink. He replied with a question, 'How old are you?'

'20 years old.'

Then he turned to his adjutant and said, 'Summon Shchukin.'

Shchukin arrived. The Colonel told him, 'You know that today Misha is 20 years old? Now then, go arrange something.'

Putting it briefly, they did some arranging. A choir was brought in from the Kiev Philharmonic. A table at the forester's home, where I was staying, was spread. By dawn I was rolling on the floor and fell dead asleep. While I was sleeping, the Luftwaffe attacked and plastered us with bombs. One of the bombs fell just 2 metres away from my window, the blast wave blew out the window frame and it fell on me, while plaster rained down from the ceiling. When I woke up the next morning, for a long time I couldn't understand what had happened. I came away from it with a light scare.

I continued to serve as the battalion's Komsorg until August 1944. On 1 September, an order from Rokossovsky came out to send all the artillerymen of the 1st Belorussian Front who were Heroes of the Soviet Union to front-line classes to make junior lieutenants out of all of us. The classes were easy – after the artillery school, they were a piece of cake. On 23 February 1945, I was conferred the rank of junior lieutenant. They put me in charge of a student platoon of Heroes of the Soviet Union. Oh, I really had my work cut out with them! They were all to a certain extent pampered and spoilt. They were going around to all the isolated farmsteads and bringing back moonshine.

I once detained two of them. They were each carrying two pails hanging from the ends of walking sticks. I said, 'You what? You've again gone out for moonshine?'

'No, Comrade Lieutenant,' they replied, 'for milk.'

I took a look and actually saw white milk. Within half an hour, the platoon was rip-roaring drunk. They had mixed milk into the moonshine – there was no need for a snack. The weather was splendid, their duties were child's play – relax! I filed a report with the commandant of the courses, with a request to send me to the front. He refused me. A short time later, I made another request to return me to the front. I received another rejection. A third request – again a refusal. A fourth request – yet another denial. The fifth time, he summoned me: 'Fool, I wanted to protect your life, but you didn't understand this!'

'You needn't,' I replied. 'My place is there.'

I don't think I was star struck because I'd been made a Hero of the Soviet Union. Perhaps some of the guys envied me. I don't know. I continued to do my duties. In the battalion, no one did me favours. The Political Department watched over me a little bit, because I was a Komsomol worker. Well, the corps commander did too. But I didn't receive any special attention. I was fed like everyone else – I received soldier's rations. Only when the command invited me to see them, there they fed me a bit better. The command always lived a little better. Almost all of them had a campaign wife. Our artillery battalion commander didn't, but all of the rifle battalion commanders had one. Each female hygienist served faithfully and with obedience ... When we arrived at the classes for junior lieutenants, I went to Front headquarters together with my comrade from a tank brigade; he was an artilleryman just like I was, but a gun commander. He was a braggart. He said, 'I've destroyed more tanks than you.'

'You didn't destroy them; it was your gunner's doing.'

'I was in command!'

'Just so, you were commanding.'

Well, God take him.

At the Front headquarters we became acquainted with girls from the communications centre. They told us where they were living, and we dropped by to visit them unannounced around 5 o'clock that afternoon. They were all well groomed and well dressed, not in simple cotton stockings, but in imitation silk stockings. After just 15 minutes, they told us, 'Guys, scram.'

'Why? We have time, and you're also off-duty.'

'What, don't you understand? We're all already claimed. Now the working day is finished and they'll be coming for us ...'

At first I didn't have anything but hostility and hatred toward the Germans. I had seen what they had done in our territory. But already somewhere in 1944, my attitude started to change a bit. I recall that once we captured several Germans and sent three of them immediately to the rear, but I kept one youngster, who was around my age and was just as green as I'd been in 1941, in one of our batteries. I said, 'Let him feel at home for a bit.' He also could play the harmonica well. On the next day, the battery commander spotted him. He immediately came to me and asked, 'Komsorg, what are you doing? Why do you have a German here?'

'But he's just a whippersnapper ...'

'It's against the rules. Send him off to the rear immediately.'

We sent him away and felt sorry for him.

Nevertheless, there was a desire for revenge when we entered German territory. The guys would sometimes enter a home and fire a burst from their submachine guns at the various portraits hanging on the walls and at the cupboards with the dishware. Yet at the same time I saw with my own eyes how the field kitchens would give something to local citizens.

But I wouldn't say that I had such favourable attitudes toward the Germans. Even today, I have no desire to travel to Germany. There is still bitterness. My best years were lost in the war with them. Not long after crossing the German border, an order was issued that put a damper on improper conduct on occupied territory. Prior to this order, though, we knew only one thing: kill the German, and for four years we lived by this. So this sudden shift didn't come easily. A lot of men were put on trial. Well, how can one judge a man, for example, whose entire family had been shot by the Germans? Of course, he marched with a feeling of vengeance! As the Komsorg, I was explaining to the soldiers how they had to behave, though in my heart I often agreed with them.

I'm convinced that someone was watching over me during the war. How many occasions were there, when I should have been killed, but wasn't? Here's another one. Once I strayed from the road by about 15 metres, not more, and I grazed some barbed wire. A metre away from me, a 'Bullfrog' [the Red Army soldier's nickname for the 'Bouncing Betty'] – a German mine – bounded into the air and exploded. By all the rules, I should have been killed or in the best case badly wounded. Not a scratch! Not even my uniform was torn! I became frightened only later … As concerns a belief in God … we were raised in a different spirit. Before the war I never once swore – in my family this was considered a sin. We had icons. We were all baptized. When we were in a tight situation at the front, not only I, but many, many of the men would whisper, 'God, let this pass!' Was this faith? After all, in a fine, good minute we never gave it any thought.

In 1945 replacements were sent to us from Central Asia. I had one Armenian, one Georgian and a Ukrainian. Later there were also Uzbeks and Tadzhiks in the artillery battalion. Let's say straight out that as fighters, they weren't much. For example, in winter, we were always running, clapping our hands and pounding each other in order to keep warm. But he's standing like a post with his arms by his side. I tried to explain to him that he needed to run. He doesn't understand why. I give him a prod, just to stir him up somehow. He says to me, 'Why, Russian, are you treating me badly?' I tell him, 'I'm not wronging you; I just don't want you to freeze to death. You need to run, move around.' They grew up in a different climate, had a different attitude toward life, a different mentality. We were fed whatever was available; for example, borsch with a bit of pork in it. They only spat it out. They wouldn't eat it. I don't think that they all refused it; one or two would eat it. The Muslims also shunned alcohol, which was laudable.

It did happen that we took plunder during the war. We seized the army dumps in Morozovskaia. All the local citizens made use of the spoils. When we entered

Germany, there were a lot of different types of food in the warehouses. Once there was the following case: A soldier walks up to a cook:

'What's for our lunch today?'

'Chicken soup.'

'Again chicken soup, can't you prepare some *pirozhki* [Russian meat-filled dumplings]?!'

That's all he could say? They were full of themselves! Before 1943, he would have gladly gone for any bit of soup!

For a long time I had no watch. Then one of my soldiers brought in some Swiss watches. I personally didn't send packages back home.[2] Even when I got my first leave of absence in 1945, the only thing I did was to buy a couple of kilograms of candy somewhere. It was very tasty candy. I had a sweet tooth myself, so there was some sense in my purchase. I brought this candy home with me. When I was travelling through Poland, at one of the stations where we stopped I purchased ten bars of chocolate at a kiosk. There wrappers were brightly coloured. They cost an incredible amount. But we had money, so I bought them. I was thinking that I'd take home both the couple of kilograms of candy and the ten chocolate bars. They would make fine gifts for my family and friends.

At first I was riding on the roof of a freight car, but when we reached Brest some guys called me down into the car. They told me that a luggage rack was free – a very narrow one. I laid on it for a half-day, with my belt tied to a pipe so that I wouldn't fall out. At some point I could no longer stand it and I thought I'd try one of the chocolate bars. I attempted to break off a piece, but it wouldn't break. When I licked the chocolate, I discovered that there was only a very thin coating of it over a piece of plywood. What, this respectable elderly woman, the vendor in the kiosk, wasn't afraid? Back then, an entire people lived in fear; you could have been shot without any ceremony for this.

22 March 1945, my fourth birthday of the war. Our command post was located beyond the Oder River, south of Küstrin in an isolated cottage with a tile roof. We removed a couple of the tiles, stuck our scissors telescope up through the opening, and observed the enemy, pinpointing targets. In honour of my birthday they spread a small table, having set out a bottle of alcohol and something to nibble. We prepared to drink. Suddenly, the vehicle of the regiment commander Colonel Shapovalov drove up. He strode into the cottage: 'What kind of outrage is this?! Why is no one manning the scissors telescope?'

It wasn't my turn; it was the turn of Lieutenant Letvinenko, who was also a Hero of the Soviet Union. He was dawdling. I was thinking that the regiment commander was only going to stay about 5 minutes, not more, and then he'd leave. I got up and clambered up into the attic to the stereoscope. Just as I reached it – a German shell! I was hurled down from the attic by the force of the explosion. I still recall Colonel Shapovalov's pale face. He was thinking that it was his fault that I'd been wounded. They carried me in their arms down to an amphibious vehicle and sent me back across the Oder into a hospital.

In the hospital I lolled around in splendid style. I didn't have to share my room. One of the guys visited, bringing with him a keg of brandy, and placed it under my bed. The other patients sniffed it out, and they would timidly drop by before lunch: 'Do you have a little left there? Can you pour me a little?' I kept giving them a taste as long as I had some left. They fed us well. There were a lot of captured foodstuffs. In the evening the clinical nurse manager would come by and ask, 'What will you have for breakfast? What will you have for lunch? And for dinner?' Why? Because I couldn't at the time eat normal food. I'd been wounded in the jaw. In general, the hospital was a paradise, but it wasn't for me. Again, I longed to return to the front, because the final offensive was being prepared, this I knew.

So again I slipped away from the hospital prior to my discharge, returned to my unit and resumed my duties. On 16 April, we went on the offensive.

In front of Berlin one evening, I was walking to the observation post with a battery commander. While I dropped into a trench and moved along it, he remained up top and walked along the surface. He said to me, 'Climb out of there.' I climbed out.

He explained to me, 'Don't you know that the German in the evenings and at night sweeps our line with grazing fire? If you walk along the surface, the bullet will hit your leg, but if you walk along the trench line, it will hit you in the head.'

Just as he finished saying this, there was a burst of fire and I was wounded in the leg. At this point I wasn't going to go anywhere. I spent three days in the medical-sanitation battalion, and then returned to my battery on crutches. My bone hadn't been hit; the bullet had drilled through some soft tissue. They patched me up and I was back on my feet quickly, but on crutches.

On 1 May I couldn't take it any longer. I was now the commander of the fire-control platoon, and it was no longer my job to be at a firing position. Itching to fire a gun again, I walked up to one of the guns, asked the guys to load it, and out in front of me (I could see it well) was the Reich Chancellery. I fired ten rounds into the Reich Chancellery and gave vent to my feelings. Two days later, perhaps, I also went to the Reichstag with the guys, and our banner was already there. All around was lime and soot; everything was burned and the buildings were half in rubble. There were a lot of scrawled signatures every-where. I couldn't resist, and I also grabbed a lump of charcoal and wrote, 'I'm from Siberia.' Beneath it, I signed, 'Mikhail Borisov'. This was the first autograph in my life. I decided that with this act my war was over. Only later did I understand that it would remain with me for the rest of my life.

Later they pulled us out of Berlin and into some woods, because the city was jammed with troops. Somewhere around the evening of 9 May, wild firing erupted beyond our camp. I was sleeping in the cab of a truck. I grabbed my submachine gun and jumped out of the truck. I thought the Germans had dropped paratroopers somewhere. From all directions, guys came running, some with a submachine gun, and others with a pistol. We didn't know what was going on. The regiment commander came running. He was smiling from ear to ear: 'Guys, the war is over! The Nazis have surrendered!' Everyone around began firing into the air. Then that didn't seem to be enough, so we deployed our guns and blasted a clearing with our shells. We each fired ten rounds. Then we opened the doors of all the storage depots. Some guys knocked together tables out of loose boards, while others carried everything out of the storage sites that they could. We took seats around the tables and celebrated Victory Day. Toasts were made freely and some drank to each and every one; others drank to as many as they were able. The peaceful, not at all easy post-war life then ensued.

Notes

1. The afternoon attack by the 1st S.S. Panzergrenadier Regiment on 11 July 1943 toward Prokhorovka from Oktiabr'skii State Farm encountered strong artillery and anti-tank fire, some of which was flanking fire from units north of the Psel River. Naturally, multiple guns were often firing at the same target, and thus it is impossible to determine how many tanks a crew knocked out with any accuracy. However, as a positive reflection on their own command and leadership skills, Soviet commanders were interested in generating highly decorated subordinate soldiers and officers. Thus, knocked-out tanks would often be attributed to a single battery, crew or even individual to enhance the prospects that a combat Order would result – especially if the individual or men involved were Komsomol or Party members. This likely happened in Borisov's case, though this doesn't diminish in the least the heroism of his actions.
2. Red Army officers were allowed to send occasional packages back home from Germany, up to 10 kg a month; soldiers were limited to 5 kg a month. These usually contained plundered items like clothing, clocks and watches, fountain pens, and other items that were abundant in Germany but scarce in the Soviet Union.

Chapter 5

A Fight to the Finish

Boris Vasil'evich Nazarov

I was born in Moscow in 1923 in the neighbourhood of Patriarshie Prudy [Patriarch's Ponds – a long-time cultural and aristocratic centre of the city]. My father worked in a factory, while my Mama was a full-time mother and housewife. In 1940 I completed my tenth year of schooling and enrolled in the V.V. Kuibyshev Institute of Engineering and Construction.

In the summer of 1941, the entire second-year class of the Institute volunteered for the Moscow militia. They assembled us at the military enlistment centre on Butyrskaia Street, created a roster, and transported us to a summer military encampment in the Moscow suburbs. There we were issued a combat blouse, a side cap and a belt – our own boots and trousers made up the rest of the uniform. In this camp we practised close-order drills, and they demonstrated to us how to use a bayonet in hand-to-hand combat. There was one rifle with a bayonet, and in turn each of us stuck it into a dummy. They told us how we ought to fire, but over the entire time of our training, we never once had any target practice.

At the end of summer we were sent as a march company to the front as replacements for a rifle regiment. In the Smolensk region we spent the night at the Semenovsky State Farm. There, we had a meal and they issued us our rifles and cartridges. One 'old man', having glanced into my rifle barrel, concluded that I'd never hit a German from it. Speaking honestly, I didn't attach any particular significance to these words. I was still thinking that the war would end soon and I was in hurry to see what it was all about.

On the next day, regular officers appeared and split our company into platoons. I wound up in one of them together with two other students. In fact, in the future we all stayed together. Soon we marched to the front in a column and we joined some unit. Where we were or what unit we joined – I don't know. The position we were occupying was not at all a good one. There was a forest out in front of us. We should have been positioned on its opposite, western side, but we were dug-in on its eastern side.

On the second or third day there, several German planes flew past over-head. Soon, a dust cloud appeared above the road that ran not far from our position. Someone said it was German reconnaissance. When their vehicles moved within range, we fired some shots and they drove away. I didn't see any of our commanders again.

Soon, Germans deployed mortars beyond the woods and they began to pound our trenches. First they concentrated fire on our left flank, and then on our right flank. Once everyone had shifted into the centre of our position to avoid the fire, they began raining down shells there. I was wounded in the arm by a mortar fragment and received a slight concussion. The blood was spurting but I had nothing with which to stop it – I had no tourniquet or bandage. My buddies picked me up and evacuated me from the battlefield. They carried me to some village, scrounged a piece of cord, applied a tourniquet, and then we set out again. We reached a road. It was jammed with vehicles and people. Where they were going wasn't clear.

With difficulty, my buddies stopped a vehicle and placed me aboard it, and it delivered me to a hospital. I was bedridden there until autumn – I received meals and good care, so I don't have anything else to say about it. My arm healed, but it took quite some time before it was fully functional. Since I was an ambulatory patient, I had to help the medical personnel take care of the more seriously wounded.

I was discharged from the hospital at the end of December 1941 and sent to a military registration and enlistment office. I tried to secure work in a factory in order to receive an exemption from active duty – the romance of war had passed and I no longer wanted to fight at all. However, my effort to avoid returning to the front failed. In February 1942 I was drafted into the RKKA [Workers' and Peasants' Red Army] and sent to the Rostov Artillery School, which trained platoon commanders for the anti-tank artillery units.

On the outskirts of Niazepetrovsk, to where the school had been evacuated, we rebuilt the factory housing that dated back to Peter the Great, adapting them to serve as army barracks. Over the summer we succeeded in furnishing them, equipping them with three-storey bunk beds and stoves for heating. However, we didn't have time to build a kitchen, a latrine or most importantly, a Russian sauna, so in the winter of 1942–1943 we badly suffered from the cold. Moreover, we were wearing shabby summer uniforms: riding breeches, a combat blouse, a uniform jacket, puttees and ankle boots. Only our caps were winter-wear. It was cold and we became lice-ridden. The 5-kilometre march every evening into the woods, from which each cadet was supposed to bring back a log for heating the barracks and instructors' residences, was particularly exhausting.

By January the cadets had begun to bloat from hunger, and one day every battery refused to leave the barracks, demanding to be sent immediately to the front. The officers attempted to force us out, but we resisted. The commander of the Urals District came to the school together with Colonel Lampel', about whom it was said that during the Spanish Civil War he had commanded the defence of Madrid. They persuaded us to fall into formation out on the drill ground. Colonel Lampel' grabbed a handful of snow and handed it to the man on the right of the line, asking for it to be passed down the line from cadet to cadet, but the snow quickly melted away. That was the way, he said, that the cadets' rations were reaching our tables. He finished his speech with the words, 'I'll set things right!'

In fact, by spring we warmed up, drills became more regular, and they began to feed us better. Colonel Lampel' personally checked the amount of food going into the pots as the cooks prepared the meals. The school began to wake up each morning to the sounds of a bugle, which roused all the cadets at promptly 0600. The day began with physical exercises. We would rush out of the barracks in bare feet and underpants, do some chin-ups, and then wash up with icy water. Having dressed, we'd form up on the drill ground for roll call, after which we would march in formation to the mess hall for breakfast, where bread, porridge and tea – well, not tea, but tinted water – awaited us. In the mess hall each cadet had an assigned spot. One cadet would stand with his back to the table while another cadet would cut off a slice of bread and fill a bowl with porridge, after which he would ask the one with his back to the table, 'Whose?' That cadet would then in turn call out the name or nickname of a seated cadet, to whom this portion would then be passed. After everyone had their slice of bread and bowl of porridge, an order would follow and everyone would start eating. The meal would have to be finished in a set time. This process repeated itself at lunch and dinner.

After breakfast was the first task – 2 hours of close-order drills. Then wc would have 2 hours in the classroom, where we studied the regulations, topical political matters, and many other things, closely following the syllabus. At the bugle signal 'Grab a spoon, grab a container,' we'd march to lunch singing. After lunch came field tactics. The instructor would be in his fur coat, while we'd be freezing in our uniform coats. Afterward, having returned to the warm classrooms, everyone without exception would doze off. The most interesting were the classes conducted by Colonel Lampel'. He would familiarize us with German tanks, their vulnerable locations and their combat tactics. I remembered his definition of 'blitzkrieg' as the combined operation of three types of troops: aviation, tanks and mechanized infantry. He said that it remained to knock-out the German tanks and the blitzkrieg would collapse. One must give him his due; he actually shared his combat experience, which subsequently came in handy for me personally; I cannot say the same about our study of the manual, which was of no use.

italy Ulianov.   Nikolai Markov.   Mikhail Borisov, 1943.

 friendly cartoon of Mikhail Borisov portrayed as the hero
 the epic saga by Shota Rustaveli, *Man in a Tiger's Skin.*   Boris Nazarov.

Комсорг батареи Михаил
Борисов сжег 7 „тигров".

Любуйтесь!
Радуйтесь!
Дивитесь!

Картина сделана
с натуры!

Пред вами комсо-
мольский витязь!

В семи тигровых
шкурах.

(из фронтовой газеты)

Soldiers of Boris Nazarov's platoon. Nazarov is sitting on the cheek of the gun carriage in a service cap.

Moisei Dorman, 1945.

Vladimir Zimakov, 1945.

Nikolai Shishkin, 1945.

...e front and back of a watch awarded to Red Army soldier Konstantinovich Shishkin.

...om left to right, sitting: unknown, Nikolai Shishkin, Potapov; standing: Avraam, Podrezov, ...hanko, October 1940.

In the so-called 'Lenin room', Nikolai Shishkin is on the left, Khanko, 1940.

Shishkin's 76-mm regimental gun crew on exercises. Standing from the left: battery political officer Nikolai Shishkin and an unknown man; sitting from the left: Klivtsov, Kiselev, Mesin, Guschin, Bur

om the left: commanders of SPG batteries Zverev and Nikolai Shishkin, commanders of Shishkin's ttery SPGs Ustinov, Murav'ev, Krasheninnikov.

From the left: ikhail Chernomordik, egimental Komsomol der Stepnevsky, chief of staff Popov.

Aleksei Voloshin.

Mikhail Chernomordik.

Aleksandr Rogachev.

Battery commander
Aleksandr Rogachev
(with binoculars) and
his soldiers.

. 45-mm gun crew during the fight in the city. The commander on the left is searching for targets while trying not to expose himself to enemy observers. All soldiers carry knapsacks. The photograph is likely to have been taken in a real combat situation.

leksandr Rogachev (left) and Ivan anteleev, 18 September 1944.

A 45-mm gun crew practising a position change.

From 1943 Willys jeeps started to tow 45-mm guns instead of horses, but sometimes they needed help.

A 45-mm gun crew moving the gun. The gun commander (with binoculars) hangs onto the barrel to balance the weight of the gun carriage.

Horses towing an anti-tank gun.

Fighting in winter. The gun crew consists of just four men.

45-mm gun in action.

Another 45-mm gun in action.

A horse-drawn battery of ZIS-3 guns on the march.

ZIS-3 crew reduced to two men during a battle.

ZIS-3 firing from a covered position.

A platoon of 76-mm regimental guns prepare to fire from covered positions.

Regimental 76-mm gun, 1927 Model.

ZIS-3 firing over open sights.

PTRD crew practise firing on a German Pz-III tank.

A PTRD crew during training.

A PTRD crew changing position.

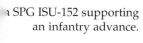
SPG ISU-152 on the
march.

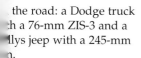
SPG ISU-152 supporting
an infantry advance.

the road: a Dodge truck
h a 76-mm ZIS-3 and a
llys jeep with a 245-mm
n.

Infantry on the march, with a 45-mm gun at the front of the column.

Somewhere in Germany: a Studebaker hauling a 76-mm ZIS-3 gun.

In addition to basic training and specialized artillery training, we were taught how to drive a vehicle and ride a horse. We were responsible for the school's security, worked in detachments and served the instructors. In general, we were busy up to our necks with studies, tasks, training and duties.

I remember one night in May 1943, when the school was raised in response to an alarm. From our formation, they called out cadets who were born in 1922 and 1923. We were issued dry rations for three days, which we consumed while we were marching to the railroad station, and we travelled to the Chebarkul'skie camps. Literally within several days after our arrival, they again loaded us into heated freight cars, which were hooked up to a train carrying tanks that was headed toward the front. We travelled for a long time; somewhere in Perm we received a good meal while our freight cars were hooked up to a different train, on the platform cars of which stood canvas-covered SU-152 self-propelled guns. Here we were divided into crews.

I was made a gun loader, and all the dirty work was dumped onto me and the radio operator, although our self-propelled gun wasn't equipped with a radio. What was the pecking order in the crew? The driver-mechanic was a god; the commander – another god; the gunner – a respected fellow; and the radio operator and I were the labourers. We had to refuel the vehicle with diesel, haul the shells, go for the meals, stand on sentry, and so forth and so on. We were always filthy and covered with oil. I don't remember the last names of these guys; I recall that the driver-mechanic's name was Grisha, the commander of the self-propelled gun was Ivanych, the gunner – Sasha (incidentally, he was a cadet just like me), and we simply called the radio operator *radist* [the Russian word for radio operator].

The platoon commander came by to see us one time. He told us that our armoured vehicles were secret, that when these self-propelled guns were brought to the Kremlin, Supreme Commander-in-Chief Stalin, having looked them over, said that this was the weapon with which we would win the war. The political worker, whom we called 'the Pope', came around occasionally, read us the newspaper and led some sort of discussion.

Once, we discovered two elderly women underneath the canvas covering our self-propelled gun. We made no effort to make them leave, and as a sign of gratitude they fed us some lard, of which they had two bags full. They success-fully reached their destination, while we received a little something extra to our rations, and it seemed to us that we'd gained some more strength.

Our commander Ivanych had a gloomy personality and he never seemed to react to anything. Grisha ran the show. He even showed the radio operator and me how to open the breech, how to load the gun, etc. Since I alone couldn't lift the 48-kilogram shell, two men had to load the gun.

After unloading, at night, we set out for the front lines. We drove all night and the following day. Despite the fact that the hatches were open, the heat inside the vehicle was unbelievable. Ivanych barred us from sticking our heads out of them, so we were sitting inside stripped almost naked. By evening we reached our jumping-off position and began to dig a revetment. Here at last the entire crew was working. Out in front of us we could hear the rumble of artillery fire. Occasionally, aircraft flew over us. That night there was a glow on the horizon in front of us.

When it became light, the sound of firing increased and in the distance, columns of black smoke rose into the sky – tanks were burning. From the hatch I could see a field, which began immediately beyond a shallow ravine that fronted our revetment. Beyond the field was a little village; a bit further on, some sort of tall buildings. The commander ordered us to move out the self-propelled gun and advance toward a knoll.

Suddenly Ivanych is shouting: 'Load!' We loaded the gun. The self-propelled gun rocked when the gunner fired. Again, 'Load!' Another shot, with scarcely time to open your mouth. With all the fumes, there was no way to breathe. The gunner began crying: 'A hit! A hit!' The vehicle commander stuck his head out: 'We hit it!' The rest of us started to move to take a look. He kicked us back down: 'Load, fuck it!'

At that moment a German shell penetrated the armour right where the driver-mechanic was sitting. Grisha was killed and rags in the fighting compartment started to burn. Ivanych shouted, 'We're burning! Bail out, fellows! . . . We'll explode any time!'

We dropped the shell that we were preparing to load and clambered out of a hatch. At first the radio operator and I dashed toward the ravine, but a Tiger was climbing out of it. We started running toward some bushes. The Tiger opened fire on our tanks, which were moving to our left. Our tanks returned fire. Everything was burning around us, ammunition was exploding, and men were leaping out of burning tanks like torches. It was sheer hell.

Bullets were whistling and armour-piercing rounds swept past us with a howl. From some unknown direction, an aircraft appeared and started to bomb – friendly or enemy, I didn't know. I was trying to run, but my legs were wobbly and the ground was shaking. I fell down several times. I looked back – it wasn't a battle, but a scene from hell! Both sides were in the process of exterminating each other. How I got out, I don't know, but I remained alive and I wasn't even wounded. When I reached the rear, I fell in with a field kitchen for anti-aircraft gunners. The battalion commander promised to add me to the roster, but soon I was summoned to regiment headquarters. A captain said, 'Listen, dear fellow, a letter of inquiry has arrived regarding you. Get moving to the Officers' Reserve.'

No matter how much I tried to convince them that I actually was Boris Nazarov, not an officer, and I had no reason to go there, they didn't begin to listen to me. NKO Order No. 0528 was in effect and it was being carried out without exception. I reached the Officers' Reserve with the letter I'd been given, making my way on foot or catching a ride on passing vehicles. The Officers' Reserve was located in a large village, where there was a sugar factory, and where we ate molasses to our heart's content. We had full freedom there, but this dream didn't last long – a major arrived and handed me a certificate verifying my promotion to junior lieutenant. I and another five men received new uniforms and shoulder tabs, and soon an instruction followed to report to army headquarters as well, and from there I made my own way to the 163rd (subsequently the 'Warsaw') Guards Red Banner Orders of Nevsky and Kutuzov Destroyer Anti-tank Artillery Regiment.

I reached the 163rd Guards Destroyer Anti-tank Artillery Regiment just after it had been withdrawn with the remnants of its gun platoons, having lost many guns and crews in a battle with German tanks in the area of the cities of Vinnitsa and Kazakin. From regiment headquarters I was immediately directed to report to the forward commander of a gun platoon, the individual gun commanders of which were Senior Sergeant Popov and Sergeant Major Liubimov. At the moment I arrived at this platoon's position, they had scrounged one divisional gun and a few shells, which had been abandoned by the infantry, plus one German light machine gun.

Thus equipped, they had set up an ambush on a road, down which German units were supposed to retreat. A short time later a column of trucks showed up which was being led by a tank. After Liubimov immobilized it and we shot up the column with the machine gun, the Germans turned back. They blew up their damaged tank and withdrew to a different back road, which bypassed our position. We pulled out of our position, gathered the soldiers who'd been wounded in the previous fighting from their hiding places, and brought them back to regiment headquarters, which was located in a village.

After these battles, the regiment's remaining personnel were withdrawn to Zhitomir for reforming. A new commander was sent to us to take charge of the battery. Soldiers with experience from the battles of Stalingrad and Kursk began to arrive from hospitals, as well as young, totally green soldiers from conscription centres.

Training began for upcoming battles. Sergeant Major Liubimov told us a lot about the 163rd Anti-tank Artillery Regiment, in which he had been serving almost since the war's start. Back then the Regiment had been equipped with horses and 45-mm anti-tank guns. In one of the battles, the 163rd Anti-tank Regiment had been completely destroyed. Its headquarters surrendered, but

Liubimov came out of the encirclement with the regimental banner and the journal of combat operations.

I learned a lot from him. One day after we'd been withdrawn for refitting, he asked me, 'Lieutenant, where have you fought?' I answered him.

'Well, then you don't know a damn thing. Go, dig yourself a hole and take a seat in it; I'll teach you.'

I dug a hole and sat down in it. He disappeared for a moment, and then a burst of submachine-gun fire struck around the hole where I was sitting.

He shouted, 'Where am I? Stick your head up, I won't fire.'

'And how should I know?' I replied.

'Listen again.'

That's how you teach someone who doesn't yet know how to determine the source of incoming fire! Such knowledge is necessary, since very often the surviving battery members found themselves in the German rear and had to make their way out of encirclement. That's how he trained me, and I had learned a lot by the time he was killed later in the war.

Soon we received ZIS-3 guns straight from the factory, and then American Studebaker trucks arrived. The gun crews were brought back up to full strength. A crew consisted of five men: the gun commander, a gun layer, a loader, and two ammunition bearers. All the crew members were mutually interchangeable. The strength of this crew was barely sufficient to hoist the gun trails and set them on the hitch of the Studebaker, and only then under the condition that the heaviest of the crew members dangled from the gun's muzzle brake as a counterweight.

I also received a personal weapon. But whereas all the command staff had TT pistols, I received a Nagant revolver, which had become so rusty that the cylinder wouldn't revolve, and no matter how hard I squeezed the trigger, the gun wouldn't fire. However, soon I procured a German Walther P-38 and life became easier. The gun crews received PPSh submachine guns. We did have to resort to them once, but it is hard for me to talk about it. Near Kovel, one day we crawled out into no-man's-land for some potatoes and bumped into a German combat outpost. The German foolishly tossed a grenade at us. Had he been smart, he would have kept down and not revealed himself. But apparently he wanted to fight, and wanted to kill us, but his grenade landed short. When he rose up to take a look, I gave him a burst. We crawled over to his position – he was lying there all bloody. I was totally shaken. I was all out of sorts ... It was unpleasant ...

Eventually I obtained an orderly, who would bring me meals from the kitchen and carry out various responsibilities. Lieutenant Colonel S.P. Arkhipov, who soon became a colonel, assumed command of the regiment. Only recently from documents did I learn that he was a Hero of the Soviet Union. He didn't wear his Star at the front and we didn't know that he was a Hero.

After the regiment was brought up to its authorized number of batteries, under its own power it joined the offensive in the direction of the city of Kovel'. On the road we were fired upon by submachine gunners from ambush positions. We quickly leaped out of the trucks, the sergeant major determined where the firing was coming from, and with several rounds we silenced it. In this place, several placards were hanging in the villages: 'Death to the Gestapo and the NKVD'.

On the road we were hardly fed, and we could only get milk from the local population; they hid everything else. But such was the atmosphere of mutual suspicions that even when accepting milk, we forced the owners to drink it first – we feared poisoning. In one farmhouse, the owner of which together with his family had left with the Germans, we found two pigs in the barn. I shot one of them. While we travelled, we ate fresh pork; even the regiment commander sent one of his staff officers, who asked for a rear leg, but we gave him only half of one.

As gun platoon commander, my task was to select a position correctly and to deploy the guns properly. After all, our shells could only penetrate the armour of tanks at close range, and this meant the tank had a chance to overrun the gun. So a position had to be selected that would enable us to camouflage the guns easily, but would also make it difficult for the tanks to overrun the guns. I loved to deploy a gun between two large trees, which the tankers knew beforehand that their vehicle couldn't knock down. In addition, I considered it my duty to fire the first shot and to destroy the first tank. If we succeeded in knocking out one or two tanks, then the rest would start to bypass our positions. Of course, they would spot us and begin to fire at us. Well, as soon as the first projectile passed over us, we would dive into holes, and wait to see if a shot hit the gun. However, they were now no longer advancing, fearing they'd lose another tank, and they'd begin to go around us. This gave us time to bandage the wounded and bury the dead. We lost men in every fight.

We created our firing positions in the following manner. We would dig our gun emplacements to a depth of around 50 centimetres and with a diameter of 5 metres. We threw the excavated dirt up around the perimeter in order to create a parapet. We would dig timber or small logs into the ground, butting them up against the gun's trail spades. If we didn't do this, the gun would roll backwards with the recoil, even if the trail spades were dug into the ground. We would then dig a magazine for the shells about 20 metres away from the gun and a trench leading to it from the emplacement. To the left and right of the gun, we dug foxholes. We set up a captured machine gun in the left foxhole, while a sentry and an observer sat in the right one. Usually they unloaded us into a firing position in the evening, and over the night we had time to dig and camouflage the position. Everyone worked, regardless of rank and insignia.

We took part in our first battle near Kovel'. The Germans were trying to free a grouping that we'd encircled in the area of the city, and we were deployed on an axis vulnerable to tanks. We moved into our firing position in the evening. My platoon was covering a road. In the place where we were positioned, the road made a sharp, 90° turn. Approximately 300 metres away from the road, there were two large trees on the edge of a patch of spindly woods. I set up the No. 1 gun of my platoon, with which I was located, between these two trees. The battery commander ordered that the No. 2 gun be deployed about 500 metres beyond the turn in the road. That night, a Guards mortar unit of *Andriusha* rocket launchers moved into that same place. On the other side of the road we could see shattered stone buildings, and a little bit behind them loomed a structure that looked like a factory workshop, from which periodically flares streaked into the sky and a machine gun fired. Behind our backs there was a ditch and a railroad embankment. The railroad had been demolished, and the rails and ties were standing practically vertically, looking like some sort of fence.

In the morning, after an enemy air attack, German tanks on our right started moving down the road in our direction, while from the front, from the direction of the factory, infantry went on the attack, taking cover behind buildings as they advanced. From long range, one of the tanks began to fire from the road in the direction of the rocket launchers and hit one of them, which exploded. As we found out later, one of the rockets, blown off its guide rail, struck the No. 2 gun of my platoon, destroying the gun and killing the entire crew. When the tanks drew even with our position, we set two of them ablaze, but a third tank opened fire at us. We had wounded. We leaped into our holes, where we sat until the firing stopped. The tanks didn't come at us, but turned off the road into a field and moved on past us.

We spent the rest of the day sitting in our position. The fighting shifted to our left, and the road became empty. That evening, the fellows carried our wounded to the rear, and I remained in the position to cover their passage over the railroad embankment. The guys returned that night with a Studebaker from a different battery. Under artillery fire, with great difficulty we hooked up the gun. I had just grabbed a hold on the truck, preparing to hoist myself into it, when I took a splinter in the stomach from a nearby exploding shell. They quickly loaded me aboard the truck and took me to the medical-sanitation battalion.

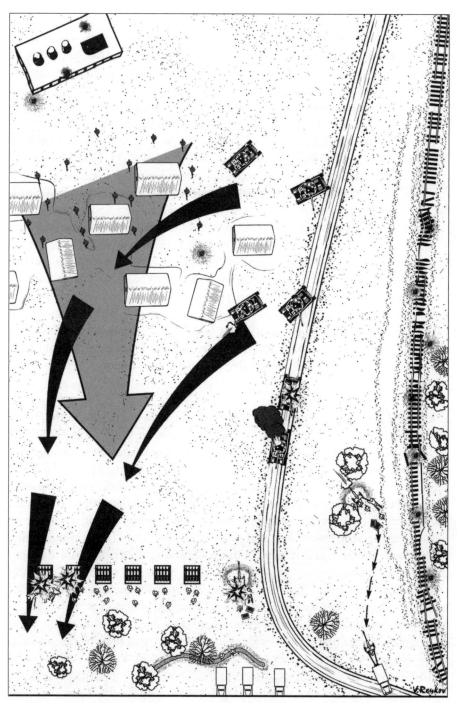

The battle of Boris Nazarov's platoon against tanks near Kovel'.

A doctor came into the room, took a look at my wound, and told the nurses, 'Carry him to the morgue.' I was trying to speak, but my mouth was foaming and I couldn't say anything though the pain was severe. After his words, I blacked out. I woke up in the morgue, when they had started to carry out the dead for burial.

One elderly nurse said, 'Take a look, this one's eyes are moving!'

The other replied, 'What do you mean, moving?! Roll him!'

However, they carried me into the operating room; a doctor came in, examined me, and said, 'Of all things, he hasn't kicked the bucket!' He operated on me.

I took rather a long time to recover, but before I was fully healed they sent me back to the regiment. I arrived all bandaged, and I had to go regularly to get my dressings changed. The regiment commander felt sorry for me, and when brigade headquarters sent a request for a combat officer to serve in the 47th Army's headquarters as a signals officer, he sent me.

In the evenings, the headquarters would organize dances, but I didn't attend them. Why? I'll tell you. On the first day when I arrived at the headquarters, I found a mirror, took off my threadbare combat blouse, my trousers, my puttees and ankle boots, washed them and bathed myself, of course without soap. Then I laid all this out to dry. Once everything had dried, I re-dressed and I felt like a million bucks! I went to the headquarters, and as I neared it I could hear music playing. Some soldier was walking nearby. I asked him, 'What's going on there?'

'They have dances there.'

I walked up, took a look, and saw that officers were dancing, and they were all such dandies. Their uniforms were spiffy, and their polished leather boots gleamed. Real prima donnas! I took another look and spotted a nice-looking female signaller. Alone. I thought, 'Well, that one's by herself; I'll take a seat next to her.' So I plopped down next to her, and then said, 'Well, you even have dances here. How fine!' I added something else and then suggested we get acquainted. She sat quietly, not saying a word. Well, then I shifted a little closer to her, put my arm around her, and said, 'Come on, let's get acquainted!' She gently took my hand, laid it back on my knee, and said, 'Listen, I have to stay on the line for commanders with multiple stars, while you've got just one little star and are groping me.' That was all! I never went back there again, except for one time when I went to see an American film, but that was it.

It must be said that I didn't feel any hatred or deep-seated envy for these well-groomed staff officers. I had an acute desire to be in their place – to sleep in a warm bed with clean sheets, and not in a lice-ridden, filthy trench; to be fed regularly and well; to be dressed so grandly. There'd also be a little less death all around. So when a month later an order arrived to return to the regiment and reassume my post as a gun-platoon commander, I felt bitter and upset. I'd become so tired of all the fighting, the filth, the blood and deaths! What kind of life is that?!

Bad news was waiting for me when I returned to the regiment. I learned that in one of the recent battles, Sergeant Major Liubimov had been killed.

In 1944 the situation in and around Warsaw was complicated. We were shifted to the area of the town of Legionowo. In one of the battles on a hill near Legionowo, I lost the gunner Mit'ka Dolinsky and the loader Tsai ... Mit'ka was a Muscovite like me. We'd become friends. How he loved to fire the gun! He was quite the fellow. He was sitting in his hole. A rocket shell came out of nowhere and landed directly in his foxhole. When I glanced in that direction after the smoke and dust had cleared, I was struck numb by the sight of this bloody mass; somehow his 'For Courage' medal glittered on top of it. That was it – Mit'ka Dolinsky was gone. So I buried him in this hole.

One day they summoned me to regiment headquarters, and the commander reassigned me to a platoon of SU-76 self-propelled guns of a then forming Polish artillery regiment. When I reached it I found three other Red Army men: driver-mechanics whose assignment was to deliver several self-propelled guns to the regiment. Within a certain amount of time, they dressed us in Polish military caps and greatcoats made from British wool.

I recall that once I entered a Polish village. I was walking down the street, and suddenly a window opened, a Polish woman leaned out and said, 'Mighty Polish soldier! Come in, come in, sir!' I went inside. She was chattering something and offered me a seat, but I was feeling uncomfortable – my boots were tracking mud into her house, and under my greatcoat I was still wearing our Red Army combat blouse. Just then she spotted someone else walking past her window – a lieutenant. Again she leaned out and said, 'Mighty Polish soldier, Lieutenant, sir!' So a real Pole entered the house. He was speaking refined Polish exclusively. She also offered him a seat. They both turned to me and said something – I couldn't catch a word of it. I thought that I needed to scram, so I quietly slipped out into the corridor. I look, and there's his cap hanging there. It was a beauty, with an eagle and a lacquered visor. I left my own cap for him and took his. I also swapped greatcoats. I stepped outside and went on my way, making sure not to pass the window. When I arrived back at my unit, the fellows gasped, 'Oh, Lieutenant, sir!' Of course, what I did was wrong ... In general, our relations with the Poles were only so-so.

Once I decided to go for a ride in one of the self-propelled guns. We entered a little city, which was still partially held by Germans. As we were moving down the street, out in front of us a German tank began to cross an intersection. From short range we set it ablaze. We stopped in front of some house. Grishka, the driver-mechanic, said, 'I'll go in and check out the cellar. I'll look for some juice.' The locals canned juice, and for us it was a novelty.

'Well, go and look,' I said.

'Let's go together, you can cover me.'

So we climbed down from the self-propelled gun and entered the house. I sensed that someone was in it. We went down into the cellar and didn't find any juice, but realized someone alive was down there. We thought it was Germans. Grishka shouted, 'Halt!' – and from behind a wall stepped a Polish or German woman – damned if we knew – and two small kids. She took a seat behind a table in front of a basement window and looked at us with fright: 'Kaput, kaput!'

I took a seat opposite her and said, 'Now the war is ending; I'll go home to Moscow and I'll get married.' She kept looking at me and looking out the window, where this German tank was smoking. Grishka asked her why she was looking out the window, and added that we were the ones who had just knocked it out.

The woman replied:

> It's only because an *Oberleutnant* was just sitting here in your spot, and he also said that the war was ending, he was going back to Berlin, and he'd get married ... Now there you are, from Moscow, sitting where he was, and you're talking about the same thing. I'm curious; is he alive or was he killed?

Grishka said, 'That can be checked.'

The woman went out with Grishka and they examined the tank, but there was nobody there, dead or living – the crew had run off. They came back pleased. We continued to sit for a bit longer, and then we headed back to our unit. The gunner with the crew of this self-propelled gun was a guy whose last name was Guiman. Soon after we returned, there was a call from headquarters: 'Guiman's father has arrived for him. He's a big-shot doctor and he's come to get his son.'

At the time, we were sitting together with him and eating porridge from a mess tin. I told him, 'Listen, your father's come for you. Report to headquarters.'

'I'm not going,' he replied, 'I'm afraid.'

'What are you afraid of? I'll give you an escort.'

'I'm afraid. I'll never reach headquarters.'

Indeed, he didn't go.

Night fell. In the middle of the night, a soldier shook me awake: 'Lieutenant, Guiman has been killed.' He had been sitting next to the self-propelled gun. A shell came in and exploded directly at his feet, taking his head off. Why hadn't he left for headquarters in the evening? Perhaps he would have reached it ...

I remember when we were shifted to a new axis; you look at the guys and all their faces were grey. They didn't look normal somehow. I recall another case.

When I came out of one battle, I dropped by a house. Mirrors were hanging on the walls. I went in, and in a mirror I saw an unfamiliar man and reached for my Walther. He did the same . . . only then did I recognize myself in the reflection, and I was just about to fire. Can you imagine that a man can be reduced to such a state?

The rear-echelon soldiers were involved in the looting and rapes. I never saw such behaviour among my guys. Those at the front, as a rule, didn't mistreat the local population, and the civilians in turn related to us not badly. What if suddenly it happens that you're wounded and surrounded? Who other than the local civilians will hide you? That's what compelled all of us, who were at the front, not to engage in looting or violence against the civilian population. Of course, we searched for hidden provisions, dug them up and, of course, devoured whatever we found. There's no way you can get by without this.

Things didn't go well with the formation of the new Polish regiment; replacements didn't arrive and there weren't enough self-propelled guns. So having gotten a bit of rest in the rear, I returned to my gun platoon.

In the winter, we were holding defensive positions, having settled into the homes and cellars abandoned by the local residents. I remember a cold, east wind was always blowing, and it snowed quite a bit. Silence had fallen over the front lines, with only rare shellfire from the enemy's side. My gun platoon received replacements: gun commander Zakharov, gunner Ermolenko, gunner Varlashkin, and gun commanders Kholetsky and Masiuk.

Two of the guns were replaced, one of which due to deterioration of the gun barrel, the other because of a direct shell hit. Over the entire time of my service in the three gun platoons, more than a dozen guns had to be written off, but not one of them was overrun by a tank or abandoned.

After the New Year 1945, the regiment formed into a column, past which the new command wearing camouflage smocks drove in review: the regiment commander, Lieutenant Colonel Bondarenko; the commissar Tsariuk; and the chief of staff Kholodenko. Soon thereafter, we launched a new offensive.

We forced a crossing of the Vistula River over the ice. We stopped in a village, which lay in ruins, on the road into Warsaw. That night I went into Warsaw in a Studebaker, because prior to this I had received a letter from home, requesting I go in search of a daughter of a close friend of my father. Her last known address in Warsaw was Building 2 on Marshalovsky Street. Warsaw was empty and burning. I found the building, but there was no one there.

As part of a tank column, the regiment moved along a road that paralleled the Vistula River in the direction of Bydgoszcz. There were a lot of prisoners. As we were approaching Bydgoszcz, the column came under fire from machine guns and submachine guns from a roadside settlement. A gun commander,

Sergeant Major Kholetsky, deployed his gun and opened fire on the cellars of the nearest buildings, but he was soon killed. After the battle we buried him at the foot of a turret of the fortress. Under the cover of tanks that had hastened up, the column entered the city. The Germans offered no resistance.

The regiment continued on toward the city of Stettin. Along the road together with us moved refugees and civilians of various nationalities, who had been working for the Germans. Having deployed in Stettin, the regiment fired from covered positions at the bridge, over which German troops were retreating from Prussia. There were a lot of families of German refugees and unarmed German soldiers who had lost their units surrounding our batteries. Our relationship with them was peaceful; they even offered us food and told us that Hitler was finished, that he hadn't been seen in Berlin since January, and that he was making no addresses over the radio. They were very afraid that they were going to be sent to Siberia, having heard what Goebbels was saying over the radio. After liquidating this pocket of resistance, we crossed the Oder River over a pontoon bridge.

We had our last combat with German tanks in Pomerania, near Deutsch Krone (present-day Wacz, Poland). We were to take a position beyond the Khlebovo Estate. My gun platoon was bringing up the rear of the regiment's column. Just a little more than a kilometre short of the estate the column was met by infantrymen, who were waving their arms and shouting, 'Where are you rolling?! Germans are there!' The batteries moving in front had time to turn off the road to the right and hide in some woods, but German tanks opened fire at our battery. The trucks of the 1st Platoon, trying to drive off the road to the right, became stuck in a roadside ditch. I climbed out of the cab of my truck and gave a sign to the No. 2 gun to turn to the left off the road and take position behind a storage bunker holding potatoes. *Katiusha* rocket launchers were already occupying a position there and were preparing to open fire on the estate.

Meanwhile I drove on a little bit and came upon an exit to the right off the main road. Under fire, we unhitched a gun, rolled it into some woods, and having taken a position among the trees, dropped off a few cases of shells. In front of us we could see a trench, with one end terminating at the road, the other end anchored on a large pond. Gunner Senior Sergeant Varlashkin, having noticed that the trench was full of Germans, opened fire on it, and taking casualties they began to run. Varlashkin and I began to pivot the gun in the direction of approaching German tanks, and at this moment a projectile tore off his leg below the knee. With Nikolai's stump gushing blood, I hoisted him onto my back and attempted to carry him away from the gun, but at this point some guys hurried up, took him from me, and carried him off in the direction of the Studebaker. Having returned to the gun, I watched as a German shell struck one of the *Katiusha* rocket launchers, and a chain of explosions resulted that destroyed them; my No. 2 gun and its crew perished there. At this time, German tanks and self-propelled guns advanced through a passage between the road and the pond and went on the attack against the positions of our infantry. Having allowed them to approach to 200–300 metres, I hit two of the armour vehicles in the flank and set them ablaze, while the remaining vehicles turned back.

After the destruction of the German panzer grouping in Pomerania, our regiment was sent on a march toward Berlin. The German Wehrmacht was disintegrating in front of our eyes. It was a repeat of 1941, but in the opposite direction. There were so many resigned German troops that we no longer took them prisoner, and they were marching in columns in some unknown direction. On this march our gun platoon lost gun commander Masiuk. One night he was standing watch at the building that housed the battery commander. A column was filing past him, and one of them approached Masiuk to have a smoke. Realizing that he was a German officer, Masiuk took him prisoner and led him into the building. While the battery commander was questioning the *Oberleutnant*, Masiuk shot himself with the Parabellum pistol that he had taken from the German officer.

During the preparations for the final offensive against Berlin, the question of converting the regiment into a heavy self-propelled artillery regiment was finally resolved. We hurried to obtain four JSU-152 'heifers', as we called them, and I became the commander of one of them. We were attached to storm groups, which consisted of infantry and combat engineers. When the fighting for Berlin began, we as part of the assault group moved down the streets, primarily using our machine guns to fire at open windows on the upper floors and at the cellars of buildings. On our axis of advance, the resistance was light and scattered.

On 1 May 1945, we were advancing toward the city centre along one of the streets. Suddenly something rocked our assault gun. I crawled out of the hatch in order to see what had happened. One of the tracks had been broken by the explosion of a shell or a mine. At this moment a shell exploded not far away, and a fragment struck me in the knee, smashing the knee cap and tearing the ligaments. I fell. Some guys picked me up and carried me into a cellar, where they bandaged my leg. The guys crafted a splint from two sticks, which they wrapped with a strand of wire, and attempted to teach me how to walk with this contrivance. However, I was unable to do so.

I continued to lie in this cellar until the evening of 2 May. The guys kept running out and bringing back cigars and French brandy. Then they returned with an entire drum of something. They were saying, 'We've brought you some ice cream!' They gave me a spoon, and when I took a spoonful and sampled it, the frozen mixture turned out to be lime sorbet. They themselves hadn't tasted it, but they dug into it with gusto – a feast of a frozen treat!

Soon I was taken to a hospital in Potsdam. German doctors operated on me and inserted a prosthetic knee ligament. After recovering I was discharged from the ranks of the RKKA in 1946 according to Article 1A. I could only walk with the support of a cane.

I went back to my institute. There they told me, 'We have no records showing that you ever studied here. We were evacuated and we lost everything.'

'Excuse me, but what can I do?' I asked.

I had to take the entrance exams again. I must say that to my surprise, even though four years had gone by, I passed the exams. I graduated from the V.V. Kuibyshev Institute of Engineering and Construction, and then worked to design and build things in the electronic industry, before switching to the aviation industry, where I worked at many of the defence industry's enterprises across the entire Soviet Union.

What was the attitude toward invalids of the war? It was a hard period. People without arms and without legs lived by begging around the subway and rail stations. Pensions were tiny. Families rejected cripples. The war invalids had to hear reproaches like 'Why have you come back? You were supposed to have been killed there, but you've returned.' There was so much hatred; where it all came from, I don't understand.

Initially after the war, films were made only about the generals and their hard-to-swallow exploits during the war. Indeed, back then there wasn't even a drop of truth in the films. There was one about anti-tank gunners entitled, *Goriachii sneg* [*Burning snow*]. Well, judge for yourselves how it would be possible to set up guns in compact rows, like in the film? Tanks would have taken them from the flanks and crushed them. They wouldn't have been able to turn and fire through each other! The general walks around, passing out Orders – nonsense! Our regiment commander never even made an appearance. Even the battery commander sought to stay with the vehicles at least 300 metres behind our positions.

I no longer dream of the war. At first, after I had just returned home, I would have nightmares about it. Everything would seemingly be fine, and I would fall asleep. I'm dreaming about a field of grass – and suddenly there's an explosion! I would wake up in a cold sweat, unable to breathe, there's no air – everything would be unhinged. For three years I was tormented like this, but then it passed. Once it had all passed, it was forgotten, and I didn't recall any of it. It is only now, in my old age, that I can say something about it.

Chapter 6

Enough Endurance Trials for a Lifetime

Moisei Isaakovich Dorman

In June 1941 I was 17 years old. Several days before the war began I graduated from the Ten-year School No. 1 in the city of Pervomaisk and received my secondary school diploma. I decided to enroll in the Leningrad Military-Mechanical Institute. On 20 June I submitted my application forms, but I didn't even have time to receive an acknowledgment before the war started. Over the first ten days of the war, we had information about what was happening at the front only from newspapers and the radio.

From the beginning of July, our city was bombed incessantly, because the headquarters of the Southwestern Front, a railroad hub, and a strategic railroad bridge over the Southern Bug River were located there. Thus, the German bombers had plenty of targets. When permits for evacuation began to be distributed freely to the residents of Pervomaisk, it was already impossible to leave the city by vehicle. There were no trains for displaced people. Only trains loaded with factory equipment and Red Army personnel were leaving the city. For several days in a row, we went to the railroad station, which was already badly damaged by bombings, but everywhere they chased us away from the trains, claiming that this one was a 'special factory' train, or that one was a 'special' train, which was inaccessible to refugees. Sometimes a train that was preparing to depart came under the next bombing raid. Any undamaged rail cars remaining after the attack were hitched to military trains. We had no success in finding a train. At the end of each day of frustrations, my parents, my elderly grandmother, my younger brother and little sister and I would return home frazzled and exhausted, but the next morning we'd head to the station again, trying to escape the city on whatever train we could take. I'll never forget that sensation of impending doom and hopelessness.

On 23 July, rumours started circulating around Pervomaisk that the city had been fully encircled. But on 26 July, I coincidentally overheard that the last factory train would be leaving from the station. The entire family ran to the station, which was 3 kilometres from our home. While we were running, we twice came under bombings. The factory train consisted of open platform cars, which were densely jammed with machine tools, machine parts, rusty beams, electric motors and roughly knocked-together boxes. No one chased us from the station platform – all the railroad command and the station security had already run off. The Germans were continuing to bomb the city. Next to us, the ruins of the bombed-out locomotive depot were smoking.

The train wasn't moving – there was no steam engine. We were praying for only one thing – that a bomb wouldn't strike the railroad bridge. Otherwise, it would be the end to all our dreams ... That night, throngs of retreating Red Army troops and some sort of wagon trains were passing hastily through the city. It wasn't a retreat – it was a stampede ... The station was bombed again and again. Those were difficult hours of waiting for some sort of miracle ...

At dawn, the ancient steam engine *Shchuka* suddenly appeared from somewhere. Our train was hooked up to this locomotive. The railroad line to the bridge across the Bug was still intact, but plainly not firmly so. The train was moving very slowly, stopping constantly. Over the first 24 hours, we travelled only 10 kilometres. Beyond, the hard road to the east awaited us. Bombings, shell fire, hard living conditions and hunger stalked us for the entire duration of the trip. Many of the people on board this train got lost along the way, fell sick or stayed behind. Many crowded us at the innumerable forced halts – encircled people and refugees, who had fallen behind their own trains ... This journey to the Volga lasted twenty days. In Rtishchevo, our train unloaded and the refugees were sent on into the deep interior of the country. Our family wound up in the town of Lys'va, and then I alone roamed around the country. Kazan', Magnitogorsk ... Enough endurance trials for a lifetime.

In the middle of 1942, I found out that the Leningrad Military-Mechanical Institute, to which I had sent my application papers, had been evacuated to the town of Motovilikha, close to Perm'. I went there. In the month of October I reached the Institute. I was assigned to the artillery department. Although the Institute was considered a military one, and even gave exemption from active duty in the army, all the students walked around in civilian dress.

I was famished. According to the ration cards, students were given 400 grams of bread a day. I studied in the Institute until the beginning of December. In my group there were only six guys, and other than me, all the rest of them were sons of the Institute's teachers.

I decided to head to the front. From the Institute I received a certificate of dismissal and a waiver of my exemption from service. I went to the local military enlistment centre and started pestering to be taken as a volunteer. Over the next half hour, I passed through all the obligatory committees and I was directed to go to the 1st Rostov Artillery School, which prepared officers for the anti-tank artillery. How had this school represented itself thus far in the war? The 1st Rostov Artillery School had taken part in the summer and autumn fighting in the Caucasus, had suffered heavy casualties at Mozdok, and at the end of 1942 it had been withdrawn into the deep rear, establishing itself in the remote Urals town of Niazepetrovsk in the north of Cheliabinsk Oblast. Now it was located in an enormous, badly dilapidated church, which had probably been built back in the time of the Demidovs.[1] The school had three battalions, each of which had three batteries. Each battery had approximately 120 cadets. The school's artillery park consisted of 45-mm and 76-mm guns and 122-mm howitzers, all of which were horse-drawn. All of the artillery training and all of the practical exercises for the cadets were conducted on the Russian '*Trekhdiumovka*' – the 3-inch Model 1902 gun.

The school selected cadets with a minimum of seven years of schooling. There were no other criteria for selection. I wound up in the 38th Training Platoon. The majority of this platoon consisted of 18-year-old guys, who'd previously been studying in secondary schools or college. Around ten of them were former criminals, young and insolent, who immediately tried to impose the prisoners' code of conduct within the battery. There was also a group of local residents from the Urals, all over age 30. In my class there were several platoons that were fully manned by veterans who'd been sent to the school for training straight from the front.

For the most part I have no fond memories of the school. Once I arrived in Niazepetrovsk, I spent several days in the school's 'quarantine'. On the very first day of my arrival, someone stole all my things, including a couple of items of great value to me: a fountain pen, which was a great rarity back then, which I had received upon my graduation from school, and what was even more upsetting, my father's heirloom 'Pavel Bure' silver watch, with the inscription 'For excellent marksmanship', which he had received back in 1916. This loss caused me enormous pain, and I took it as a bad omen.

On 15 December 1942, the newly arrived students were taken out of quarantine and sent to a bath house. At the instruction of some officer, we 'voluntarily' turned over all of our civilian clothing to the Defence Fund, and in return received some receipt written on notebook paper. They gave us a shabby cotton fabric uniforms, short threadbare coats, and well-worn ankle boots with puttees. Rags, not uniforms ...

The winter of 1942/1943 in the Urals was very harsh. Quite often the temperature fell to –50° C. [–58° F.] At night, the temperature inside the church where the cadets lived never rose above freezing. Water in a bucket turned into ice overnight. Under Soviet power the church had been converted into an agricultural storage facility; the building had fallen into disrepair and was very drafty. Each night before we slept, we had to run 8 kilometres into the nearest woods, gather logs at a cutting site, and haul them back to the school. Each cadet was obligated to bring back a log of 2 metres length. The church had rows of three-level bunks, each with a sack-mattress stuffed with straw.

We were constantly hungry. The wartime rations were meagre; the typical meal consisted of cabbage soup and a frozen potato. The bread, I'm ashamed to say, was divided up according to prison custom. One of the cadets would turn around and call out the name of the cadet who was to receive the next portion. To be assigned to a work detail in the stables was considered a stroke of good fortune; there you could eat a little linseed meal! When out of the barracks and not in formation, the cadets were forced to move only at a run. The discipline in the school was draconian. We were pressed into work details for the slightest demerit for a violation of regulations or for the most insignificant breach of rules. There were no leaves of absence, no free days or any sort of diversions.

The daily drills were mind-numbing. Each day consisted of 12–14 hours of intense drills, exercises and studies. The cadets, their moods low from the cold and the hunger, eagerly awaited graduation from the school as a deliverance from their suffering. Those who washed out from the school were sent to the front with the rank of sergeant. So it was against this backdrop that nine months of my training went by in the 1st Rostov Artillery School.

My platoon leader, Lieutenant Shornikov, who had survived the fighting in the Caucasus and was striving to return to the front again, was respected by the cadets and behaved commendably. A good man, he repeatedly filed requests with the commandant to be returned to the active army. We admired his longing. My battery commander Prishkura also made a good impression. He was an experienced and fair-minded officer. The deputy chief of the school, the German Colonel Lampel', also elicited respect. Our school commandant was an imposing figure, a brigade commander with the last name of Kudriavtsev, it seems. He was a former Tsarist officer. The commandant had a high-bred, noble face with a goatee and an attentive, stern appearance. He comported himself in a suave, dignified fashion.

As far as the training we received at the school went, the volume of knowledge we acquired was of course not even close to being adequate for the front. At the front we had to learn much all over again. We had little gunnery practice. Only a handful of men from each battery went through qualification firing. I was the gunnery officer, who corrected the fire, only once. We fired at wooden mock-ups of tanks that were towed by a long cable only twice. We saw German tanks only in illustrations. But obviously in order to fight in the anti-tank artillery, experience is necessary. After all, combat against German tanks, even for those serving in a destroyer anti-tank artillery regiment or a separate destroyer anti-tank battalion, was not a constant job. Experience at the front demonstrated that in addition to destroying German tanks, a no less important task for the anti-tank gunners was to support the infantry by 'fire and wheels'.

An understanding of the combat situation, the dynamics of combat, as well as a 'sense of terrain' comes only through real combat experience, and unfortunately, not right away. As for all these school drills in tactics ...

They taught us how to lay indirect fire from defilade positions. Over my one and a half years at the front, I never once fired indirectly; it was always over open sights.

Theoretically, it only required three or four days to train a gunner. The gun layer watched the range dial, and sets the sight taking into account the necessary deflection for movement. Seemingly all quite simple, but ... Not everyone could become a gun layer. It was a demanding position that required speed, accuracy, even precision in actions, but most of all, coolness under fire. He had to aim the gun at a moving target quickly and accurately, even when shells are falling all around him with a howl, bullets are rattling against the gun shield, and the tanks are brazenly heading straight toward the gun emplacement, firing on the move. Any lack of accuracy or a moment's delay by the gunner could cost the crew dearly. A good gunner in training sessions could hit a tree trunk with his very first shot at a range of 700 metres.

Only the friends that I made in this school helped me to overcome all these hardships of cadet life. We kept together: Nikolai Kazarinov, Kostia Levin, Valentin Stepanov and I. As it happened, after graduation from the school, at the front Nikolai and I wound up in the same anti-tank battalion, while Kostia and Valentin were assigned to a different one. Nikolai Kazarinov was killed in 'fighting of local significance' on 25 June 1944 in the village of Pistyn'. The battery in which Kazarinov served was repelling an attack by Hungarian infantry. After the battle, there was a sudden artillery strike and Nikolai was cut down by a shell fragment. I personally buried my friend in an apple orchard on the outskirts of the village. The soldiers saluted him with three volleys from their carbines, while I mechanically fired off the entire clip from my pistol.

On 28 April 1944 at Iaºi [Jassy], my other friend and classmate, the Muscovite Valentin Stepanov was killed by an exploding mine. At the end of April 1944, also at Iaºi, a German tank overran Kostia Levin's gun. A shell fragment nearly removed Kostia's leg at the knee. It remained attached by only a few tendons. He attempted to cut it off with a pocket knife, but because of the loss of blood, Kostia didn't have the strength to do it. Slipping in and out of consciousness, he managed to crawl off the battlefield, where a medic found him and rushed him to the medical-sanitation battalion. My closest, my last friend of my youth passed away on 19 November 1984. I've kept fond memories of Nikolai, Valentin and Kostia for all my life.

Let's return to the school. In the summer of 1943, we were transferred to a military encampment on the outskirts of Cheliabinsk, to the so-called 'Red

Barracks'. There, upon completion of our accelerated training, we became officers and acquired the rank of junior lieutenant.

In the final week before graduation, they began to hound and push us around less; we had a certain feeling of empowerment, liberation from the crude daily oppression. On graduation day, the school commandant gave us a speech. I can still recall verbatim his parting words to us:

> I congratulate you on your first officer's rank! The Motherland will soon entrust her sons to you. Remember, the soldier should see in you not only his commander, to which he must subordinate himself unquestioningly, but also an example for imitating. Your every action will be in full view; the attentive soldier's eye will notice everything – valour and cowardice; concern and neglect. If you even once show cowardice or display dishonesty, you will lose the respect of your soldiers, your comrades-in-arms, besmirch your name, and cover your officer's uniform with shame. It is better to die than to be so dishonoured!

Before our departure for the front, we were given new officers' blouses, leather boots, soldiers' belts and greatcoats. The first to graduate and to be sent to the front were the platoons consisting of former front-line veterans.

In October 1943, they loaded us, the approximately 300 freshly baked junior lieutenants, into cattle cars and sent us into the acting army. We travelled by rail to the shattered city of Khar'kov. Here we joined the 38th Separate Battalion of the Officers' Reserve under the command of Major Titov. This battalion was the source of replacements for officer losses in the artillery of the 38th Army. I spent one and a half months in reserve. We lived in this time according to the principle, 'They will not send us anywhere worse than the front, and we will still command the platoon.'

I didn't reach the front until December 1943. I was assigned to the 14th Separate Guards Airborne Destroyer Anti-tank Artillery Battalion of the 2nd Guards Airborne Division. Thus began my front-line service.

The battalion consisted of three batteries, each of which had two gun platoons. Only battalion headquarters had an operations platoon. Each battery had four 45-mm Model 1942 guns and approximately twenty-five to thirty men, including the drivers. The guns had mechanized transport; we had Willys jeeps to tow them. In the autumn of 1944, the 45-mm guns were replaced with 76-mm ZIS-3 guns, and instead of the Willys jeeps, we were given Dodge ¾-ton trucks. The batteries did not have their own signallers or scouts; they were all located with the battalion's operations platoon. The battalion's TO&E included an anti-tank rifle company of twelve anti-tank rifles, but in our battalion this company served primarily as a source of replacements for the anti-tank artillery crews, and they were rarely used for their designated purpose. There was also an ammunition supply platoon of approximately ten men with the battalion headquarters.

The battalion was commanded by Guards Major Fedor Kuznetsov. Since our battalion was separate, the commander had rights equivalent to those of a regiment commander. The battalion headquarters also had several more officers – 'executives' – deputy political officer Kudriavtsev, senior adjutant Makukhin and deputy commander Vishnevsky. There were also the chief of ammunition supply, the chief of finances (who was also the chief of general stores and of ration and forage supplies), the technical assistant, and the medical chief, who was a combat paramedic. Of course, there was also the staff 'collective' – clerks, a mail clerk, the chemical instructor, two female medical assistants, the Party organizer, procurement officers and other 'lame-brains'. The battalion had two radios, but they never worked, and I can't even recall whether we had any radio operators at all. In total, we had approximately 180 personnel.

As I've already mentioned, the battalion was equipped with the long-barrelled 45-mm Model 1942 anti-tank gun, designed by General Krupchatnikov. We called this gun the 45-mm/68 calibre. It was light, weighing only 570 kilograms. Two or three men could easily manhandle the 45-mm across a field. It was a smallish gun; we had the saying about it that it could 'turn the soil'. It had hinged shields, one central and one on each side. The gun's rate of fire was twenty rounds a minute. The nominal range of fire at tanks was 1,200 metres. The 45-mm gun was notable for its accuracy. It had a normal sight, not a dial sight. The crew consisted of five or six men – a commander, a gunner, a loader, and two trail handlers, who were also shell carriers. The 45-mm gun were nearly useless against tanks. The probability of knocking out a German medium or heavy tank from the 45-mm gun was close to zero. With its very first shot, the gun gave away its position, and if at this moment a German tank fixed its sights on the crew, the crew had no chance of survival; not a single man …

We always had the guns ready for action; the battalion might at any moment shift us to the next axis vulnerable to tanks, and from the move we immediately joined battle. On the defence we checked the guns and prepared them very thoroughly. But on the offensive we often had no time for the meticulous alignment of the sight. Therefore our guns were always at full readiness. It was always necessary to keep the barrel clean.

Our guns were intended only for direct fire. Therefore we were always positioned close to the Germans, in the very front line, in open positions among the infantry's combat positions. Our guns were fine in almost every regard – small, light, accurate, easily camouflaged and not prominent, as long as they didn't fire, of course. They had one shortcoming – their lack of hitting power.

We rather effectively suppressed firing positions at close range and lightly armoured vehicles. With our presence alone we emboldened the infantry, bolstered their fighting spirit, which is to say that we supported them with fire and movement. Each crew had a reserve of anti-tank grenades and a PD machine gun to combat enemy infantry, and each member had a rifle, carbine or pistol. That, in principle, is all the characteristics of a separate anti-tank artillery battalion in brief.

Our first serious encounter was during the Germans' successful breakout from the Korsun–Shevchenkovsky pocket. We were positioned on the outer ring of the encirclement in the vicinity of the village of Kobeliaki. It was snowing. The German tanks were firing from hull-down positions in a ravine and taking shelter behind buildings. In a short period of time, two guns of our battery were destroyed. I was with a gun beside a road that was buried under snow. A platoon of SU-76s came up. The platoon commander asked me, 'Where's the road here?' Everything around was covered by a blanket of snow. From behind some buildings, a German self-propelled gun appeared. We fired three rounds at it, but the shells merely chipped the armour and ricocheted away. One SU-76 moved forward about 10 metres, and right away a shell from the German self-propelled gun drilled cleanly through the SU-76, and then the Germans gave it two more rounds. Our self-propelled gunners were killed. I ran over to the gun mount; I wanted to remove the dial sight from the gun. I glanced inside ... and there I saw someone's severed arm. Everything was burnt out, smoking ... and gory. The dial sight was jammed and I couldn't remove it. Just then I realized that I had to get away from the vehicle urgently; one fuel tank was still full and if the German took another shot now, there might not be even a remembrance of me left. I made a dash away from the self-propelled gun, dropped into the snow and crawled a few more metres, when yet another German shell punched through the SU-76. Then another ten shells came flying in. It was a terrifying moment ... The Germans poured machine-gun fire into our position, and a heavy mortar barrage began. The cases of shells behind our firing position caught fire from a machine-gun burst. I was ordered to withdraw several hundred metres to a point behind a ravine. We got the gun away. As we began to withdraw, high-explosive shells started dropping around us; front-line veterans know what sort of 'treat' that is ... Suddenly the gunner, a young Tatar, remembered that he'd left the gun sight back in the firing position. He refused to go back for the sight, saying 'I won't go! Germans are there!' I had to force him. That was what my first experience with combatting enemy tanks was like.

I don't remember that there were any restrictions on the expenditure of rounds for the 45-mm guns. No one created an untouchable reserve, and I didn't need the battalion commander's permission when opening fire. I don't recall that we ever had a catastrophic shortage of shells. The supply of high-explosive, armour-piercing and armour-piercing discarding sabot shells was adequate. We sought to conserve our canister shells, since we had to encounter German infantry face-to-face quite often. Canister and armour-piercing dis-carding sabot were shells for close-range combat. An end cap screwed onto a high-explosive shell converted it into a fragmentation shell. Eight cases of shells were normally loaded onto the Willys – half of a combat load, among which there had to be canister shells!

One could fully picture the preceding combat by the expenditure of shells. Here's an entry about the expenditure of shells per gun in a battle on 25 April 1944, which I've preserved from Kostia Levin's notebook. Altogether the gun fired 66 rounds, of which 28 were fragmentation shells, 7 were canister (which means the German infantry was quite close, not more than 200 metres away), 21 were armour-piercing, and 10 were APDS (which means they had to try to repel a tank attack from close range). At the end of a battle we were required to collect and turn in the shell casings; non-ferrous metal was in short supply in the country.

Some soldiers couldn't stand the strain. I remember in the Carpathians, a soldier, a young fellow named Burakov arrived as a replacement. Outwardly he appeared calm, though he was extremely quiet. Everything seemed fine, but at nights he would wake us up and frighten us with wild screams, like some sort of dying wails. It turned out that one night, Burakov and three of his comrades had fallen asleep in a combat outpost, and German scouts had caught them com-pletely by surprise. Burakov managed to hide in some bushes, having covered himself with a tent half. The Germans immediately gagged one of his comrades before carrying him away. But the Germans spent a long time strangling and knifing the other two. Either their knives were dull, or the Russians were putting up strong resistance. Burakov lay in the bushes, and nearly fainting from fear, took in this terrible scene, as the bodies of his dying friends twitched and he listened to their death rattles ...

Each night he relived this ordeal in his dreams. He began to fear darkness almost in a total panic. With time these night fits became more frequent, and Burakov's mind finally snapped. They took him away to the medical-sanitation battalion, and he never returned to us.

No one ever abandoned a gun in combat without an order. There were no pathological cowards in the gun crews.

The first time I had to take command of a battery was in March 1944 at Proskurov. During a battle, a 'ChP' [an accident or extraordinary event of some sort] occurred, when the commander of the 2nd Battery Senior Lieutenant Saltykov suddenly disappeared. Several hours later he was found in a haystack. He was not responsive and babbling something incomprehensible. They took him to a hospital to find out whether he really had lost his mind, or whether he was playing the fool in order to hide his desertion. But it was easy to go mad in the anti-tank artillery. Saltykov never returned to us from the hospital. I was appointed battery commander, but in June 1944 I returned to my duties as a gun-platoon commander, and didn't become battery commander again until several months later.

The new battery commander arrived from the reserve. He had previously served as a commander of a howitzer battery in a regiment of the Supreme Command Reserve, but at Kursk he'd been severely wounded, and after a year of roaming from hospital to hospital and in the reserves, he was returning to the front lines. The battery headquarters was occupying a position at the foot of an elevation that we called 'The Mare'.

Suddenly I saw the battalion chief of staff Captain Makukhin approaching in a Willys. I was more than surprised. Staff officers never showed their nose at the front, and the last time I'd seen Makukhin at the battery's position was in February, and moreover, it was during a lull in the fighting. Seated next to him was a tall, handsome, mustachioed middle-aged captain. He was wearing a sparkling new uniform, brightly polished calfskin boots, and a cavalryman's sword belt that was a rare sight at the front. There were combat Orders and two medals on his chest. His appearance was no-nonsense and inspiring. As was my duty, I briefed the chief of staff – the situation was quiet, we had full ammunition, there'd been no losses in the battery, and that we were holding firing positions along the spine of the ridge, and so forth.

Makukhin gave a dismissive wave of his hand and said, 'I've brought you a battery commander.' The new battery commander started to take over my duties. However, from the outset my Jewish name, Moisei Isaakovich, disturbed him, rather than the Russian Mikhail Ivanovich, for example. Then he asked me to point out the battery commander's bunker to him. When he learned that I didn't have a separate bunker, and that I was sleeping together with the crew of the No. 2 gun in their trenches around the emplacement, he was totally shocked. His reaction to what he'd heard was the following: 'You're undermining discipline and the officer's authority! Never mind, I'll restore order here!'

Our new battery commander assembled the battery's personnel and in a well-staged command voice warned that he would not tolerate any violations of military discipline or regulations. That same day the battery's soldiers got to work building an enormous new bunker for the new battery commander, with separate compartments for the orderly and switchboard operator.

Indeed, this battery commander started to live like a lord and master, striking everyone with his arrogance and unreasonable exactingness. He almost never made an appearance at the firing positions … He regarded the men in a condescending manner, with a clear air of disdain. All of his captious fault-finding was strictly by the book. The men began to grumble that some sort of prison warden had been sent to oversee us. The battery's soldiers grew to despise and hate the battery commander.

At the time, it was quiet at the front. Suddenly the battery commander went absent and returned to the battery with a woman! He brought to the front a young village woman about 19 years of age, who'd already had time to bear him a child in the rear! He'd met her in the hospital, where she had been working as a nurse. Just think of it – bringing a civilian to the front! Later this battery commander went completely off his rails.

He became jealous of one of the gun-crew commanders over the attention he was paying to his lady, and one night, finding a moment when he thought no one was around the gun, he surreptitiously stuffed the gun barrel with sod. The gun barrel was supposed to burst with the very first shot, killing or maiming the entire crew. And for that, I'd have been shot or sent into a penal battalion. It's a good thing that the guys had noticed the battery commander screwing around in the gun emplacement.

We quickly cleaned the barrel. Soon an order arrived from the battery commander's observation post: 'Reference point "X", a German observation post in some woods. Open fire!' This scoundrel and cold-blooded killer wanted to watch as the entire crew together with the gun was blown into the sky.

We fired four rounds, three of which were right on target. Soon the battery commander showed up at the firing position, and through his teeth hissed:

> So, Dorman, it turns out that we have a clever guy in you! However, you're too young to test your strength against me and not man enough to do it. Never mind, I'll get back at you; no one escapes me!

Thus I had to serve alongside this piece of shit. The artillery battalion commander Kuznetsov knew everything that was going on; likely had had an 'official snitch' in our battery. Aware of the growing conflict within the battery, Kuznetsov transferred me to take command of the operations platoon in place of the recently killed commander. This battery commander continued to create a lot more trouble 'behind the scenes'.

Later, when the general offensive began, the following event took place. In the autumn of 1944, now in eastern Slovakia, the battery's soldiers quietly shot this battery commander during an artillery barrage. He had driven the guys into a state of absolute fury. They reported that the battery commander had been killed by a shell fragment. The battalion commander was fully aware of what had actually happened and who had fired the shot (as did, incidentally, many of the artillerymen), but thank God he didn't let on that he knew.

After the death of the battery commander, I was ordered to return to the battery and again take command of it. Then the division's SMERSH deputies arrived to investigate. They were unable to uncover anything. So they sat in the battalion headquarters and started to haul in witnesses for interrogation. At the time, we were in the front lines, in a lowland area, while the Germans, occupying stone buildings of a large estate, were keeping our positions under machine-gun fire. A call came over the telephone from headquarters, demanding that we urgently send witnesses back for questioning. The guys had to crawl to the rear under a torrent of German machine-gun fire. One of them, who just might have cracked under the questioning, was wounded in the leg on his way back to headquarters, and he was immediately taken to the medical-sanitation battalion instead.

In the battery, everyone sighed with relief. In fact, such things happened at the front.

An anti-tank gun commander must have certain qualities. Our entire war was nothing but laying direct fire on targets. So the role of the gun commander in the anti-tank artillery was even more important than in the heavy artillery, where fire was conducted from defilade positions or from covered positions, where commanders don't see the enemy and received all the firing data from the observation post or through signals from the commander of the operations platoon. Ours was a different job. The gun commander had to determine the data for gunnery himself, had to control and correct the fire, and while doing so make sure his men remained calm and confident, even when enemy tanks and submachine gunners were just 100 metres from the firing positions. Thus, the gun commander in the anti-tank artillery had to be a brave man with nerves of steel who was able to think on his feet.

I remember almost everyone who I happened to serve together with at various times. In December 1943, when I arrived at the front line and took command of the gun platoon, Volovik and Baturin commanded my two gun crews. Volovik, a guy from Moscow who was 26 years old, commanded the No. 2 gun; he was an educated and highly cultured man, who before the war had managed to finish his schooling and was preparing to teach in Moscow's Liuberetsky District. He was a very courageous fighter. Senior Sergeant Baturin, a former lathe operator in the Cheliabinsk Tractor Factory, commanded my No. 1 gun. He was an old-timer with the artillery battalion, having fought with it since the summer of 1943. The commander was knowledgeable and charismatic, but he was a very bull-headed character. As a man he was coarse and vain, with a surly disposition; he was always trying to emphasize his pre-eminence, and behaved arrogantly, rudely and at times, insolently. It wasn't easy to command such a man. Both Volovin and Baturin returned to the battery after being wounded, which in itself was a heroic act. After all, no one came to us voluntarily.

My Senior Sergeant Stukach, my assistant platoon commander, knew how to handle people. I could always rely on him.

Junior Lieutenant Volodia Pir'ia came to us at the end of 1944. He was killed absurdly, accidentally blowing himself up on his own grenade.

Gun commander Mal'kov – he was a kind man, but he knew how to be strict. The soldiers loved and trusted him. He called his own and other soldiers 'Tootsie', so everyone in the battery called Mal'kov, 'Tootsie'. He was killed at the end of 1944. The Germans were attempting to infiltrate the battery's positions and Mal'kov was mortally wounded by an explosive bullet in the neck. He didn't make it to the medical-sanitation battalion.

My orderly and signaller Nikitin seemed like an old man to me at his age of 46. He was a simple man, distinguished by his natural tact, wisdom and unfeigned kind-heartedness. He had a son at the front, a guy my own age, so he fussed over me like his own natural son.

The gunner Kovalev before the war had worked as an assistant chef in a Khabarovsk restaurant. He was knowledgeable of both the French and Chinese cuisines. He carried around a beautiful wooden box that held an assembly of culinary tools which we'd never seen before. He was always dreaming about becoming the personal cook of some general. However, Kovalev made no effort to get out of his front-line assignment, and he conscientiously served as a 45-mm gun layer. This was a noble act.

I also recall Rakhmatullin, from the Tatar Autonomous Republic, who commanded the No. 4 gun and was killed at the end of the war. Then there was the driver Zaiko, a former sailor. He was a splendid soldier and comrade, one of the best drivers in the battalion. He returned to the battalion after being wounded. It was a rare case when a chauffeur, who was always in great demand everywhere, wanted to return from the hospital to a unit, where he almost daily had to drive up under direct fire. He often came under German fire as he moved up to a position and pulled away from it.

I remember Lieutenant Volosov, who had served in a howitzer regiment until he'd been wounded, but after the hospital he'd wound up in a destroyer anti-tank artillery battalion. With us, he was wounded again. I hope he survived.

I recall so many other men; a battery sergeant major Alimov, who came to us from an anti-tank rifle company; he was a cheerful, brave, boisterous Regular who joined the Army in 1940. Then there was the experienced gunner, a former schoolteacher from Kazakhstan's Chimkent, Khairulla Kerimbekov, with whom I was friends. Sergeant Kokotov was a unique personality. Before the war he'd been a docent at a pedagogical institute. In the war he'd been a captain who had served as the commander of the anti-aircraft battery that guarded army headquarters. An imposing, stately, intelligent man, he outwardly seemed like a general. He wound up in a penal company, but survived his time as an orderly to a penal company commander. He came to us as a sergeant.

Doshly was a clever man. Something always seemed to be going wrong for him – either the muzzle brake on his ZIS-3 gun would malfunction just before a battle, or his tow vehicle would run out of fuel. This comrade knew how to survive.

There was the Kuban Cossack Sinel'nikov, a gun commander who was also a cavalier with two Orders of Glory. He was a superb hunter. Once a column of prisoners was passing us, and among them Sinel'nikov spotted a 'Vlasovite', who'd been serving as a wagon driver for the Germans. It turned out that this guy had been a former village neighbour of Sinel'nikov's. Sinel'nikov beat the hell out of his traitorous neighbour, but he didn't kill him – and he didn't allows others to do it either.

I do recall many others. But if I continue to list them, you'll quickly tire of it.

The losses among the destroyer anti-tank gunners were heavy. After one-and-a-half years of service in the battalion, not more than 25 per cent of its initial complement of men remained, and this includes the command staff. From among my own soldiers, of those who arrived in the battalion in December 1943, only Volovik, Nikitin, Baturin and Zaiko served out the war in the battalion and survived. Of the seven platoon commanders who were serving in the battalion at the beginning of 1944, I was the only one to survive. Our platoon lieutenants were very frequently killed.

In January 1945, we were engaged in 'fighting of local significance'. The battalion was in bad shape. Only one gun and seven men remained of my battery. In making the crossing of the Oder, we lost four guns and thirty men, and these were considered light casualties in that operation. When on 1 May 1945 the battalion entered Moravska Ostrava, it had only eight ZIS-guns and fifty men. In fact, we continued to suffer combat fatalities in the first days of May 1945. A battery lost several men killed in action on 5 May, when searching for the lost banner of a rifle division in some Czech woods and they encountered Germans that were retreating to the west.

At the end of the war, the infantry was not at all pitied, nor were we, the anti-tank gunners. The ethical level of many of the senior commanders was low. It was useless to search for kindness, humanity or unselfishness among them. It was these militarily incompetent commanders, who for the sake of Orders and their own careers repeatedly hurled their subordinates into the very jaws of death. It was senseless, heartless, and for nothing.

The destroyer anti-tank artillery battalion began to be used as a shock unit; we no longer felt any difference from the infantry. We would joke, saying that perhaps we could weld a bayonet to the radiator of our trucks. They frequently used us even without the support of rifle teams. How many times the artillery-men had to engage in rifle combat with their own personal weapon!? Let's just say that one could realistically have a chance to survive only in the heavy artillery of the Supreme Command Reserve.

Death was always nearby. So many times I had narrow escapes from death without even realizing it. I understood this only after the war. It would have been shameful to be a coward; after all, the battery's soldiers were watching me. I managed to fight the fear of death, but I was certain that I wouldn't escape alive from the battles. Many men in the depths of their souls concealed the hope of returning alive from the war, or at least meeting a quick death, without prolonged agonies. I was ready for the worst.

We were under constant stress. It was especially hard to return to the front after a short break. Then when you're sucked into the fighting, there's no longer the inner or physical strength to ponder the possibility of death.

I was often lucky. Fair enough if you were killed in combat, but death was everywhere and always stalking us. I remember once we were driving through the Carpathians. The sappers had already checked a narrow road and had given the all-clear sign for our passage. My truck was leading the column. Suddenly there was an explosion of a mine beneath a wheel. The truck blew apart, killing everyone on either side of it. Only the driver and I by some miracle remained unharmed. Another time, I was sleeping in a slit trench at the front, together with two other soldiers. It was cramped. Nearby there was a haystack. I got up, walked 15 metres toward the haystack, and suddenly behind me there was an explosion. It was a direct hit on the slit trench. I got away with merely a shell splinter.

There were other incidents. In Czechoslovakia, in street fighting I once ran into a burst of machine-gun fire at almost point-blank range. I remained alive, but my field service cap had a bullet hole in it. Another time there was a combat action in some cemetery and I was running along a wall. A sniper fired . . . and the bullet just singed my chin.

In the Ukraine at the end of March 1944 I dreamed that I'd been wounded in the stomach by a shell fragment and that I was dying. I woke up in the middle of the night in a cold sweat. I took this dream as an omen and decided that it was going to take place. So until the very end of the war, in combat I constantly tugged my map case in front of my stomach, thereby protecting myself from the fragment that had been predestined for me. That's how I tricked fate ...

There were also a lot of absurd, unexpected deaths. There might not be any fighting going on, but people were still getting killed. In December 1944, soldiers of the battery were cooking something in a pot for themselves. In place of firewood, they were using empty ammunition cases. They failed to check one thoroughly and tossed it onto the fire, without noticing that it still contained a shell. There was an explosion and three men were badly wounded. At Shepetovka, on the outskirts of the village there was a still smouldering, smoking house. We went inside to get warm, but also at the same time to drive away lice. One wall collapsed suddenly and one of our comrades died from the burns he received.

I remember a couple of times when a soldier attacked a panzer with grenades. Once, a German tank became immobilized in front of our positions. But both guns of my platoon had already been destroyed by German panzers, and the crews were totally exhausted. A drunken soldier from the anti-tank rifle company went after the tank with a bundle of grenades. Just 20 metres short of the tank, he was cut down by a burst of machine-gun fire.

No one could escape his fate. Our postal clerk Volchkov, a man who never took part in fighting, was marching on foot in the column. He laid his sub-machine gun under the canvas of the anti-tank rifle company's wagon. When he later reached into it to retrieve it, the breech-mechanism lever apparently caught on something. There was a shot, and Volchkov took a bullet in the stomach from his own submachine gun, which killed him.

We had a guy named Zabrodin, a former welder in a tank factory. He was conscripted into the army in 1942. Zabrodin's wife found out that there was an order about recalling defence-industry specialists from the front; she spent a long time running around the rear area making appeals to chiefs, and she eventually reached a chief designer, from whom she wangled a summons for her husband to a factory in Cheliabinsk. The factory was in need of qualified specialists. Zabrodin soon had all the documents required for demobilization in his pocket. He needed to 'shove off', but he wanted to make sure he procured some new boots first. Zabrodin went running to the storage depot, but on the road to it he was severely wounded. He died on the way to the medical-sanitation battalion. Such is fate ...

There was no staff deputy of the Special Department in the battalion, but 'these guys' never left our battalion alone without oversight. All the soldiers hated the Special Department deputies, and the old soldiers called them '*Gepeushniki*', or

GPU-men.[2] But we all sought to avoid saying anything superfluous in the battery. The snitches were as thick as blackberries around us.

Once we were holding a defensive front in the Carpathians. We had no infantry in front of us. There was no intact front line. There were numerous gaps between our batteries and their gun positions. All around was wooded, rough terrain, with hills, valleys and ravines. It wouldn't have been difficult to penetrate into our rear, and one could have likely passed through the entire division – no one would have noticed. It was almost a half-kilometre between our No. 1 gun and No. 4 gun.

At night there were artillerymen crouching in listening posts surrounding the guns in an all-round defence. On one of these nights, a team of German scouts broke into the positions of the 3rd Battery, which was positioned on an adjacent hill to our right, and they quietly slaughtered the crew of the left-flank gun and took the gun commander Samylin prisoner.

Immediately, Special Department officers arrived in vehicles. They accused gun-platoon commander Junior Lieutenant Znamensky of criminal dereliction of duty, saying that he hadn't checked his outposts at night, and they put him in front of a tribunal. The sentence busted Znamensky down to private and sent him into a penal company.

There and then they took steps to 'strengthen' our combat spirit and vigilance. They arranged a public execution in the neighbouring 115th Rifle Regiment. Two men, a sergeant major and a soldier, were shot for fraternizing with the enemy. There was a rare, isolated farmstead that hadn't been devastated out in no-man's-land, and our guys were going there for milk and butter. The Germans also fell into the habit of going to the farm to get some food. There, they peacefully conversed with our soldiers, and both sides observed a truce. These two Red Army soldiers were accused of betraying the Motherland. I still recall how they were shot.

In the autumn of 1944 we received ZIS-3 anti-tank guns. These guns were twice as heavy as the 45-mm guns and it was much more difficult to handle in the direct fire mode. They were unwieldy guns with a large rectangular shield. They were visible with the naked eye from a range of 3 kilometres. Because of this, in one way or another we drew a lot of enemy fire – machine-gun, mortar and artillery. We didn't require any special training in order to fight with these guns. We had one gunnery practice, and that was all.

Back in action, as always, we leaped out into our positions, deployed the gun and began firing. After the third round, the trail spades are shifting in the loose soil, but we didn't bother digging them down into the earth. We simply chocked them with logs.

The first tank we knocked out with the ZIS-3 was in Poland. An infantry company, around 40 men, was dug-in around 300 metres in front of us. A German medium tank popped out from behind the lee side of a hill and began to overrun the infantry. We hit it with our first shell. The tank began smoking and rolled behind a hillock, where it burned out.

The infantry regarded the anti-tank artillerymen with respect, because we were a shield and a big help for them, an additional chance to survive in the slaughter-house of war. On the march whenever we drove past the infantry, an exchange of traditional greetings would begin: 'Don't kick up the dust, infantrymen!' In response we'd hear, 'Eh, Farewell, Motherland! Your barrel is long but your life is short.'

In combat at the front, the infantry was always happy when we were deployed next to them, but at the same time, all the infantrymen preferred to be occupying positions a little removed from our guns, understanding quite well that with the first shot the 45-mm artillerymen would draw fire and become goners. To be positioned next to us was a great risk. It also happened that because of our proximity to the Germans, our own artillery would take us as the enemy and we'd receive 'gifts' from them.

It has been said that before each battle, regimental staff officers and political workers would arrive at the firing positions as replacements for those crewmen who'd become casualties. But it is hard for me to believe that such a process ever existed anywhere. No one would ever come to us during combat – neither staff officers nor any kind of Party organizers or deputy political officers. No one wanted to be around us during a fight. If such a thing did happen in some anti-tank artillery regiment, then most likely it was the result of a direct order from the regiment commander.

I never saw the battalion's chief of staff anywhere near our firing position for four or five months. The same could be said about the others. Our deputy political leader was a former newspaperman from some regional office. We also had a Party organizer, a Georgian. They knew how to deliver fiery speeches eloquently, but they didn't take part in the fighting.

The hardest episode of the war for me was in March 1945, at Lake Balaton. We were making a fighting retreat; there were around 50 of us, infantrymen and artillerymen. The Germans encircled our wounded men, who were located in a shallow depression in the ground about 100 metres from us. We were unable to break through to extract them. For a long time, the wounded were yelling to us, 'Finish us off, brothers!' This cry has haunted me through my entire lifetime.

For me, war is the most significant, the most powerful experience in life. In it I learned the value of human life, and witnessed how cruel and pitiless a man becomes in war. War cannot be forgotten. I still often dream about it ...

Notes

1. The Demidov family was an extremely prominent and wealthy Russian family in the late 18th and 19th Centuries, well connected politically to the Tsar, and which used its wealth to promote science, culture and public infrastructure across Russia.
2. GPU stands for the Main Political Directorate of the People's Commissariat of Internal Affairs, the dreaded NKVD.

Chapter 7

'We've Always Fought with Our Fists . . .'

Vladimir Matveevich Zimakov

I learned that the war had started only when German aircraft began bombing Smolensk, where we were living at the time. It was either on 22 or 23 June. Our family was evacuated, but in 1943, upon reaching 18 years of age, I was called up into the Red Army.

We were first taken to Morshansk, which was in the Tambovsk region, and then, having loaded us onto trains, we were sent to the Melikessa camps in Ul'ianovsk Oblast for training. We were given new underwear, but an old uniform, which had apparently been removed from our dead – neatly mended bullet holes and shell-fragment tears were visible. But how cold it was there! We still had nothing, no greatcoat, no warm cotton underclothing, and no ankle boots with warm puttees. Yet we were sent Uzbeks – oh, such unfortunates! They were allowed to wear smocks under their coats. Even so, there was no real danger that you'd freeze to death – rehearsed attacks, runs, and forced marches of up to 20 kilometres once every ten days. They'd pour 16 kilograms of sand into the rucksacks, you'd grab a rifle – and off you'd go. That's how it went from January to March. In March they called us into formation and said, 'Those here with seven grades of education or higher – take three steps forward.' I stepped forward, since I had eight years of schooling. Primarily, we had peasant fellows with five or six years of schooling, or else even men with no education at all. A hundred of us were selected and sent to an officers' school.

We grabbed our things and off we went. Well, what sorts of items did we have?! A pair of underwear, black household soap and a towel. No one even had a toothbrush: it wasn't routine. You could look in a German's rucksack and see a toothbrush, powder, and ersatz soap – for the German, everything was neatly done. Even this ersatz soap was kind of abrasive: it seemed to have sand in it. Before long you were clean.

From Melikessa, it required three days of travel to the town of Kinel', which was near Samara. We were assigned to the 3rd Kuibyshev Infantry School, the barracks of which were located 140 kilometres from the Volga. Our uniforms were just like those that cadets wore prior to the war – calfskin riding boots, wool tunics and twill trousers. After a six-month period of training, we were to be sent to the front, and once there, acquire the rank of junior lieutenant. Oh, how many of these lieutenants fell at the front! Few were those that survived! As soon as he arrived at the front, he'd wind up in the sights of a sniper. We couldn't protect the man: officers wore a different tunic and service caps with visors, not garrison caps. The German snipers were superb marksmen.

So, for two months we studied, and then suddenly an order arrived to send the senior class to the front. No problem, except that their uniforms hadn't arrived yet. So we were told to take off our uniforms and turn them over to the senior class. We were given back our old civilian clothes, but instead of boots, which for some reason were missing, they gave us bast shoes[1] and white puttees.

So we were going around in bast shoes for two months, until uniforms arrived for us. We had trained for a total of three months in this school, when it was disbanded and we were sent to a 'production mill' for junior command staff in Inza, where sergeants were being trained. It amounted to an enormous camp in a pine forest. There we found three-level bunks and rats the size of horses! The camp had a training brigade, which consisted of a machine-gun regiment, an artillery regiment, an anti-tank rifle regiment and a tank regiment. So I wound up in the anti-tank rifle regiment. The training we received wasn't bad: we did a lot of firing from rifles, submachine guns and, of course, Degtiarev and Simonov anti-tank rifles. The Degtiarev anti-tank rifle would give your shoulder a strong kick, while you could hardly feel the Simonov's recoil; moreover, the Simonov PTRS-41 had a clip of five 14.55-mm rounds with a semi-automatic action. We fired the anti-tank rifles at moving plywood mock-ups of tanks.

There wasn't such a thing as a telescopic sight for our anti-tank rifles. More-over, the rifle was ineffective at long ranges. For example, at 200–300 metres, perhaps out to 500 metres, the lack of an optical sight presented no problem; the tank was visible: you just let fly and immediately you'd see the slug's impact! But any further out, it couldn't penetrate the armour.

We had to aim at any tiny vulnerable spot on a German tank in order for our round to be effective. If the tank was approaching directly toward you, then you had to hit a vision slit or just under the turret, in the hope of jamming it. But just try to hit a vision slit at a range of 500 metres! A few cadets were able to do it, but I wasn't. Yes, it was also possible to break a track if you managed to hit it. That would immobilize the tank, and either the anti-tank riflemen or the anti-tank artillerymen would finish it off. If a tank showed its flank to you, if you managed to hit its ammunition, you could obtain a splendid sight – a huge explosion and great fireworks. The tank would blow into pieces and the turret would go flying off ... it was beautiful! The soldiers would start shouting, 'Hurrah!' and fling their caps into the air. Indeed, that's how we destroyed our 'Ferdinand', but more about that later.[2]

They literally gave us three months of training. Upon completing it, we became sergeants and were dispatched to the front by train. It took us around two months to reach it. While we made our way to the front, approximately twenty to thirty of us were killed by mines. The route was heavily mined. One idiot of a sailor triggered a 'Bouncing Betty' mine. Like a fool, he had gathered some of the young, green soldiers around him and said, 'Watch how it jumps; I'll catch it and it won't explode.' Of course, the mine bounded into the air and exploded. The sailor's arm was blown off and he was disemboweled. One of the onlookers was killed and several more were wounded.

Some guys were superstitious and carried good-luck charms, but I didn't have one. However, whenever I was extremely stressed or in danger, I would consciously appeal to God: 'God, let this pass! God protect me! God, deliver me!' That was all.

We reached a point near Staryi Oskol, but there we came upon a blown-up bridge and we became stuck. The Battle of Kursk had ended just a couple of weeks before, so while the train was blocked, they unloaded us and forced us to find and bury the dead. We removed the corpses from knocked-out tanks, both German and ours. The stench was terrible! Later we became accustomed to it, but at first we were nauseous. But we had no choice. Oh, there were a lot of burned-out, derelict tanks there. Some had collided directly into one another and were standing on end. Whose knocked-out tanks were more? We didn't count them ... perhaps the Germans had left a few more. We buried the corpses in fraternal graves. First, of course, we searched their pockets for documents. If we found some money or a locket on one of the Soviet dead, we sent them back to their families. Sometimes we found notes in case of death. But many of the dead had no papers, nothing. Of the tankers, only charred effigies remained. How could we identify them? It was surprising, but they didn't smell. We buried the Germans and our own guys together. We simply wrote on the grave markers, 'So many Russians and so many Germans have been buried here.' As one political worker said, 'Even though they were indeed fascists, they were still people.'

Our 202nd Rifle Division of the 53rd Army remained in the reserve and didn't take part in the fighting prior to the beginning of 1944. Then we were transferred to Korsun-Shevchenkivsky. We spent likely a week en route to there, marching about 70 kilometres over each long January night. We badly wanted sleep. But the January weather was warm and the roads had dissolved into mud. You'd march, and seemingly pounds of the black Ukrainian soil would stick to your boots and puttees. You'd scrape it off, take ten paces, and again find the same enormous clod of mud clinging to your boots. Oh, did we trample the land there!

As I recall, in the winter we didn't wash our clothes at all. In the summer, yes; we'd set up saunas. Once when I was with the recon, the Jijia River was flowing past our position. The river itself was muddy, but it had a clear tributary. Our guys would dam up the tributary to create a pool, and there we would bathe. We didn't so much wash our clothes as steam-treat them. For this we would pour three or four buckets of water into a drum, place a grating across it, lay our uniforms and underwear on the grating, and then light a fire beneath the drum. Not a louse or flea survived that heat! Then you could walk around in your uniform for a couple of months.

We got sick, of course, but not seriously. Occasionally someone would get a sore throat or something. Well, a guy would lay around in his dugout for three or four days, regain his health, and then he'd emerge, good as new. Occasionally a medic would come around and ask, 'Any sick men?' That was it – we were all young and healthy.

Our dry rations were pea concentrate. They were in little bricks, and when you added boiling water, you'd get pea soup. We also had buckwheat bricks that contained a little fat or margarine. You'd just add boiling water and have a meal. Some of the guys simply chewed on the dry bricks – they didn't bother to dissolve it into boiling water. When we had dry rations, it wasn't so bad; otherwise we had nothing to eat and it would be impossible for the field kitchens to get food to us – it seemed artillery barrages were always dropping around us. If the sergeant major was a bit cowardly, you'd always be hungry. Actually, we'd always get something to eat at night. When we were in the front line, they'd deliver a hot meal at least once a day.

I was in an anti-tank rifle company. Together with my team member Malyshev, a tall Siberian who was born in 1925, we had a Simonov PTRS-41 anti-tank rifle. At first we carried it assembled, but then the company commander permitted us to remove the gun barrel and carry the components separately. Just imagine, the weapon weighed 22 kilograms, while the forty clips of five-round cartridges weighed another 28 kilograms. In addition, I had a Nagant revolver (the No. 1 of the team was armed with a Nagant, while the No. 2 had a submachine gun), while Malyshev was armed with a PPSh submachine gun and three drums of ammunition for it. In addition we lugged the rest of our gear, our rations and a change of underclothes.

There was a halt. Scouts reported that Germans were nearby. We received an order to dig in on the outskirts of the village of Komarovka, or in Ukrainian, Komarivka. We were directed to construct the trenches so that they extended toward the village. Our regimental headquarters was located there, as well as the regimental reconnaissance. We started to dig in. We created a horseshoe-shaped trench beneath a windmill and set up our anti-tank rifle. Then we waited for further orders – for 3 hours. In the meantime we continued digging – water was seeping into the trenches.

Well, did the Germans really give it to us then! This was the only time over my entire war that this happened. It turned out that the Germans were concealed in a nearby ravine on the other side of the village, and once our infantry had completed their work on the trenches extending to the village and things had more or less quieted down, they began mortaring the village. Unbeknown to us, there was also a German heavy machine gun positioned in the windmill right above us, and it began to pour fire down into the village. Our trench was just 5 metres away! Why didn't they think to toss a grenade down into our position? Perhaps they didn't have any? Malyshev waited a bit before saying, 'Volodka, I'm going to climb up there and shoot them. Give me your Nagant.' I gave him my pistol and he still had his submachine gun. He crawled away. Within a short time I heard an exchange of fire. The Germans were firing, and I could hear Malyshev returning fire.

'Well,' I thought, 'that's the end of Malyshev.' Nothing like it! I see him crawling out of there. He had killed both of the Germans that had been there.

'That's it,' he says, 'I've finished them off.'

Then such a nightmare began! I didn't see an officer again that night. We opened fire from our anti-tank rifles. But we didn't know where to fire – we couldn't see anything! It was pitch black, damn it! We fired at gun flashes. Malyshev and I expended twenty or thirty rounds.

As it became clear later, there had been only around 500 Germans. We had two battalions confronting them, sitting in trenches, and one more in reserve. Most of us were still untested in battle, but even the seasoned veterans that were among us lost their composure.

A senior lieutenant, I don't know from which company, came running by, shouting, 'We're retreating, guys! Get the hell away from the anti-tank rifle, just remove the breech.' That's just what we did. We dismantled the anti-tank rifle and tossed it into a trench, while Malyshev covered it with his quilted jacket and stuck the breech into his pocket. We saw this officer fall, wounded in both legs. We grabbed his arms and we started hurrying away as best we could. The Germans were raining mortar shells down on us. The other guys were also running, and men were falling, falling. The Germans were firing. Most of our retreating men turned off into a swale to take cover from the bullets. Our officer said, 'Run straight toward that hill! Run toward that hill! Don't even think to enter that swale – there will now be a slaughter there.'

It was true – the Germans shifted their mortar fire to the swale and concentrated their fire on it – body parts of men went flying. Can you imagine?

Meanwhile we crossed over the hilltop and sat to take a rest. The officer spoke up, 'Wait a bit, I can't go on – my heart is in my throat.' He looked young, but he'd been wounded in both legs. Fortunately no bones had been hit; the bullets had passed completely through the fleshy parts.

So there we were, sitting in tall grass. It was getting light. Two Germans were moving below us. The lieutenant was the first to spot them: 'Quiet, Germans! Get down and I'll kill them; you might miss.' He cocked his pistol – he had a TT – and took aim. The pistol fired. Immediately, the second German fired a burst from his submachine gun in the direction of the shot. Their reaction to the sound of a gunshot was nearly instantaneous and accurate! The lieutenant killed the second one with a single shot. He did it so calmly – he was a real warrior! We were scared nearly to death. We were thinking it was already the end for us. Nevertheless, it was our baptism of fire.

Well, we fell back. But the reserve battalion came up, drove out the Germans, mopped up the village and proceeded on its way. In contrast, we – two battalions – had taken to our heels. In fact half of those who had taken shelter in the swale were now lying dead there. So they consolidated the remnants of our two battalions into one composite one. A battalion had approximately 500 men. A company consisted of 125 men. We had three companies, plus a machine gun, a submachine gun and a mortar platoon.

In the morning, we arrived at division headquarters. We turned the lieutenant over to the medical-sanitary battalion. We reported to the command about what had happened in the swale, and they promised to send men with horses there to bring out the survivors. The lieutenant spoke up, 'The boys should get a medal – they saved my life.' We said in response, 'We didn't save him – he saved us!' Everyone was laughing – we were totally unseasoned men.

They immediately placed the senior lieutenant on an operating table. They operated on him. They cleaned his wounds out, and the lieutenant endured it without any anaesthetic. Brave fellow!

Then came the questions:

'Where is your sidearm?'

'Here.'

'Who are you?'

'Anti-tank riflemen.'

'And where's your anti-tank rifle?'

'We left it there.'

'Go back and get it!'

We went back for it. There'd been a frost overnight and we had firmer footing beneath us. As we passed the swale, we heard moans! We kept moving – we were afraid. Devil take it! There was no one else around – we were moving down the road alone. Well, great. We arrived at the place where we had abandoned the anti-tank rifle and found it was still there. We entered the village – there seemed to be not a living soul there. Then an old man emerged from a shed. I asked, 'Old man, how did you manage to stay alive?'

'Oh, I don't know, boys,' the old man replied. 'Your guys were shooting back at the Germans from that hut over there all night long.'

We walked over to it and peered inside – they were our scouts. They'd all been killed. There you have it. That was our first battle.

A bombing was the most frightening thing at the front, because you didn't know where the bomb would explode. Even if you were huddled in a slit trench, you might get blown to pieces – your arms, legs and guts would go flying in every direction. They bombed us a lot! They would also choose a moment when our fighters were absent. You'd think, 'Where are ours? Where have they gone?' In the meantime the Germans are diving, releasing their bombs, and pulling out over and over again – the earth would shake. This would go on for 10 to 15 minutes – and then they'd all at once make their getaway. Well, our own ground-attack aircraft would also give them a taste of their own medicine. Once at an observation post, I watched as our aircraft came in just above ground level, and then saw explosions and explosions – they'd accurately plastered the German trenches with rockets. There was also this 'Vaniusha' – the German six-barrelled rocket launcher. As it howled, 'Oo, oo, oo', everyone knew what was coming! You'd look – and all the guys were burrowing more deeply into their foxholes or trenches.

We sometimes fired at infantry, but in general we sought to save our ammunition in case tanks appeared. True, there was such an incident. It happened just three days after we arrived at the front. It seemed that the Germans had detected our arrival and had decided to test us under fire, so they really let us have it. The barrage was heavy. Artillery shells and mortar rounds were exploding, while we lay prone in the bottom of the trench. Apparently one shell landed on a neighbouring fighting position: someone was killed, but one Uzbek received a concussion; he leapt out of the position, spun around a couple of times, and then headed straight toward the Germans. At that point, our battalion commander came running, yelling 'Shoot him! Shoot him!' He ran up to us, shoved Malyshev aside, took aim with our anti-tank rifle and shot him, hitting him right in the back of the head. Later we went on the counter-attack; we stopped and turned his corpse over and his face was gone. The shell had blown it away. What else could you expect? The 14.55-mm bullet weighed 70 grams and hit with devastating force.

There, at Korsun, we spent another week in the trenches. That's where Malyshev and I knocked out that 'Ferdinand' self-propelled gun.

Our position was quite poor – the Germans were holding the high ground and we were in a small hollow. The distance between our two lines was approximately 300 metres. There was a village atop the slope. We could see a self-propelled gun was concealed behind one of the buildings – its long barrel was sticking out. Apparently, they also had an observer there, because one could see the evidence of their work. Our 45-mm anti-tank guns had been standing on a hill behind us, but obviously the main thing was the position they'd selected – wide open ground! Not a single artilleryman survived. When we arrived, we looked and saw two guns standing there with their dead crewmen surrounding them, already covered with snow. No one had collected their bodies.

Even after we moved into our position, we saw how the self-propelled gun would roll out from behind the house, fire an accurate shot, and pull back behind cover. Right in front of our eyes, five T-34 tanks erupted in flames. One shot – and done. One shot – and done. Then another and another. The Germans, the swine, were clever and strong warriors. There was no one in the world stronger than them, except for us Russian fools. We've always fought with our fists. We constantly ram our heads into brick walls.

The company commander had already sent up three pairs of anti-tank rifle-men – and they had all been killed there. Whether a sniper had got them, or other tanks had killed them, I don't know. He says to us, 'Let's go, guys. Crawl under the first knocked-out tank, don't be afraid.' My Malyshev – he's a young devil. Hoo-boy! He was a hunter, a Siberian. I was a bit more gutless; even though I'm the No. 1 in the pair, he always did the firing. So he says to me: 'Come on, Volod', don't be afraid. We'll knock it out.' So that night we made it to the most advanced knocked-out tank, the one closest to the German-held village, and crawled beneath it. It was about 150 metres to the hut.

Just as it began to grow light, we started firing. We were aiming at the barrel or a track, because only parts of those were visible. It noticed us and fired a round at the turret. My God, what a noise! The turret was blown off of our tank! It is good that the shell didn't hit underneath the tank, or else we would have been finished! I couldn't hear anything. I was deafened. This self-propelled gun crawled out from behind the hut in order to finish us off. 'Well,' I think, 'that's the end of us.' Any moment it's going to kill us. But Malyshev didn't lose his cool – he pointed the anti-tank rifle at the exposed flank of the German vehicle and planted five heavy calibre bullets into it, one after another, resulting in a tremendous explosion. Our 'Ferdinand' blew into pieces.

On our way back, the Germans blanketed us with mortar shells. We were already close to our trenches as the rounds started dropping. I see the shells are exploding nearby: one lands a bit short, the other goes long. We're bracketed! I urged, 'Malyshev, let's go, run!' Why was he tarrying? I didn't know; perhaps he'd been wounded or had lost his hearing too. I gave his leg a yank, 'Let's go, come on!' That's the last thing I recall. I regained consciousness in a trench –

the firing had already ceased. The guys told me, 'A shell almost made a direct hit on you both.' I was wearing a cuirass and a quilted jacket under my great-coat. The back of my coat was now tattered, but I didn't have a scratch on me. However, Malyshev's right leg had been torn off.

Why hadn't we waited for nightfall? Because the company commander himself had said to us, 'Once you've finished your job, get back right away. Otherwise, it will be curtains. The Germans will creep up and kill you.' We had with us the anti-tank rifle, my Nagant revolver and a submachine gun with one drum of ammunition. Malyshev didn't take anything more – he was hoping everything would go smoothly.

For knocking-out this self-propelled gun, at the end of the war we received the medal 'For Courage'. For destroying an armoured vehicle, we were supposed to receive 500 rubles and the Order of the Red Star. Well, the first and best medal was the 'For Courage', and after that the Order of Glory.

When all the dust had settled, we didn't have much left of the company. There had been sixty men – thirty anti-tank rifles, a regiment's full-strength anti-tank rifle company, but now there remained, God forbid, only ten pairs. A platoon commander had been killed. Well, approximately a week went by, and we received a small batch of replacements from the local population – men born in 1926 and 1927. They were all rounded up and sent to the front. We called them 'Blackshirts', because they were all wearing dark shirts, as well as grey coats. They hadn't been given uniforms.

Then we marched onward and arrived at fine dugouts that had been prepared by sappers. It was here one day that I was knocked unconscious. When I came to, there was no one else in the dugout and one of the corners of it had collapsed. Good heavens! I couldn't figure out what had happened. Had there been an artillery barrage? Supposedly, the Germans had no shells. Perhaps a bomb had fallen? I didn't report to the medical and sanitary battalion.

We set out on a new march. Again, we moved only at night. On this particular night, the moon was shining brightly. The German reconnaissance planes were in the air, and we were marching. Whenever a 'Rama' appeared, the command would ring out: 'Company, halt!' The entire regiment would stop and remain still. Once it had passed overhead, we'd resume the march. I was marching alongside my team mate – I had a different partner after Malyshev's wounding – when suddenly, splash! He and I had fallen into a water-filled crater. The water in it was at ground level and its depth was over our heads. We didn't know whether to laugh or cry! We barely managed to scramble out and we were sent straight to the medical and sanitary battalion. They checked my partner; he had no temperature and showed no other problem, so they returned him to the front. I had a concussion. I had an earache and it had become difficult to speak.

I was hospitalized and I remained there for two weeks. Then some of the other patients were saying, 'Let's head back to our unit. What can we do sticking around here? It is merrier there!' We tricked the nurse into giving us our uniforms, and we told her, 'Masha, goodbye!'

'Where are you guys going?'

'We're bound for the front. We're going to catch up with our unit.'

'I'll write you up!'

'Go ahead, write, write.'

It was close to Passover. We walked and walked and came upon a village. The female owner of the hut where we stopped spread quite a table for us on the occasion of the holiday: fried potatoes, boiled grits, ham, salted lard, and pickled cucumbers and tomatoes. She also procured some moonshine. My Lord! We hadn't seen such a feast for years! Now that was a holiday! We drank down so much of their Ukrainian distilled spirit that we spent the next two days sleeping it off.

The time came to move on. Four of our group came up with a little scheme and said, 'You go on ahead and we'll catch up. We won't be long.' So I and another guy started off, but we didn't know which way to go. We waited and waited, but our fellow travellers never showed up. Then a man came along who was wearing German boots and carrying a German submachine gun. He came up to us: 'Well, boys, from which division are you?'

'We're with the 202nd.'

'Oooooh, the 'Turn-tail Division'! You're better off joining us, the 180th Division's reconnaissance.'

'How so? We're anti-tank riflemen.'

'The devil you say! Enough banging away at those tanks with your pop guns! Join the reconnaissance – its better there!'

That's how I wound up in the 180th Rifle Division's 90th Separate Reconnaissance Company.

Notes

1. Bast shoes were a traditional Russian and Ukrainian style of footwear made from the woven bark of linden or birch trees.
2. Red Army soldiers routinely called any German self-propelled gun a 'Ferdinand'. It should not be taken literally that the term refers to the German Elefant heavy tank destroyer.

Chapter 8

'The Beast-Killer'

Nikolai Konstantinovich Shishkin

In 1939, I graduated from tenth grade with honours in the Kazakh city of Petropavlovsk and applied to three institutes of higher education: Moscow's Aviation Construction and Architectural Institutes and the Sverdlovsk Polytechnic Institute. I was accepted by all three institutes – honour graduates were admitted without entrance exams and I decided to enroll in the Metallurgical Department of the Sverdlovsk Polytechnic Institute. Two months after the start of my studies, simultaneously with the outbreak of the war with Finland, a voluntary call-up of students to military service was announced. One could refuse to join the Red Army, but we were all patriots and almost my entire class decided to sign-up in defence of the Motherland. Guys from other nearby higher education institutes also responded to the call to service.

We thought we would immediately be sent to the West, but we wound up in the city of Achinsk in Siberia's Krasnoiarsk District. At the beginning of November, there was already snow on the ground there. We arrived at a transit point, where we cleaned ourselves and donned our uniforms, which altered our appearances so much that at first we didn't recognize each other.

We were called into formation on a drill ground and formed two ranks, down which 'shoppers' walked, choosing soldiers for their particular units. I and a handful of other soldiers wound up in the regimental artillery. That's how I became the gunner of a 76-mm Model 1927 gun. With this gun I went through the entire Winter War with Finland and the beginning of the Great Patriotic War. My platoon commander was Lieutenant Orel, and my gun commander was Sergei Semin, who achieved the Hero of the Soviet Union Star for heroism in action on the Karelian Isthmus. The Finns had broken through to our regiment headquarters, and although our gun was disabled – the counter-recoil mechanism wasn't working – we deployed it and opened fire on them, returning the barrel of the gun to its firing position with our hands. It was because of this that we saved the regimental headquarters, and Semin was awarded the title Hero of the Soviet Union and promoted to captain and battalion commander; he was killed in 1943.

As part of the 90th Rifle Division's 613th Rifle Regiment, I arrived on the Vyborg [Viipuri] axis. The combat was very hard. In the month of December 1939, the snow was up to our belts. True, we Siberians had been well trained and were well equipped. We were dressed in short sheepskin coats, winter fur caps with earflaps, and fur mittens that came up to our elbows. I can't say that the –40° C. weather was trifling, but we didn't sense it so acutely. We could lie prone (and did lie prone) in the snow for several days. Back in Siberia we had become inured to this and also accustomed to running through the snow. Our platoon leader, thanks to him, had trained us well. We'd haul a gun into position. He'd give the command, 'Ranging mark 1, right 20, a machine gun, two shells. Fire!' Then he'd shout, 'To cover!' This meant we had to run through thigh-deep snow for about 200 metres. You'd run and then drop into the snow. Barely having caught our breaths, the command would already come, 'Man the gun!' You'd struggle back over those same 200 metres back to the gun at a run. That's how he in fact saved us from the frost and trained us. On the Karelian Isthmus, oh how this helped us! We could quickly open fire, and then make a run to take cover from counter-battery fire or a mortar barrage.

Over the entire Winter War, we perhaps fired several times from defilade positions, since we spent nearly all our time manhandling the guns forward behind the advancing infantry, always firing over open sights. We'd take a ridge line, advance 100 to 200 metres, and then make no headway for about a week. We'd then make another 100 to 200 metre advance and again come to a grinding halt. That's how we broke through the Mannerheim Line. Even though I do believe the regiment command was competent, nevertheless, the regiment was replenished with troops more than once before we reached Vyborg.

The regiment's last battle was for possession of Vyborg itself. During the assault on the city, our regiment lagged behind in the advance. The neighbouring regiments managed to break through, but the Finns had our infantry pinned down in front of some barbed wire by flanking machine-gun fire. Yet just 300–400 metres remained to the city's outskirts! The regiment commander assembled everyone who was still reporting for duty, took half of the battery's personnel, and led them all to the barbed wire. There, he himself got the men up and moving forward. Although we lost a lot of men, we broke through to Vyborg's outskirts. On the night of 11 March 1940, when it became known that a peace treaty was to be signed the next day in Moscow, all the artillery fired in the direction of the Finns. We were in a forested area, with little clearings, so the guns stood in rows with just 3 metres between each gun, and all night long we pounded the Finns without any concern for conserving our shells.

In the summer of 1940 we were shifted to the Hanko Peninsula as part of the 8th Separate Rifle Brigade, which had been formed on the basis of our division. The regiment took up defensive positions along the Petrovsk corridor, over which, according to legend, Peter the Great dragged his galleys from one part of the harbour to the other during the war with Sweden. By June 1941, we had thoroughly entrenched our positions.

Prior to 17 June, there were only 6 wooden shells per gun that we used to rehearse the loading procedure, but on this day an order arrived to man the defences, and in place of the imitation shells, we were given 200 rounds of live ammunition. The earth and timber emplacement for our gun still hadn't been finished: two side walls had been embedded, and the wall that protected the gun from the front had been thrown up, so that only the barrel of the gun protruded over it. We had covered the emplacement with metal beams, covered them with rocks and logs, and then shovelled dirt over this entire structure. A large mound resulted, and although we had camouflaged it, our emplacement clearly stood out against the backdrop of the terrain. A ditch had been dug in front of us, along the bottom of which three strands of barbed wire had been laid under tension. In front of the ditch, two machine-gun pillboxes had been constructed with overlapping fields of flanking fire. Everything had been mined. Our regiment engineer was Lieutenant Repnia – a master of his craft and a big extemporizer as well. He placed not only mines, but also built remote-controlled demolition bombs and stone mortars. The latter consisted of a conical hole dug out of the ground, in which first gun powder and then a sack of rocks were placed. We were told that something was going to happen and were given an order to not allow the enemy to penetrate our line. We could fire only in response to an enemy attack, but also had the strictest instruction not to fire first, in order not to trigger a war.

On 22 June we heard over the radio that the war had begun. On this same day, two of our fighters shot down a German Ju-88 reconnaissance plane over Hanko, but it was quiet on the ground. We didn't know the situation. We were told, 'If it starts, fire and drive them back.' On 25 June the Finns for the first time opened artillery fire on us, but they didn't go on the attack. But at 0300 (remember, at this latitude it was bright as day!) on 1 July, a preparatory artillery barrage began, which continued for 2 hours. The entire forest was burning! They also pummelled our gun emplacement. The crash of the shells and the subsequent explosions were terrifying! The rocks were shattering and fragments were flying in every direction. We were sitting in a bunker for the crew, but the gun was standing on a platform, protected by a concrete parapet. Our guys were firing in reply. After the preparatory barrage ended, the Finns went on the attack in dense lines. In front of my gun and a bit to the left and right of it were the pillboxes, which could direct flanking fire on the attackers, while our gun, as it were, was covering them, situated at a certain distance behind them and at the apex of a nominal triangle. It must be said that in front of the machine-gun pillboxes, a listening post had been thrown out closer to the border. On this day, Sergeant Sokur and Private Andrienko were manning it. Everyone thought that they'd been killed – both our artillery and the enemy's artillery were falling around it, and moreover the waves of attacking Finns were passing over them. However, after the battle they returned, prodding several captured Finns in front of them. For this action Sergeant Petia Sokur received the title Hero of the Soviet Union, while Private Andrienko was awarded the Order of Lenin.

As soon as the Finns moved out, we started firing at them. We were working on our knees, in order to keep behind the gun shield. The Finns began to climb toward the emplacements. We were firing canister at point-blank range, more than anything because we didn't have time to select a shell. The adjuster Sasha Klevtsov, a powerfully built Georgian longshoreman, was chucking the gun back and forth to the left and the right; it happened more than once that we fired while he was still holding it. We were now firing without aiming it, only because there was no way to miss. They shoved another round into the gun. I fired – but there was no report! We opened the breech and the casing tumbled out, but the projectile remained in the gun barrel. The attacking Finns were approaching and there were bursts of machine-gun fire. That's when Sasha Klevtsov performed an amazing feat. He grabbed the bore cleaner with the attached brush, whereas according to regulations, in case of a jammed shell, you were supposed to force it out carefully with a specialized gun swab, which avoids the detonator as you drive out the shell, whereas the bore cleaner has a blunt end that strikes the detonator directly. But where is the other one? Sasha jumped up under fire and drove out the jammed shell with the bore cleaner; thank God, it didn't explode! Sasha survived and after the battle he was decorated with the Order of the Red Star. In general, such exploits always ended with medals. I, the battery commander and the gun layer were recommended for the Order of the Red Banner. The battery commander received it, but we didn't.

Likely, our recommendation got lost somewhere on its way up the chain of command. You see, only an army commander could sign a recommendation for a higher Order, while the guys who were put up for the Order of the Red Star and the 'For Courage' medals received them, because just the regiment and division commander could sign off on those award lists. So those men got their decorations within just a couple of weeks. Later, after we arrived in Leningrad, we checked, but I had no award, so they gave me a 'For Courage' medal.

Returning to our story, the fighting went on for 2 hours and the Finns repeated the attack twice. They even managed to close to within 20 metres of my gun, but we stood firm, having killed in the order of 200 soldiers and officers. At the end of the fight I only had six shells left; the ammunition bearer Ozerov had been wounded, the gun had been knocked out of alignment, and we were bleeding from the nose and ears. These metal beams, with which we had covered our earth and timber emplacement, rang so loudly that we were completely deafened. Later it became clear that we had received the enemy's main attack. After this battle the entire crew was replaced, while we were sent to the hospital, where we spent approximately a week recovering. Our eardrums had ruptured; we'd say something, but couldn't hear each other. We rested in the hospital for a week before returning to the front lines.

We found our gun emplacement had been smashed, all the camouflaging had been blown away, and the stones had been broken up and scattered around. We changed positions, creating a new earthen and timber emplacement in the direction of a village, and concealing it within a large shed. Generally speaking, we frequently had to change our position, practically after every battle.

That's where we held out for 164 days. The Finns dropped leaflets over us, which stated, 'You are heroes, but your situation is hopeless. Surrender!' They dropped so many that the ground became snowy white with them. But we also scattered our own propaganda leaflets over their lines. I recall that one of them had a depiction of Mannerheim on it, licking Hitler's shaggy ass. We laughed uproariously over the image! Music was played for us: 'Sten'ka Razin', 'Katiusha' and other songs, but we also didn't forget to fight.

On 1 December, an order was given at midday to cease fire. Our regiment was the last to withdraw. At midnight we were instructed to abandon our guns, throw away the latching mechanism, and withdraw on foot. They rolled away only my gun as the heroic cannon that had started the war. They say it is now on display in a museum in St Petersburg. We boarded ships, and ours led the convoy of the last ships that were abandoning Hanko. With our arrival in Leningrad, the 136th Rifle Division (subsequently the 63rd Guards Rifle Division) was formed on the basis of our brigade. Colonel Simoniak assumed command of the division. He was a competent commander with a tremendous amount of experience and practice, who knew how to prepare the troops and to promote sensible officers.

The fighting on the Leningrad front was hard. People were dying not only in battles, but also from hunger. We were defending the banks of the Neva River near the village of the Novosaratovka colony.[1] I recall the owner of the house in which we spent our nights. During a lull in the fighting, he went outside, walked 50 metres, and there he dropped dead from hunger; in his pocket he still had a small piece of bread that he was conserving and hadn't eaten. The people were emaciated. You'd walk to the mess, they'd ladle you out a half a mess tin of so-called pea soup – a yellowish broth with a single pea swimming in it – and you'd add a little snow to it before eating it. Yet after this, you'd still have to haul your gun through the snow. In the summer you'd lie around the gun and pluck blades of grass, until you came across one with a tender, whitish section. You'd eat that and then pluck another one. Over the course of the day, you'd eat your fill. They'd distribute pieces of bread. You'd cut your portion into little cubes and slowly chew these pieces. If you got a full slice to eat, you'd feel kind of stuffed. Never mind ... we still manhandled our guns into firing positions and fought.

On 2 September 1942, our 136th Rifle Division broke the blockade in the vicinity of the village Ivanovskoe near Ust'-Tosno, in the so-called 'Valley of Death'. We had moved into our jumping-off positions; the infantry had dug approach trenches to within about 100 metres of the German barbed wire. There remained 100–150 metres to the enemy's trenches. We also rolled our gun right up to the infantry. Sappers cleared lanes through the minefields. The offensive was to begin at 0800 after a 2-hour preparatory artillery barrage, at a time when the fog still hadn't lifted. I don't know why, but the artillery barrage began 90 minutes late. By this time the fog was already dissipating and the Germans, noticing our infantry that had been massed for the attack, opened up a hurricane of fire. The trenches became abattoirs covered with blood and human flesh. It was a horror! We sat there for 2 hours while they poured fire into our trenches. When the bungled artillery preparation came to an end, the infantry moved out, but the losses in its ranks were already enormous. As a result, a breakthrough didn't result, and we became bogged down in positional fighting, advancing just 200–300 metres per day.

The terrain was boggy and sandy. We moved about on our bellies. Rifles wouldn't fire – they became jammed by the sand and mud. There was a heavily damaged, enormous grey concrete building in the valley, from which a railroad embankment extended. The infantry would assail the Germans with grenades – they'd fall back from it and we would take it. We'd run out of grenades, and then they'd throw us back. This embankment changed hands repeatedly. The casualties were staggering ... but the regiment kept attacking. On one sector we made a penetration of 1 to 1.5 kilometres. We were rolling our gun forward directly behind the infantry's battle lines. Just then a Ju-87 dived on us, and the bomb exploded almost right next to the gun's left wheel. I remained alive, three of us were wounded, of which only one was still mobile, and the rest, including Sasha Klevtsov, were killed.

At this time, a group of Germans moved up from the right, intending to strike the company I was supporting in the flank. A company! Today we normally talk about larger formations: armies, divisions, regiments and battalions. But we had only 100 men left in the battalion, instead of the normal 500, and just 20 in the company. The Germans, likely, were also attacking with only a company, but it also had no more than thirty to fifty men. My gun was behind our infantry. What could I do? The gun had a smashed dial sight and wheel, but it could still fire. From somewhere we found the strength. I pivoted the gun by the trail, and we slaughtered the counterattacking Germans, firing all my remaining shells, likely not more than ten, at them. We didn't kill all of them, of course, but the main thing was that we broke up their attack. Simoniak later said, 'That's Shishkin for you! Again he was successful. He repelled the attack!'

I spent the next couple of days in bed, recovering my strength. I felt shivery. Then I received a new gun, and with it we pressed on. It was later also disabled during a bombing.

For this fighting, for the first time I was put up for the title Hero of the Soviet Union, but the battles were unsuccessful. Our losses were enormous and after the operation ended, the Front commander assembled all the sergeants who had distinguished themselves in it and told them, 'With my authority I can give you all the rank of junior lieutenant, or I can give you documents for three to four months of training in a specialist school back in the "Big Land" [in the expanses of Russia in the rear area].' Some guys chose to remain, but I and a few others accepted our tickets out of the front line. Probably I had lost a bit of my nerve, but I had fought honourably over the preceding year and I was simply tired, and I wanted a break from the war, the hunger and the cold.

We were sent to Saratov to the 2nd Artillery School, where we studied and trained for the next three to four months, losing one of those months to cutting firewood and digging trenches. But what could they teach us? We all had combat experience, and we knew the ins and outs of the artillery better than some of the school's lieutenants. Thus in April 1943 we hastily acquired the rank of lieutenant and were sent to Cheliabinsk, in order to pick up SU–152 self-propelled guns.

At this time, the 30th Urals Volunteer Tank Corps was forming up; its 244th Tank Brigade, commanded by Fomichev, was in Cheliabinsk. In the oblast, a motorized rifle brigade was also being formed on a volunteer basis. There were 100 applications for each place. First, there was the awareness that it was shameful to sit in the rear, when others were pouring out their blood; secondly, conditions were hard in the rear. At the front you'd be fed, but here there was nothing to eat.

One, let us say, overzealous officer was placed in command of our 1545th Heavy Self-propelled Regiment. He, for example, could dress down any officer with a healthy dose of swear words in front of the assembled rank and file. Yet this was the crudest violation of the Regulations! What was it like for the soldiers to hear their commander be disrespected in such a manner?! My fellow lieutenants would say, 'When we reach the front, he'll get his.'

Before its departure to the front, the regiment was located at the Self-propelled Artillery Centre. This regiment commander on the day we were to embark on the trains drove off somewhere. The regiment received the order to load onto trains, but the chief of staff reported to the Centre that it had no regiment commander, that he had gone off somewhere unknown. Literally within an hour, a bulky man showed up on the platform of the Mamontovka Station, which as we later found out was the new regiment commander Tikhon Efremovich Kartashov. He approached, didn't question anyone about anything, and only watched: who, how and what was being done. That's how he took command of the regiment. Another one would have started giving instructions. There were those like that – they were constantly directing how a tank should be loaded, but for this there are lieutenants and sergeant majors. I'll tell you a bit later about our first battle, but when we came out of it, we learned that the neighbouring tank regiment, which by a whim of fate was being commanded by our former regiment commander, had lost almost all its armour. Later we were talking with guys from that regiment, and they told us, 'Well, how was it like to fight under our idiot? He only knows one thing, "Forward!"' But Kartashov told us, 'If you're grabbing a bull by its horns, I'll be the first to latch on! Here's some scrub brush, here's some ravines, here's a haystack; use the terrain, the factor of surprise and concealment.' It is with such commanders that we in fact won the war.

Both the higher command and the troops thought highly of our commander, because the regiment was always prepared for both combat and for marches. The first orders after a combat were, 'Inspect your weapon, calibrate the sights, load the vehicles with ammunition and fuel, and test the traverse.' Only then were we allowed to grab something to eat and to get a bit of sleep. Thus we had a lot of damaged tanks, but our losses were not large. Of course, regarding the light losses in our regiment, they can also be explained by the fact that we were used in a supporting role. We only helped the main combat units – the tank and rifle units to which we'd been assigned – to carry out their assignments, and we didn't have our own independent missions.

Our first battle took place at the Nugr' River, beyond which on a steep bank sat the village of Bol'shaia Chern', which the Germans had converted into a strongpoint. From there, 88-mm anti-tank guns were firing at our tanks and infantry that were attacking across a large field of rye. Amid the rye, one couldn't identify where the fire was coming from. Tanks were burning. My gunner Bychkov was superb. In this battle he left two enemy tanks in flames. At some moment we took a hit. There were sparks, smoke and the smell of red-hot metal in the fighting compartment. The driver-mechanic Nikonov quickly drove the vehicle into a depression. I crawled out of the hatch and began to look around. With difficulty I spotted an anti-tank gun on the edge of the field in a patch of bushes. We moved out of its field of fire, and it redirected its fire against the tanks. I decided to turn and aim the gun at a landmark in line with the German anti-tank gun, and to drive out of the depression toward it for a shot. If our first shot didn't hit, we'd be toast. Barely had we emerged from the depression, when the anti-tank gun began to pivot in our direction. Bychkov shouted, 'Shot!' and simultaneously the sound of the gun firing rang out. I barely had time to shout, 'Nikonov! Reverse!', but this proved to be unnecessary – Bychkov had hit the target.

The tanks were crossing a shallow stream, outflanking Bol'shaia Chern' from the left. We covered their manoeuvre with fire. Suddenly three or four Panthers emerged on the flank of the attacking tanks and opened fire. I will say here that if an enemy tank appeared at a range of 1.5 kilometres, then it was possible to distinguish its type only through binoculars, and at that only a motionless vehicle from a halt, and even then not always. Well, given the battlefield situation and through the dust and smoke, we didn't scrutinize them. Anyway, we fired at them from a range of 1,000 metres and left them burning – or at least three of their burned out hulks were still there when we passed by them a little later as the advance resumed. I looked over at them and my hair stood on end – they were our T-34s. We would all be sent in front of a tribunal! Only having passed them and looking back, when I spotted crosses on the turrets, was I able to calm down. The tanks were German. I was correct – they had been firing at our tanks, but if they had in fact been our tanks, I would have hardly been able to make a case for myself . . .

In these battles I happened to encounter the army commander. We had reached the area of Shemiakino. From the gardens on the outskirts of this settlement, the Germans greeted us with fire, knocking out several tanks. We had suppressed one gun and had caught the next target in our sight. I shouted, 'Aladin, load!' At this moment there was a blow – the radio flew from its place and the gun's breech suddenly dropped – a projectile had punched through a trunnion. I shouted, 'Nikonov, reverse!' and a second round struck but failed to penetrate the armour. The self-propelled gun rolled back about 20 metres and stopped behind a mound. The gun barrel was hanging loosely, the spent German projectile was in the breech assembly, and just then there was a rapping sound on the armour. I opened the hatch and looked, and found the commander of the 4th Tank Army General Badanov standing there with a pistol in his hand: 'Where are you headed, son? Are we staying on course?'

I replied, 'I have a shell in the breech assembly and the gun is hanging loose.'

'Ah, OK,' said the General, 'but let's go, get moving to a repair station.'

But he might have given me a cuff, if I had been retreating to the rear undamaged. In a nearby forest, a repair team replaced my main gun with one taken from a different self-propelled gun, and soon we were already catching up with the regiment.

A couple of weeks later, in one of the battles the battery commander was wounded and I took command upon myself. After all, I had combat experience from two wars, while many of the self-propelled gun commanders were newcomers to the front. Things went well for me, and subsequently during a re-forming period, I was confirmed in this post.

In the Battle of Kursk, our 30th Urals Volunteer Tank Corps received the honourific title of a Guards unit, while I was awarded the Order of the Red Star. I never drank in the war with Finland or to this point in the Great Patriotic War, but this time I couldn't resist. In the regiment there was a tradition to drop an Order into a full glass of vodka; the recipients would have to drink it down to the bottom before he could attach his own Order to his combat blouse. I recall the regiment commander seating everyone around a table, before he got an Order and placing it in the glass. Everyone took a swig as it was passed around the table, but I moved it aside without partaking. The regiment commander looked and said, 'I'm giving him an Order, but he isn't drinking! The hell ... Get with it!' I had to take a swig. I set down the glass and quickly reached for a snack. The commander exclaimed merrily, 'And he said he doesn't drink! He downs glasses!' One can say that this was my Vodka-Order baptism.

Incidentally, there we also liberated the regiment commander's home village. Only scorched chimneys remained of the village, but Kartashov's parents were alive, hiding in a nearby wooded area. Around this time we were withdrawn from combat for refitting. So we spent it cutting logs for several new cabins and building stoves. To put it briefly, we put this village back on its feet. When we departed, we left behind everything necessary for the villagers.

In addition to medals and Orders, a crew received a cash award for destroying tanks – 2,000 rubles for each one. Usually over an operation the battery as a rule added more than one tank to its score, normally three to five, and sometimes even more. In my crew there was no permanent scheme for distributing the money. Sometimes we split it equally, sometimes we gave a little extra to the gunner or, if we knew, for instance, that the grandparents were still in Aladin's house, we'd give him a little more to send back home. Sometimes the money was shared even with those batteries that hadn't taken direct part in the fighting. For example, sometimes some bonus money was given to the mechanic or to someone else – they also contributed to our common cause. The officer's ration – biscuits, spam and sweets – was always shared with the entire crew and never eaten somewhere on the sly. We all worked together, which is why the crew and the submachine gunners attached to our vehicle regarded us, the commanders, very warmly.

There was the following incident in the Kursk bulge. For several days we stood down, bringing ourselves back into order. Several former prisoners arrived at this time in the platoon of submachine gunners. On the next day one of them reported to me that one of these guys had stolen a loaf of bread. Although we were not starving, our sustenance was limited, and how could we pillage and plunder our own people? I told him, 'Dig a hole deep enough so that only his head sticks out.' I ordered the thief to be placed in this hole and for a sentry to be posted, thereby creating a unique sort of brig. Everyone walking by could see him sitting there – it was deeply shameful for him. Within several hours, he was begging, 'Battery commander, free me from this shame. I'll redeem myself with my blood!' I replied, 'Fine. But, just look, you've made a promise.'

Several days later the regiment again entered combat. We were driving through a village, seated atop the self-propelled gun. Suddenly he gave me such a blow that I flew off the turret head over heels and struck the engine compartment with a thud. I jumped up and went after him, 'What the hell?!' But he was wounded – he had spotted a German submachine gunner who was crouched on the roof of a barn, and he had managed to knock me off just before the German fired. For saving the life of an officer, a soldier could be recommended for the Order of the Red Star, which I indeed did.

From the end of 1943 until early 1944, the regiment went through rest and refitting in the vicinity of the city of Karachev. We received new self-propelled guns, repaired the old ones, and engaged in daily training, particularly for the new personnel. I, as a former gunner, paid particular attention to training our crews in gunnery, and without false modesty I will say that my battery fired with the most accuracy.

In January–February 1944, our regiment was transferred from the 4th Tank Army to the 5th Guards Tank Army, which in the spring was redeployed to the Ukraine. There was very hard fighting around Targu-Frumos. In May 1944, I was wounded near this city. We were standing in one of the positions, ready to attack. The Germans were pounding us relentlessly with artillery fire, and then several dozen German aircraft appeared overhead just as I had popped my head out of the commander's hatch to take a look around. Just then an artillery shell or bomb exploded near the vehicle. I dropped back inside the fighting compartment and felt like I had banged a rib against the edge of the hatch. I felt a bit sick. I passed my hand over the spot that had taken the blow and looked – it was all bloody. A fragment had struck me in the back. I said aloud, 'Guys, I've been wounded.' They quickly patched me up and the regiment's assistant commander of the administrative unit took me to a hospital. There was no X-ray machine, and the fragment was deeply embedded. Where to find X-ray apparatus? They decided not to operate and merely stuck a gauze compress into the wound. It would become saturated with blood, and then they would pull it out. That's how I went around for the next two weeks until the wound had scarred over. Later after the war, when they took an X-ray, I found out that the fragment had almost reached the heart. It is still sitting there today.

There was another memorable incident that took place near Targu-Frumos. I had summoned all the self-propelled gun commanders to my vehicle, in order to give them their orders. They took them and started to run off back to their vehicles, but one of them, Iura Krashennikov, delayed a bit. At this time a group of Ju-87s appeared and began to bomb us. The infantrymen who had been assigned to me scattered and dropped prone. Whenever a bomb was falling, I would watch to see where it would land, and then I would run and kick the prone men, so that they would move to the opposite side of the self-propelled gun, instead of lying there like logs. They would get sprayed with fragments, while I always managed to take shelter behind the vehicle. This time we were running from the bomb, and then we saw that it appeared as if it was going to drop right into the open hatch of the self-propelled gun commanded by Iura. Shocked by the realisation that he'd been saved by a miracle by lingering next to my vehicle, he immediately went grey and began to stammer. I even had to send him to a hospital for treatment.

What am I driving at? If a man is watchful and sees where to turn, where to jump, and where to fire – then he'll have success and he'll survive. Well, luck also means a lot. I, in all likelihood, had been born lucky.

In June we redeployed to Belorussia. Our regiment was assigned to the 3rd Guards 'Kotel'nikovo' Tank Corps under the command of General I.A. Vovchenko. My battery practically always served with Grigorii Pokhodzeev's 19th Guards Tank Brigade – the best brigade in the corps. These were skill-ful commanders, from which I learned a lot. Brigade commander Colonel Pokhodzeev was an eagle. He was a hard-driving, taciturn man. You'd report to him at a conference in order to receive your orders before a battle, and he would ask, 'So, artilleryman, do you know your mission?

'I know.'

'Do you understand what you need to do?'

'Understood.'

'Dismissed.'

That just reminded me of one combat action. Three tanks of the brigade's spearhead, which had emerged from a forest and were climbing a low ridge, were destroyed by a Tiger, which was standing out in the open on the opposite side of the clearing. It was impossible to bypass this clearing, so the brigade commander ordered: 'You're a beast-killer, right? So go destroy this tank.'[2]

My self-propelled gun moved forward, reached the bottom of the slope and began slowly to climb it. I was standing in the hatch, exposed to my waist. At a certain moment I spotted the German tank, which was positioned with its aft end up against the trunk of an enormous tree. The Tiger fired. The vortex of air created by the shell as it whizzed over my head almost tore me out of the hatch. While I was pondering what I should do, it fired another round or two, but since only a fragment of the superstructure was visible above the crest of the ridge, it failed to hit us, even though the trajectory of the shells fired by the Tiger was flat. What to do? If we advanced over the crest, we'd surely be killed.

So here I decided to make use of the possibilities of our 152-mm howitzers, which fired shells in an arched trajectory. I noticed a bush on the slope. Looking through the barrel of the howitzer, I had the driver manoeuvre the self-propelled gun to a position where this bush was lined up with the crown of the tree, under which the German tank was sitting. I took a seat behind the gunner, from where I could see this bush in the optical sight, and I lowered the gun barrel to a point where I knew the shell would have to strike the enemy tank. There were millions of calculations, but it has taken me longer to narrate this than it required doing all this. We fired. I stood at full height in the hatch, and I could see the Tiger's turret lying next to it – we'd hit it right below the turret! Later in the brigade newspaper it was written, 'Shishkin shoots like the Good Soldier Svejk – on the sly.'

In June 1944 the corps went on the offensive with the task of reaching the Berezina River in the Borisov area, and then to move on Minsk. We didn't advance along the Minsk highway, but stuck mainly to the woods. We in our columns would cover 15–20 kilometres before bumping into a rear guard detachment; we'd deploy, drive it away, and then resume our forward move-ment. In the vicinity of the settlement of Bobr, the corps collided in a meeting engagement with a German division. We managed to smash the division, but I was wounded in the stomach by a shell that exploded directly in front of me as I was dashing between self-propelled guns. I fell. Next to me was a foxhole, in which as I later learned the corps' commissar, who had been the commissar of my brigade back at Hanko, was sitting. They bandaged me and then took me to a field hospital in a staff vehicle.

The hospital consisted of a dozen small soldier's tents, in each of which stood an operating table. There were a lot of wounded. They laid me on some straw. I laid there and was silent, and because I was silent, they didn't place me on an operating table. So I laid there for a day; no one even took me to processing!

Battle of Nikolai Shishkin's ISU-152 with Tiger tank.

It is a good thing that the regiment commander arrived and demanded that someone examine me. They laid me on a table, gave me an injection, removed the fragment, sewed me up, bandaged me, and literally within a week I was back with the regiment. We took Minsk, but then again I was hospitalized, because my wound hadn't healed.

I returned to the regiment only after Vilnius had already been captured. Savage fighting was going on in Lithuania. There we were shifted from one axis to another, from Siauliai to Tukkum. The front lines were changing with kaleidoscopic rapidity. We were attempting to cut off the German Courland grouping. We were told that the commander of the unit that first entered the city of Tukkum would receive the title Hero of the Soviet Union. A lot of people were killed, but no one managed to become a Hero. We forced a crossing of the Dzelda River. A gently sloping rise with a length of 200–300 metres extended from the mouth of the river. The Germans had taken up a defensive position in a patch of woods about 300 metres behind this rise. My battery and the tank battalion of Hero of the Soviet Union Captain Penezhko, being in the vanguard of the brigade's main forces, managed to cross the river on the heels of the withdrawing Germans. The tanks attempted to make a further advance, but while they were climbing out of the river valley onto level ground (during which time it was impossible to fire because the gun was pointing skywards and nothing could be seen), they were being shot up at almost point-blank range. Having lost three or four tanks, we rolled back. We requested artillery support, but it was still in the process of deploying. The tank commanders climbed out of their tanks, and each of them selected a target. We repeated the attack, knocked out several German tanks, but we lost two more tanks and fell back again. We spent all day spinning our wheels in place like this. It began to grow dark. On the opposite bank the brigade's main forces were concentrated, the headquarters came up, and with it the regiment commander. My vehicle was parked next to Penezhko's tank. I heard him say, 'The brigade commander has ordered that within 20–30 minutes, after the artillery gives us some fire, we all in concert climb that rise and attack.'

The artillery fired a barrage. We went on the attack, lost one vehicle and again fell back. By now it was dark. The order had to be carried out. We started our engines, clattered up to the crest of the rise, but stopped before fully revealing our superstructures. We could see Penezhko's tanks; they weren't going anywhere. We requested another artillery barrage, and the artillery again blanketed the German positions. The commander is shouting at me over the radio, 'Penezhko is reporting that he is attacking and has reached the road. And you? Why are you silent? What are you doing?'

'I'm in my jumping-off positions.'

'Get going, advance! Penezhko is attacking.'

'Penezhko's tanks aren't moving; they're simply gunning their engines and firing into the sky.'

Penezhko was being clever – just running his engines and firing, while he was reporting, 'I'm attacking; I came out onto the road and met strong enemy fire. I had to fall back and re-occupy my jumping-off positions. We will repeat the attack right away.'

The regiment commander cursed me up and down before saying: 'Well, OK; do whatever the tankers are doing.'

The next morning the brigade's tanks crossed the river. All the artillery came up. They fired a powerful preparatory barrage, and we broke through the German defence, losing just two or three tanks.

There was a lot of fighting after this breakthrough, but I particularly recall one battle near Memel. At the time, I was now fighting with the 18th Guards Tank Brigade. The brigade was concentrated in some woods, and I had deployed my self-propelled guns on the edge of it among some bushes. A field stretched out in front of us, and beyond it I could see Hill 29.4, which was overgrown with bushes. The brigade at that time had not more than twenty tanks – in essence, a tank battalion. The brigade commander summoned the battalion commanders and issued an order to attack the hill. While the attack was being prepared, we managed to spot several German tanks in a patch of woods to the left of the hill. At my command the self-propelled guns moved into firing positions and destroyed the detected targets – one or two shots and a tank would be destroyed. My gunner Bychkov hit one tank at a range of 1,000 metres with his first shot; I had trained the others to shoot not badly, so over the 24 hours before the tanks attacked this hill, my battery had destroyed approximately ten tanks, and this meant 20,000 rubles!

Well, and what about the tankers? They popped out into the open field, and the Germans began to lay into them. One burst into flames, then another ... and a third. They came back. No one was eager to burn to death within a flaming tank. A certain amount of time passed, and then again the brigade commander called a meeting: 'Repeat the attack.' Again they went forward, again they took losses, and again they came rolling back. A third time: 'The Motherland must today fire a salute in our honour! We must take Memel. Our neighbours have already broken into Memel, while we're spinning our wheels! A green flare – launch the attack!' The brigade commander loved this business ...

The guys were saying, 'Again we're going to be lit up. First we must work over the Germans with artillery. But he's recklessly driving us to attack.'

We attacked a third time. Some tankers were unbolting the bottom hatch and the crew would tumble out, while the tank kept rolling forward until it was consumed in flames. Over the three attacks, a company of tanks was knocked out. When this commander tried to hound the brigade into a fourth attack, one battalion commander grabbed his pistol and said, 'If you send us once more into the attack, I'll shoot you. It's all the same to me – burn to death now or be sent to a penal company later.'

At this time my battery was ordered to conduct a lateral march along the front and assemble on a different axis. I gathered the men and told them to leave their positions covertly and to assemble behind a copse of trees in our rear before moving further. When we had assembled on the road and were waiting for an order, a German fighter flew past low over the column. The pilot shook his fist at us and flew away. I think that he had radioed that the heavy self-propelled guns had pulled out of the area. Suddenly instead of a signal to move out, an order arrived to return to our previous positions and to restore the situation there. That was the entire order. Today they write large orders that run for two to five pages. But back then, it was nine words: 'Return to your previous positions and restore the situation.' Looking back toward the copse of trees that we had just left, I saw some major running and shouting, 'Stop, stop!' I stopped. The major said excitedly:

> The brigade has been used up, the Germans are attacking there. When you left, anti-aircraft gunners took over your positions, they were overwhelmed and Tigers are on the move there.

I looked and saw one tank emerging from the woods, followed by another. One's main gun was smashed; the other's mud guards were battered. In total five or six tanks came out. I gave the order, 'Load the guns. To our former positions! At the attacking enemy tanks – Fire!' We loaded the guns, returned to our previous firing positions, and saw five Tigers at a range of 400 metres that were heading directly toward us. Well, what of it?! With our first volley of shots, four of the Tigers were destroyed. We muffed the shot at the fifth Tiger, on the extreme right, and missed. It stopped, and then pulled back behind a house. I had Ustinov's crew on the right flank. I ordered him to move out, keeping concealed by the bushes along the ditch, and to finish off the Tiger. That's just what he did.

I returned to the edge of the woods and reported to the regiment commander that the situation had been restored. Just then the brigade commander walked up: 'Oh! See, with you we hold the defence.' For this action I was recommended for the Order of Suvorov 3rd Degree, but I didn't receive it. The recommendation got lost or they simply didn't award it to me – after all, Memel hadn't been taken and a half of a brigade had been destroyed. One can always find a reason. Yes, if all the deserved Orders had been received, there would have been nowhere to hang them all!

In October or November 1944, an order was given to entrain at Vainod Station. There are some places that you remember for a long time … It was 20 kilometres to the station, but the mud was such that the road wasn't a road, but a swamp. You take a step, and your boot gets stuck and your foot comes out of it. Your foot popped out of even tightly laced boots! It was forbidden to climb up onto the railroad embankment – for this you might even have received a bullet! Only cars were allowed onto the corduroy road that had been laid down. We had to move along a hastily improvised road through the woods. It took more than 24 hours for the regiment to move 20 kilometres! The self-propelled guns sank into the mud up to their underbellies, to a point where they were unable to move. Each had a log to assist with this which was attached to the front of the track. Slowly you'd progress across the bog the length of the hull. Then the log would disengage and you'd have to repeat the process. A tow cable would snap, or the log would wrench free, or a track link would break.

Well, nevertheless we entrained, which took us to Warsaw. We began to attack toward Mlawa in the direction of the city of Elbing. We deployed into combat formation at night. Nothing was visible. There were seemingly random gunfire, flares and the flashes of shots and explosions. To put it briefly, we took Mlawa. Our 19th Tank Brigade was moving in the forward detachment. We moved on toward Preussisch-Holland (modern-day Paslek). I was advancing on the highway with the task to reach the northern and northeastern outskirts of Preussisch-Holland, while the tanks were swinging around to the left. We rolled past Marau Station. It was a little way off the highway we were taking. I thought, 'I wasn't told to take the station, but I should check out what's over there.' I walked up to it and saw trains parked there and a big crowd of people. I stopped the column and ordered them to swing their guns around toward the station. As an interpreter, I took a boy who'd been taken by force to Germany, who one day had drifted into our camp somewhere along the way. He spoke German fluently. We walked up to the station. There was a crowd of German civilians standing there, and German soldiers en route to some place – it was a troop train. I attempted to clarify who was in charge. I ordered the soldiers to surrender. At this moment, there was a burst of automatic weapons fire from out of this crowd. The boy crumpled and fell, while I ducked around a corner of a building. I gave the signal to open fire, and we fired a couple of shells at the train. I don't know who it hit. The principle was: if you fire at me, I'll fire back. I returned and again ordered that the German troops surrender or they'd all be killed. At this time, the crowd led the Germans who had fired at us to our vehicles. I turned them over to the submachine gunners, who tied them up, and then left behind several men to wait for the arrival of our main forces. We patched up the boy as best we could and sent him to a hospital. We had no medics. Meanwhile, a throng of civilians encircled the self-propelled guns, shouting and pointing at the prisoners, 'Don't shoot us, don't shoot ... They're the fascists!' I said, 'Guys, let's get away from this crowd as soon as possible.'

From this station we moved off toward Preussisch-Holland. The road travelled along an embankment, on both sides of which were 5-metre-wide shoulders. It was jammed with refugees and enormous wagons that were just like in the movies about the Wild West. They were all moving toward Preussisch-Holland, filling both lanes of the road. A little to the right of us, there was another road that angled toward this city. I looked over at it and saw that some German unit – artillery, self-propelled guns and trucks – was moving along it. If they managed to reach the city before we did and fortified themselves, there was nothing I could do with them. I issued an order: 'Keep to the left side. Close the hatches. Forward!' We had to crush these wagons. Whoever didn't turn off the road fell under our tracks. Nevertheless I managed to win the race to the outskirts of the city, where I turned my SU-152s around, allowed the German column to approach to within 500–600 metres, and then we opened fire. The column dispersed, and at this time the brigade arrived. That's how we took the city. I believe that I seized it. It wasn't just the tankers who took objectives!

The next day I received orders to move on to Elbing. En route we took other little towns. The adversary was primarily occupying the villages and towns. You'd move up close to a town, pick out the largest building, fire a round at the bottom floor, and it would collapse; if there was no obvious structure, you'd fire a couple of shells into the gardens in the sector of attack. After all, if you moved in without firing, you yourself might be knocked out. We, of course, were conserving our ammunition.

We arrived at Elbing somewhere between 20 and 25 January. We took the city at night. Music was playing in the restaurants and there were pedestrians out and about. Our regiment was given the order to take the villages of Baumgart (Ogrodniki), Trunz (Milejewo) and Gross Stoboy (Kamiennik Wielki) in order to block the road to Elbing to the German units retreating from Konigsberg. My battery was positioned in Gross Stoboy, Captain Zverev's battery was in Baumgart, and one more battery was in Trunz. We also towed two abandoned Sherman tanks up to our position – apparently they'd been unable to climb the ice-covered road leading up a slope and had been abandoned. Later their machine guns would really help me out.

The Germans attempting to break out of encirclement at Konigsberg initially attacked to the right of the highway, where they ran into Zverev's battery and recoiled. They decided to try again along the highway. They had no other options – it was impossible to break out across the muddy fields. Somewhere on the morning of 29 or 30 January, they came at me. In the course of the day, we destroyed those tanks that tried to escape along the road. The next day they made another attempt to break out. Once again we repulsed them. We fired at attacking infantry, but my shells were running out. Each SU-152 had only ten to twelve rounds left. The German infantry reached our positions, but thank God, they had no grenades or anti-tank mines. We had to defend our positions with submachine-gun fire and grenades. Somehow, we managed to drive them back.

We even took prisoners – we rounded them up and placed them in a barn. They were standing and trembling – they thought we were going to shoot them now. However, we didn't have the desire to shoot them ...

At some moment, from my vehicle I saw several German tanks that had turned off the road into a ravine, trying to turn our left flank. My radio wasn't working, and I decided to go in person to deliver orders to my self-propelled guns on the left flank to shift further to the left in order to block the exit from the ravine. I leaped out of my vehicle, next to which was standing our motor mechanic Sergeant Major Aleksei Semin. Actually, he was the brother of my machine's driver-mechanic, Technician-Lieutenant Nikolai Konstantinovich Semin. We walked away from the SU-152 about 20 metres. My vehicle fired. The round flew short or overshot its target. I thought it would now fire a second time. Instead of a shot, the vehicle exploded. Aleksei appealed to me, 'Battery commander, keep silent! Don't report anything to my home. My mother would die from grief.' Recently his pilot brother had been killed, and now another brother had burned to death in front of his eyes ...

What had happened? The loader had evidently been careless and bumped the detonator of the shell he was loading against the breech. However, that isn't even the real cause. If the detonating fuse had been functioning properly, then it wouldn't have ignited. It turned out that in one lot of fuses, the inertial safety device had already been triggered and was no longer effective.

For this battle I was again nominated for the title Hero of the Soviet Union. For three days we held the highway leading into Elbing from Konigsberg. But instead I received a 'Red Banner'. Why? A short time later the Germans broke through to the encircled forces in Konigsberg 30 kilometres to the right of our position. The army commander seemingly said, 'What kind of heroes are you?' But what did that failure have to do with me? I'd been assigned a 3-kilometre sector, and I had held it for three days, allowing no German to pass. The recommendation was made a month later, after the Germans had broken the encirclement. If it had been put in right away, they probably would have given it to me.

After this battle I was appointed as the regiment's deputy chief of staff to replace Shipov, who'd been killed. A month later, I was promoted to regiment deputy commander.

The nickname for the JSU-152 self-propelled guns was 'Beast killer'. We didn't call them 'Heifers'. The JSU-152 had a separate load of ammunition. The shell weighed 48 kilograms and the casing weighed 16–20 kilograms – more brass and less cardboard. For the loader, this demanded unbelievably hard work. We sought to pick guys of a corresponding build – no taller than 160 centimetres, so they wouldn't bump their heads on the roof of the fighting compartment, but with arms and legs like a weightlifter.

I always had five men. A gunner, a loader, a radio man, the commander, and the driver-mechanic. I'll say it was a true brotherhood. The crew was one family. Of course, a lot depended on the commander and on the character of the crew members, but in the majority of cases, the absolute majority, the crew acted as one. It never happened that one or two would be doing something, while the others sat around watching and smoking. Everyone worked together. Let's say the vehicle was gassed up, but ammunition had to be loaded. Everyone would go to fetch and load the ammunition. Or, let us say, the vehicle still had to be fuelled. Then one would ready the hose, while another would open the drums. Work was allocated in a way so that it would be carried out with maximum speed.

Of course, there was a superior-subordinate relationship. I would give the orders, which was my job, but I would never tell the gun commander, 'Comrade Sergeant, I'm giving an order!' I never once even uttered the words, 'I order ...' Instead I requested. Or I wouldn't be saying, 'Well then, button up!' or something else, if combat was imminent. That's hogwash!

In the self-propelled gun there are two officers – the commander and the driver-mechanic. These were the two primary members of the crew. Of course, there was a hierarchy. But also, we passed through battles together; we'd sit together, eat together out of the same pot, and share the 100 grams of vodka [a normal combat ration in the Red Army to boost morale]. If there was free time, the soldiers and sergeants had their own yarns to spin, while the officers had their own tasks, their own professional matters to which to tend, and their own circle of responsibilities. However, as soon as a common task appeared, this hierarchy immediately vanished. The vehicle commander could always take over the driver-mechanic's role.

We had heavy casualties – how could it have been otherwise?! Over six months, almost all of the self-propelled gun commanders had to be replaced.

It is hard to distinguish between the SU-152 and the JSU-152. Even today I won't tell you that there was a difference in anything but their designation. The main gun was 152-mm, the shell weighed 48 kilograms, but I could care less about whether it had seven rollers or only six, or carried twenty or twenty-two shells inside it. The vehicles were green. They did have code symbols on them that belonged to the regiment. The letter 'K' or painted squares. In winter our vehicles were never repainted white.

Unfortunately, the JSU-152 had no machine guns. Although they later mounted a DShK machine gun on it, my battery never received any of these. This circumstance forced us to procure a captured machine gun on the sly, and we almost always had one with a supply of ammunition for it. It was usually lying in a case carried on the armour outside the fighting compartment. In general, in addition to the machine gun we always had four or five cases of shells there as well. Behind the fighting compartment on the outside of the vehicle there was a fuel drum. The vehicle moved toward the battlefield always with this camel's hump mounted on top of it. In our jumping-off positions, we would transfer the fuel from the external drum to the internal tanks and toss the empty tanks aside. Sometimes we discarded the auxiliary tanks, but we never got rid of the shells – they were always atop the vehicle. The vehicle always carried one and a half standard ammunition loads. Twenty shells were plainly too little. During a pause in the fighting, we might take the next shell not from the internal store, but from the external cases.

For those times the radio communications were good. The radio sets kept pace with the times. Sometimes, we even bandied words with the Germans. Although it was precisely the loss of radio communications, as I've already mentioned, that saved my life.

We used armour-piercing shells against tanks – they were more reliable. The T-3 or T-4 – they broke up when striking armour, but the slug would punch through heavy tanks. If in doing so it detonated the on-board ammunition, it would rip off the turret. The distribution of the bunker-busting, armour-piercing and high-explosive shells in the ammunition load differed. Whatever they had at the dump, they'd distribute it in that proportion. It was fine to fire a solid shot at tanks, but if you had to collapse a building, here you couldn't get by without a high-explosive shell.

Self-propelled guns suffered malfunctions, just as with any mechanism. The running gear would break down or the track idlers would fly off. The motor might conk out. If you maintained and serviced it well, it would run just fine. The crew took care of minor repairs themselves. Sometimes we required the assistance of a field repair shop for jobs we couldn't handle ourselves, but we never had to turn in our vehicles for major repairs.

The entire crew took part in maintenance and repairs, including the commander, without exception. There were some commanders that didn't want to get their hands dirty. Here we're talking about officers who had uniforms with white linings and high-necked tunics made of imported fabric ... Such officers didn't last long. Who needs a guy like that? Such guys were replaced or learned to change their ways.

I had to escape a burning vehicle a couple of times. Once out of sheer stupidity – oil-soaked rags ignited inside. We had to bail out. The guys quickly covered the flames with canvas and smothered the fire. But one time, it was in combat. A shell penetrated the armour and the gunpowder caught fire. But it burns slowly and it was a simple matter to bail out. However, it happened repeatedly that a shell penetrated without igniting a fire. It happened in Lithuania once that a large-calibre shell struck the self-propelled gun, when we were inside. There was a shower of sparks, like from a welder. I still don't know what it was, but it gave the impression that a conflagration had started. True, this passed very quickly.

Primarily the self-propelled guns were used to support the tanks. We usually moved a bit behind them. We never had independent assignments, but helped the main combat units – tank and rifle units – carry out their tasks. Since our regiment served in a tank army, it was broken up and each battery was assigned to a tank brigade.

In each column there was always a variety of vehicles, which are driven by drivers with the most diverse levels of training and abilities. God willing, the brigade column moved at a speed of 20 kilometres per hour. On the whole, we were no hindrance or burden for the T–34s.

It was important for me to know how many enemy I had in front of me, or whether they had tanks and artillery, but as to which formation they belonged, that wasn't important to me. Let those who work out the operational plans think about this.

I can't speak for everyone, but among my guys there was no rancour against the Germans when we entered German territory. There was a well-defined hatred toward their soldiers. But toward the civilian population? I wouldn't say that somewhere something came out in us with respect to them. I didn't witness this. We were in combat, and we had no time to engage in mistreatment of the civilians, and we almost never saw them. Coming out of combat, we had no contact with the population. We'll say that in the very first East Prussian town of Neidenburg that we entered, the guys did scatter to check all the homes, but the population had already departed or was in hiding. But no one searched for them in order to take revenge against them, even though some of the men had lost family members.

I can pass judgement on the old ladies and mothers. After the war, German prisoners were constructing a road next to my home, and they would often ask my mother: 'Mother, can you share some bread or water?' Then Mum would bring out both bread and water. We're a charitable and kind people.

We didn't take trophies back to our vehicle or to place on the baggage train. If you got killed, they'd say about you: 'He was a packrat.' In the area of Marau Station, a motorcycle with a sidecar drove up to meet me. It stopped, a German hopped off the motorcycle and he handed me a pouch. Evidently, he thought that our column was German. We took him prisoner, and in the motorcycle sidecar we found chocolate and some bottles. We, of course, analyzed them. Later, near Elbing, we knocked out several vehicles. We searched them and found chocolate and whisky, which we also took. So our trophies were all like this – anything we came across while on the move. We took Marienburg, and I said to the soldiers, 'Take off, go and see what you can find.' One brought back a long case, like for a rifle; inside it, tinted crystal stemware was nestled against velvet. I asked him, 'Why did you come back with this?'

'It's for you.'

'I don't have anywhere to put my pistol, and you bring back stemware. Take it away.'

I don't know what he did with them, but the beauty of those crystal glasses have stayed in my memory.

I don't know how many tanks I knocked out in total. How to count them? I myself didn't fire the gun. I gave the orders. But my self-propelled gun knocked out probably two or three dozen tanks, and well, the battery, of course, even more.

Notes

1. This colony was founded in 1763 by ethnic Germans from the Volga region, who had come to the St Petersburg suburbs. There they also built St Catherine's Church with the help of a large donation from Catherine the Great. Today, the church and its grounds are a Lutheran theological seminary.
2. Designed as an assault gun, the SU-152 with its massive gun was capable of knocking out the heavily armoured German Tiger and Panther tanks, so it often acted as a heavy tank destroyer and received the nickname 'Beast-Killer'.

Chapter 9

Ordered to Knock-out a Ferdinand
Aleksei Prokhorovich Voloshin

I was born in 1920. My parents were living in Tambovsk Oblast. In 1921, as the Russian Civil War raged, my parents fled to relatives of my mother near Kanev. I graduated from the 10th grade in 1938 and applied to the Sevastopol Naval Specialist School. I passed all the entrance exams, but at the medical board they detected a heart murmur and rejected me. That same year I enrolled in the Odessa Institute of Water Transport.

The war caught me in Bessarabia. At first the talk was that we had to go to sign up, or else the war would end without us. This didn't last for long. We returned to Odessa and headed voluntarily to the military enlistment centre. As students of a technical higher education institute, we were assigned to train at the Odessa Artillery Specialist School, which prepared artillerymen for the super-heavy artillery. Then there was an evacuation. At first we went on foot to Nikolaev, and then by railroad to Kamyshlov. My training continued until February 1942. I acquired the rank of lieutenant and soon found myself as the commander of a platoon in the 54th Heavy Artillery Howitzer Regiment of the Supreme Command Reserve. I was commanding a battery's only howitzer, for which there was not a single shell.

In March 1942 I was wounded in an artillery barrage, but already in April, after recovering, I became the commander of the operations platoon of a battery of the 62nd Army's 1104th Artillery Regiment, which was equipped with 152-mm howitzers. Soon I became the battery commander. On the Myshkova River I destroyed my first tank. Having noticed a German troop concentration, I requested four shells from the regiment commander. I prepared the firing data and with these shells I blanketed the enemy. One of the shells landed squarely on a German tank, which burst into flames. The regiment commander had a drink together with the army commander in a dug-out to celebrate the regiment's first destroyed enemy tank, but they didn't even summon me. I thought that I would get the 'For Courage' medal, just like the battalion commander was wearing, but they awarded me the Order of the Red Star. I wasn't pleased.

We crossed the Don in retreat. A small ferry carried the guns across the river, but we had to swim. The chief of staff, who had served back in the First World War, said, 'Take apart a fence, place your stuff – your trousers, combat blouse, pistol and belt – on a board, and swim. Don't rush to save someone drowning, because he'll take you down to the bottom together with him.' We agreed that someone would help me if I was lightly wounded, but if I was badly wounded they'd keep swimming and leave me to drown.

Soon after we crossed the Don, I was transferred to the 10th NKVD Division's 271st Rifle Regiment to take command of a battery of 76-mm infantry support guns … I can say with complete confidence that my most terrible memories of the war are from the fighting withdrawal to Stalingrad and the defence of the city. The Germans had an overwhelming superiority. Their airplanes were constantly overhead. Our air force never made an appearance, while our entire anti-aircraft artillery was wiped out at point-blank range in ground combat. Thus, you had to find any sort of little hole or depression and you'd try to burrow your way even more deeply into the ground with your chest. Even so, I was wounded in the middle of September, and didn't take part in the brutal, inhumanly savage street fighting, in which nearly our entire division perished. True, though, over the time I was with the division, I once participated in a bayonet charge … there were only sixteen men left in the battery, and only eight came back alive from the attack.

I was wounded in the leg just above the knee. They brought me out of Stalingrad across the Volga aboard a ferry. I heard later that when the division was withdrawn to the east bank of the Volga, only 191 men remained of the 10,000 that had entered the battle.

They brought me to Tomsk. There I spent three months recovering from my wound. I very badly wanted to return to the front, because I was bored and hungry. Each week they showed two films for the patients: *Chapaev* and *Svetlyi put'* [*Shining path*, but also known as *Tanya* – a socialist Cinderella story about the rewards of hard work and loyalty to the state]. I received my discharge from the hospital in January 1943. On that same day, the hospital director had received a telegram from Lieutenant Colonel Tsygankov, the artillery chief of the 10th NKVD Division, or as it was now designated, the 181st 'Stalingrad' Rifle Division, with a request to return me to the division after I healed.

With difficulty I made my way to Cheliabinsk, where the division was in the process of reforming. Soon we were loaded onto troop trains and at the end of February we disembarked in the vicinity of Elets. From there we conducted a ten-day rapid march to a point near Sevsk, where the Germans had encircled a cavalry corps. The regimental battery that I was commanding was being towed by horses, but we had only two horses per gun instead of the requisite four. At times the crews had to help haul the guns through the snow. It was hard. Snowdrifts blocked the roads. The local population was mobilized to clear the roads. Once we met Colonel General Rokossovsky. He was driving by and stopped. He shouted, 'Who's the commander?' I went running up to him and reported, 'Lieutenant Voloshin, commander of a regimental battery of the 271st Rifle Division.'

'What's this? Why are you moving so slowly?'

'We don't have horses, and there are snowdrifts.'

He drove off. The next day an order arrived: 'Get horses from the state farms. Give them a receipt, stating that their horses will be returned.'

I remember going up to one collective farm chairman. He told me, 'We only have three horses.'

'We're taking them.'

He pointed at one: 'This one's lame.'

I ordered a soldier to lead the horse around. It in fact was lame. I told the chairman, 'We'll take two horses. Here's your receipt.' He had tears in his eyes. What was that slip of paper worth to him? He had to plough the fields within a month. That's how we scraped together horse teams for the battery.

We approached Sevsk. Along the road we began to encounter dead horses on the left and right of it, all upside down – they'd frozen. We began to take the saddles from them. Our boots were now badly worn and in lousy shape. So we removed the saddles in order to make boots from the leather. That's what we did.

The regiment took up defensive positions to the right of Sevsk. While on the defence, once the battery had to make a combat probe to obtain intelligence. In general, both we and the Germans fought poorly there. We were louse-ridden. In the rifle companies, half the men came down with typhus. I had eighty men in my battery, and half of them became sick. The spring was a cold one. The soldiers packed the available houses to the point where they were almost sleeping in several layers. At the end of March 1943, I also became sick. I spent the entire month of April bedridden in the medical-sanitary battalion. My hair fell out. But nevertheless by the end of April I was on my feet again and began to walk around. I remember I wanted to jump over some fallen branch in my path, but my foot caught it and I fell – my legs were so weak. I was hungry all the time. There was meat, because there were a lot of dead cows and calves, but there wasn't any salt, and beef without salt isn't tasty. So at one point, I and another battery commander went to see the battalion commander. He treated us to some tasty meat.

'Nikolai, where did you get the salt?'

'This is horseflesh.'

The other battery commander ran outside and threw up. After all, before the war, horsemeat was considered inedible.

I remember once the battery commissar left to get some additional training. So I wrote him a letter asking him to send me some salt. He managed to obtain some and sent these large granules of very coarsely ground salt. I remember you'd take one of these granules into your mouth and you walked around sucking on it. It was such a delicacy!

In general, our living conditions at the front were satisfactory. Or one could say they were mediocre, though the command thought things were fine. But back in 1942, we had to forage to stay alive. We begged for food from the local population wherever it was possible.

In May 1943 we were pulled out of the front lines, and in June we were withdrawn into the rear of the 13th Army. The German Kursk offensive never reached us – they were used up, and already on 15 July we went on the offensive. My battery was supporting a rifle battalion. It advanced somewhere about 3 kilometres and got tied up in combat. I decided to catch up with them. We crossed a small brook that flowed in the bottom of a ravine, and climbing a hill on the opposite side, we spotted two German tanks advancing in our direction. We quickly deployed the guns, camouflaged them, and when the tanks had approached to within about 200 metres, we set them ablaze. I decided that the job had been done and that we could move on up ahead. We limbered the guns and climbed to the top of the hill, where we fell into an ambush. The German tank with its first round smashed the No. 1 gun. I only watched as the arms and legs of the gun crew went flying in different directions. A shell struck the No. 2 gun's carriage limber. I started to run over to the No. 3 gun in order to stop it. I was shouting, 'Stop!' My orderly stuck out his leg and tripped me. I fell. Dropping down beside me, he said, 'That's all, Comrade Lieutenant; you won't make it in time.' In fact, the German tank also destroyed the No. 3 gun. The No. 4 gun was still below the crest and remained undamaged. We laid there for a little bit, and then hauled away the No. 2 gun.

After thinking over the situation for a while, we decided to knock out this tank. One platoon commander had been killed, but I ordered the remaining one to take the two guns and bypass the tank. It was beginning to get dark. In the twilight we managed to slip past the tank and deployed the guns approximately 100 metres away from its shelter behind a mound. After a few minutes, it started up its engine and started to back up toward us. We fired a volley and it burst into flames. The Germans tried to clamber out, but we shot them down. We then limbered up our guns and moved on a short way before stopping for the night. We set up a hasty defensive position.

In the morning, the regiment's artillery chief came driving up.

'Where are the knocked out tanks?'

'Over there.'

'Good man! How many guns did you lose?'

'Three. One is only lightly damaged.'

'You'll go before a tribunal!'

'A tank was in ambush. We knocked it out.'

'Then why did you fall out here? Your job is to support the infantry!'

At that point the division commander Major General Aleksandr Andreevich Saraev came driving up: 'Who knocked out those tanks? Where is this fine fellow? Come here, son.' He kissed me on both cheeks and told his chief of staff, 'Put this man up for the Order of Lenin.' My immediate superior had been threatening to send me before a tribunal, and this commander was recommending me for an Order! In fact, they replaced the Order of Lenin with the Order of the Red Banner.

Soon we advanced to the southern outskirts of Chernigov, having forced a crossing of the Desna River. There was a large German garrison in the city, supported by tanks. Scouts reported that they had counted approximately 100 armoured vehicles. It was decided to organize an assault battalion of Slavs in each regiment. (In the vicinity of Slutsk the division had received a large batch of replacements from Central Asia. These soldiers fought poorly – if one got wounded, twenty of them would bring him off the battlefield.) These assault battalions were reinforced with all of the division's artillery and combat engineers.

On the evening of 19 September we formed them up, and at 0100 we attacked. We had made an agreement with the infantry that we would tow the guns with the horses up to the nearest buildings, and then unhitch the teams and lead them away, while soldiers would take over and help the crews manhandle the guns further. In general, the infantry loved it when the artillery was nearby. If a gun is beside them, they aren't so afraid and will hold their positions. In this night battle my battery knocked out five tanks. We liberated the city by 0600. We rested, reorganized and moved on toward the Dnepr. By now I had become the regiment's artillery chief.

We forced a crossing of the Dnepr River at the village of Gliadky, advanced another 4 kilometres, and seized the large village of Kolyban'. We deployed the guns so that several guns could fire at the same tank from multiple directions. Just beyond the village ran a railroad embankment. The sappers mined it.

On the morning of 28 September, the Germans counterattacked. I ran over to the 1st Platoon of my former battery; it wasn't where it should have been. It had pulled out and the infantry had followed them. The platoon commander had recently arrived from a cavalry regiment. That's the sort of fighter he was. I chased him down: 'Why are you fleeing?'

'The position is better here. If the tanks come, I'll knock them out.'

'Go back! I'll shoot you!'

We hitched infantry to the guns and hauled them back toward their previous positions about 500 metres. At this moment tanks appeared. We allowed them to come a little bit closer and then opened fire. We knocked out three Pz-IVs. Two panzers attempted to cross the railroad embankment and hit mines that immobilized them, and we finished them off.

The German attack shifted a bit to our left and hit the neighbouring 292nd Regiment. I was ordered to send a battery of 76-mm guns to their assistance. The Germans managed to penetrate the 292nd Regiment's lines and overran the command post. We deployed the guns and opened fire. I directed the fighting, running from gun to gun. I was running through a ravine with a sergeant, the battery's Party organizer. There was a haystack in the ravine. We ran around it and nearly bumped right into two Germans with rifles. In my shock, I pointed my submachine gun at them and then froze for a moment, before instincts took over and I gave them a burst – they fell, but I continued to fire at them.

In this action the battery knocked out another six German tanks. Altogether over the day, we destroyed eleven tanks. For this I was nominated for the title Hero of the Soviet Union.

I remember, we drove to a Komsomol conference. I gave a speech, and then one battery commander spoke up and said, 'You think that he knocked out eleven tanks, but he was just in the right place at the right time. The tanks came at him. If they had attacked my sector, I also would have knocked them out. This isn't his achievement; it belongs to the Germans who launched the attack.'

In the summer of 1944, I knocked out a Ferdinand[1] north of Lutsk in the vicinity of the village of Rozhishche. We were holding a defensive position, and it was camouflaged on a hill about 2 kilometres away. It knocked out several of our machine-gun nests and a 45-mm anti-tank gun. Suddenly the regiment commander is summoning me and he tells me that the division commander had decided to introduce an attached battalion of Valentine tanks into our sector, while I was to secure its entry with my artillery. The tank battalion commander, a captain, came up to me. I cautioned him, 'Be careful, there's a Ferdinand out there.'

'What's that to me? I'll get it. I have fifteen tanks.'

'Oh, yeah?! A Ferdinand can destroy any tank at a range of 2 kilometres.'

'So what, I'll outflank him there on the left.'

He promptly formed his tanks into a column and moved out. He had gone approximately a kilometre when the Germans opened fire. It allowed the first two tanks to pass into an area of low ground and started with the third Valentine. At that point, it was simply 'Boom' – and a tank would go up in flames, 'Boom' – and there would go another one. It walked its fire down the column and destroyed thirteen tanks! The division commander roundly cursed the regiment commander: 'Where is your destroyer of tanks? He's lost thirteen tanks and a gun! If he doesn't destroy this Ferdinand, I'll strip him of his Star.' Even though at that time I still didn't have a Star.

So that evening I set out with one gun platoon to go around this hill, before deploying the guns about 300 metres from the self-propelled gun's presumed position. When it became light, we opened fire at its tracks and undercarriage. We fired five or six rounds. It attempted to move, but lost its tracks. Now immobilized, combat engineers crept up to it, set an anti-tank mine beneath it, and blew it up. They said that later, someone wrote '181st Division' on it and sent it to Kiev to be put on display.

In June 1944, I received a grazing wound to the belly. At first I lay in Kiev, before the doctors decided to send me to Moscow. Directly at the train station, I began bleeding from the wound in my stomach and I wound up in a hospital. There they found me and invited me to the Kremlin to receive the Star of Hero of the Soviet Union. After the ceremony I was received by the Chief Marshal of Artillery Nikolai Nikolaevich Voronov. The Marshal proposed to enroll me in the Artillery Academy. I didn't even begin to refuse. That autumn in the Kremlin, the American president's close adviser Harry Hopkins, the US Ambassador in Moscow W. Averell Harriman and a military attaché presented me with a Silver Star, which had been bestowed upon me by a decree of President Franklin D. Roosevelt.

Note

1. Translator's note: from the details in his story, this does appear to be a German Panzerjäger Tiger (P) Elefant heavy tank destroyer, so I have not placed the title Ferdinand (the heavy tank destroyer's original name) in quotation marks.

Chapter 10

'Our Fate was not Envied at the Front ...'

Mikhail Aleksandrovich Chernomordik

I was born on 31 December 1922 in Smolensk. In June 1941 I had finished my tenth year of schooling and was waiting to be called to Leningrad to take the entrance exams for the Frunze Higher Naval School. The romance of the sea, the handsome uniform, the cutlass and the young ladies' admiring eyes taking in this resplendence ... you yourself can understand. Before the war simply frenzied agitation had been unleashed among the older classes, exhorting the young men to enter military schools. Indeed, my generation, which had grown up on the hoorah-patriotic slogans and was loyal to its citizens' duties, gladly enrolled in military schools. But the war disrupted the donning of the sailor's striped vest. On 22 June I went to the military enlistment centre and requested the papers I needed for my enrollment in the Frunze Higher Naval School, but instead they proposed, or more accurately ordered, that our group, which numbered thirty men, enroll in the Smolensk Artillery Specialist School. It trained officers for the howitzer artillery.

Already within two weeks, the Germans were approaching Smolensk, so the school was urgently evacuated to the city of Irbit in the Urals. The 700 cadets went with the school, but in Irbit we were informed that our period of training had been reduced to 6 months (before the war, cadets studied and trained for almost 3 years in the specialist school). We were busy in the school for 14–16 hours a day, and over the six months of training, they made 'men' of us. Only the gunners had the opportunity to do field firing exercises with live ammunition, but overall the training, including the basic training, was on a high level. I even fired a Maksim machine gun at the target range three times, and once the Degtiarev light machine gun.

Already on 4 January 1942, I graduated from the school with the rank of junior lieutenant, and with a group of other 'freshly baked' artillery commanders I was sent to the Altai, to the city of Biisk, where the 232nd Rifle Division was forming up. We were split up among the artillery units. I and three other junior lieutenants wound up in the Separate 214th Anti-tank Artillery Battalion. Thus, it didn't happen that I served with the howitzer artillery.

The battalion consisted of three batteries equipped with 45-mm anti-tank guns. Senior Lieutenant Vostrikov commanded the battery, and Motenko and Shamshiev were the political leaders. I was appointed to the post of deputy battery commander, but the platoons were commanded by lieutenants, guys who outranked me, who were graduates of the Rostov Artillery School, which prepared commanders for the anti-tank artillery units that were equipped with the well-known 'Farewell, Motherland' [a common nickname for the 45-mm anti-tank guns].

As you can imagine, it was January, with frigid temperatures, and we lived in the woods in tents. They fed us according to the extremely miserly rear area norm and we had no short sheepskin coats or felt boots, so our primary concern was not to freeze to death. They began combat training only at the end of April, and we focused on the interchangeability of assignments in the gun crews, so that each member could do the other members' jobs as well as his own. The men that arrived for the division's forming-up were primarily Altai peasants and former prisoners from Krasnoiarsk District, who had been released early and designated for the front. The atmosphere in the division's units matched this contingent of personnel. I don't even want to talk about it.

There was a shortage of commanders in the division, particularly in the rifle regiments. The division was commanded by Major (!) Ulitin, who by the end of the war became a general. Vostrikov was selected for the post of division chief of staff, so I had to assume command of the battery.

In June 1942 we were loaded onto trains and sent to the city of Voronezh. My friend, Il'ia Eidinov, who was killed later, in 1943, told me before our departure to the front, 'I know that you will survive.' For some reason, he was certain of this.

Our first battle went well for us; we didn't have any casualties. About 300 metres from us, two tanks emerged from some woods in the wake of yet another column of retreating Red Army troops. A red banner was limply hanging above one of them. Suddenly a gust of wind unfurled the flag, and we saw a white circle with a black swastika on it. Everyone was momentarily startled by the sight ... The fire of the battalion's guns chased the German tanks back into the woods.

For the next half-year we held a line along the banks of the Don River, approximately 20 kilometres from the northern outskirts of Voronezh. All this time, the battalion was positioned immediately behind the infantry's trenches. There was a catastrophic shortage of shells. As the battery commander, I didn't have the right to open fire without first receiving the approval of the battalion commander! Our infantry was constantly being used up in attempts to seize a bridgehead on the opposite bank of the Don. The river in this place was not very wide.

I recall the fighting for the village of Khvoshchevatka in August 1942. There was a terrible incident that took place here – two of our rifle battalions broke into this village, but approximately one and a half dozen German tanks encircled them, and the majority of them were taken prisoner. The Germans led the prisoners out of the village with an escort of their tanks, which surrounded the column on all four sides. We received an order to open fire at the receding column, even though it was plainly clear these men were our comrades being led into captivity, not German infantry. I fired a volley to one side of the column. The battery's political leader kept silent. But the neighbouring battery fired a salvo that was squarely on target …

My battery knocked out its first tank a month later, in fighting for the bridgehead next to the village of Novopodkletnoe. It was a medium tank and the '45s' could cope with tanks of this type. Although it is said about the crews that served the 45-mm anti-tank gun that they were doomed men, it was still possible to fight with these guns, though usually not for long – until you were killed. Our fate was not envied at the front, so no one came to us voluntarily.

The 45-mm gun was low, light, and almost toy-like; it was mobile and manoeuvrable. It could easily be pivoted in any direction and could be rolled forward by manpower alone, advancing from place to place behind the attacking infantry. We had these 'toy cannons', which were being produced even before the war. But precisely because of their construction, they were extremely vulnerable. The short and narrow shield offered little protection to the crew from enemy fire. It was extremely awkward to fire the '45s' – when firing, the artillerymen had to be either on their knees, or hunched over almost double. Until 1943 we could fight relatively successfully against tanks, but any bobble by the crew – someone was killed or wounded, or the gunner muffed a shot and the shell missed – as a rule threatened the artillerymen with death. Without exaggeration … tanks would succeed in overrunning the gun's position, and with their tracks they would grind both the crew and the gun into the dust. It really was the case, 'Farewell, Motherland'. Even when positioned in a static sector of the front, the battalion constantly suffered substantial losses, though during this period there were not a lot of German tanks in the area of Voronezh.

In January 1943 we went on the offensive. I recall fighting for the village of Kochetovka for several days. There our 605th and 712th Rifle Regiments lost almost their entire personnel in frontal attacks. Afterward, with uninterrupted fighting, we reached the borders of Kursk Oblast. At the end of February 1943, I was reassigned to a destroyer anti-tank artillery regiment.

Experienced artillerymen were chosen for the destroyer anti-tank artillery regiments, who had performed well in preceding battles; in addition, only Communists and Komsomol members were selected. However, for example, the regiment in which I was fighting at the end of the war was formed from new conscripts, primarily those born in 1925, who didn't know the smell of gunpowder. I'm not aware of any other selection criteria. No one looked at the personnel questionnaires or ferreted out people among the kinfolk who'd been repressed or dispossessed. I wound up in the anti-tank artillery after a rather unique affair which will seem unjust to you, but which was part of my lot at the front.

In February 1943, my battery got stuck in a village in the Kursk area because two of our vehicles had broken down. Prior to this, I hadn't slept for two days. I collapsed in sleep on the floor of the nearest hut, when suddenly my platoon commander Malyshev woke me and said, 'They've caught a Nazi police goon. What should we do with him? Shoot him or turn him over to headquarters? The local residents want to execute him.'

The only thing I managed to say in my grogginess was, 'Lieutenant, go to hell; do whatever you want, just let me sleep.'

A couple of minutes later there was a burst of gunfire out in the yard. I went outside, and on the snow were the dead Nazi collaborator and a crowd of villagers, intermingled with my soldiers. The peasants were shouting, 'A dog's death for a dog!', and saying what vermin the dead German hireling had been.

A week passed, when suddenly an authorized agent of the Special Department called me in for an interrogation and began to question me about the circumstances of the event that had taken place in the village. I told him what had happened, and the Special Department agent, smiling affably, shook my hand and wished me combat success.

But a couple of weeks later, I was summoned to division headquarters. I took a horse from a rifle battalion commander and rode to the headquarters, which was located in a rural school building. A captain walked up to me – a lawyer, and peremptorily ordered, 'Follow me!' He led me into a classroom, and sitting there was a session of a divisional tribunal! Three rear-area loafers were sitting there, and without listening to my explanations, they accused me of taking justice over a civilian into my own hands, asked me again the same questions from the Special Department agent's report, and about 10 minutes later announced that the tribunal was retiring for deliberations. They returned and the chairman pronounced the sentence: 'Eight years imprisonment.' I exploded, 'For what?!' But he continued to read from the paper in a monotone voice: 'If courage and heroism are shown in fighting for the socialist Motherland, the sentence can be reviewed and lightened at the recommendation of the command.'

That was it! There were no words about the commutation of my term in the penal battalion, or how the implementation of the sentence was postponed until after the war. There was nothing more! They turned around and walked out of the room. I sat there for two more hours, waiting for when the guards would arrive – they would tear off my shoulder boards and take away my belt and pistol. But no one came. I didn't know what to do. I stepped outside, mounted the horse and quietly returned to my battery with no interference from anyone. I was seething inside, thinking 'Chekist swine! If only you were all sent to the front, you *osobist* [the Russian nickname for the Special [*osobyi*] Department officers] assholes!

The battalion commander arrived; I told him what had happened, and he said in reply, 'Fight and don't think about this hogwash. We'll try to look into it.' If someone else had been in my position, likely, he would have likely gone AWOL or would have gone over to the Germans ... but I was a Jew, a Communist, and a patriot, and the word 'Motherland' for me was not empty of meaning. Such a choice didn't appeal to me.

Two weeks later, an order came down over the telephone – I was to turn over command of the battery and to appear at division headquarters. Now I was utterly confident that there was one path in front of me – to Siberia, to a prison camp. The battery's sergeant major packed a rucksack full of food for me. I said my goodbyes to my combat comrades, passed out all my prized possessions to my friends, and headed on foot to headquarters. There I found four other artillery commanders, and we were all offered the choice to serve in the Supreme High Command's destroyer anti-tank units. There were no rejections. I don't know what happened further with my 'criminal' case. When I was demobilized, there were no tribunal documents in my personal file. But I wasn't particularly afraid to wind up in a penal battalion; after all, I'd spent my entire war to this point in units where the slogan was, 'The barrel is long, but the life is short.' What difference did it make where I was killed? But let's return to my story.

I wound up in the Separate 1660th Destroyer Anti-tank Artillery Regiment, which was under the command of a splendid man and courageous officer, Lieutenant Colonel Ivan Vasil'evich Cherniak. The regiment consisted of five batteries. These regiments didn't have subordinate battalions, but there were destroyer anti-tank regiments that had six batteries, and among them there might be one battery of 45-mm guns, one howitzer battery, and one equipped with ZIS-2 57-mm guns. Our regiment was armed only with the ZIS-3, which had the long nickname of 'Seventy-six millimetres' in the army.

There were four guns in each battery, all towed by Studebakers. The four guns were divided between two fire platoons with two guns each. Each crew had seven members. The operations platoon consisted of a scout squad (a commander and six scouts), a signals squad (a commander, two radio operators and five signalmen-wiremen) and a logistical support and ammunition supply squad (the sergeant major, his artillery mechanic, and drivers); we didn't have ammunition supply platoons. Altogether, the battery had around sixty men. Each battery was supposed to have six vehicles. All of the artillerymen were armed with carbines; only the scouts carried PPSh submachine guns. Each battery was supposed to have two light machine guns for defence against German infantry, but through the entire war I also had a Maksim heavy machine gun with a large supply of ammunition belts, which more than once bailed us out of difficult situations.

But there were a lot of differences between the destroyer anti-tank artillery regiments and regular artillery regiments. For example, we went around with the emblem of the tank destroyers sewn to our sleeves – two crossed gun barrels on a black background. In the 1186th Destroyer Anti-tank Artillery Regiment, its officers wore this emblem on their astrakhan fur caps. The same emblem was stencilled onto the cabs of the trucks. Yet the battery didn't have its own field kitchen, although the men of the destroyer anti-tank units received increased rations. In some of the batteries they would drag around an anti-tank rifle, but this was more for reassurance as a 'last chance'. I had a nest egg of two cases of anti-tank grenades, so that 'If you're going to die, at least do so with music.'

The artillery regiments of the Supreme Command Reserve had no rifle companies; these existed only in the anti-tank artillery brigades. All the soldiers and officers received double the regular wage, and for each year of service in a destroyer anti-tank artillery regiment, we were credited with one-and-a-half years of service. We were supposed to receive monetary bonuses for destroy-ing a German armoured vehicle, but we transferred all of our bonuses to the Defence Fund.

In distinction from the regular artillery batteries, we had two radios, because very often, you know, the regiment operated in separate batteries on different sectors in order to cover tank-vulnerable directions, and communications with the headquarters could only be maintained by radio. Combat training was arranged so that in each crew there were at least three men capable of replacing the gun layer in case of necessity; after all, we did take grievous losses ...

There was one more important detail: A battery commander in the destroyer anti-tank artillery could at his own discretion expend shells from the 'untouch-able' reserve (twelve shells per gun barrel) without seeking the permission of the regiment commander. Our standard ammunition load was at least double that of the regular artillery. We had 140 shells per gun, while the load in the regular artillery units was always much smaller. We usually had thirty to forty high-explosive shells, two boxes of canister shells, but most of our load consisted of armour-piercing and armour-piercing discarding sabot. I can still think of a number of other distinctive features unique to the destroyer anti-tank artillery regiments.

The regiment had its first fight in May 1943, but we were being used only to provide fire support to the infantry. During the Battle of Kursk, the regiment was in the second line of defence not far from Prokhorovka, and the Germans were stopped only 3 kilometres short of our positions. We had already prepared ourselves to die heroically. At the end of July 1943, our regiment took part in a hard fight with German tanks. My battery knocked out three of them, but German dive bombers simply pounded our positions into the ground with bombs and we were left without guns. In addition, just a handful of the soldiers survived.

However, my most terrible memory of 1943 is the crossing of the Dnepr River. We crossed at night by battery together with the infantry. The Germans spotted the start of our forced crossing, and with their illumination flares they turned the night into day. The surface of the river was literally boiling from the falling artillery shells and mortar rounds. Such a hurricane of fire was opened from the high, right bank of the Dnepr that no one was lucky enough to cross the river that night. Only around ten smashed boats and ferries with dead oarsmen made it to the opposite bank. How many people were killed or drowned there! The Dnepr's current indifferently swept everyone and everything downstream – the living, the dead, fragments of boats, empty fuel drums and logs. The inhuman screams of drowning soldiers rose above the river.

Although I had wanted to become a sailor, I was a very poor swimmer, so before the crossing I knew full well that this was going to be the last day of my life. To enter this hell with the hope of surviving was a stupid illusion.

We had cut logs and made the rafts ahead of time, but when we were rolling the guns down the plank ramps onto the rafts, the Germans gave us a salvo right on the riverbank from their six-barrel rocket launchers and tore us to pieces – both our rafts and our gun crews were shredded. We, about fifteen men who had survived intact, together with some infantry soldiers rolled the two operable guns away from the bank. Over the radio I contacted the regiment commander, briefed him on the situation, and received the order to halt the crossing. Meanwhile, German fire was killing everything living on the riverbank; it was piled with the bodies of our soldiers. It is terrifying even to recall it …

On 19 October 1943, we were shifted to a bridgehead north of Kiev. Just at the time I was suffering attacks of malaria. One day I'd be commanding the battery, on the next day I'd be sprawled in a bunker, incapacitated with fever. I kept refusing to turn over command to someone else. Later I gradually got better.

On 3 November, we launched our offensive to liberate Kiev. The nervous stress from the realization that battles were forthcoming, and all the fuss before the coming offensive proved to be the best medicine against the attacks of malaria – they went away as if by magic. On 5 November the battery entered Sviatoshino. Further ahead lay our path to Zhitomir.

We approached Korostyshev. The battery was running low on shells, except for the untouchable reserve, and over the radio I received the order to stop next to some village 5 kilometres from the city and wait for shells to be brought up. The regiment's remaining batteries went on ahead. Suddenly we saw a German truck with infantry and an armoured personnel carrier moving along a by-road. We destroyed them with our first volley. Our infantry came running to join us. A lieutenant among them walked up and appealed to me, 'We seem to be surrounded; there are a lot of German infantry near the village and about twenty tanks. Take us with you, or we'll fall into the Germans' hands.'

We couldn't abandon our own. We had no time to send scouts into the village. We heard the sound of a motorcycle engine and saw a German riding by in the distance. Fortunately, he didn't notice us. I understood that if there were Germans in the village, we'd have to slip past them at high speed before they realized what was going on, but the sounds of our engines would give us away even before we reached the village. I decided to move toward the village at extremely low speed, thereby creating as little noise as possible. I deployed the infantry on both sides of the Studebakers and cautioned that in case the Germans appeared, they were to open up a storm of fire, leap into the trucks, and we would plunge on ahead at top speed. This was an extremely risky manoeuvre, but there was no other alternative; without shells, we could not successfully duel with the enemy tanks.

We approached the outlying huts. The large village was seemingly deserted. The atmosphere was so tense that I was certain that the Germans were lurking in ambush, ready to spring the trap on us, and that it would all begin at any instant.

We went into the first hut and found an old man sitting inside, trembling from fear. I asked him, 'Are there Germans in the village?'

'Yes, a lot, and with tanks.'

'Show us a road where the Germans won't see us.'

'I won't do it; the Germans will shoot me for this!'

I reached for my pistol and said, 'You're afraid that a German will shoot you, but not that a Red Army soldier will? If you don't guide us out of here, I'll kill you right here and now.'

This worked. The old man led us down a side road and we slipped out of the noose.

We reached the Kiev–Zhitomir highway; our regiment slipped out of the encirclement with few casualties, simply by luck. Over the radio, the regiment had been informed of the most suitable route for exiting the pocket, so it was able to escape the ring. But many thousands remained forever there, killed in the encirclement.

The next day I was laid low with malarial fever and I was sent to the nearest medical-sanitary battalion. While I was lying there, I heard the trample of many feet, as if dozens of people were running past. I glanced out the window and saw our soldiers, who were fleeing head over heels away from something. I looked out a different window and saw a German tank sitting about 40 metres away. I leaped out a window and started running toward the forest. I was running, stumbling, falling, and running once again. Only when I reached the woods did I become completely exhausted. Somehow I found my regiment. It was better to be sick 'at home'.

Our regiment received replacements and was given a short time to rest, and then the 'condemned men' resumed their march to the west. For the Kiev–Dnepr River fighting, only two men of our regiment – I and Isaev – were nominated for Orders of the Red Banner. Isaev received his Order several months later, but instead of the 'combat banner' I received the Order of the Patriotic War 1st Degree.

In January 1944, with constant fighting, losing men and equipment, replenishing them both and then losing them again, we approached Shepetovka, close to the old border of the USSR. Just 12 kilometres short of Shepetovka, on the outskirts of a village called Velikie Derevichi, the battery's advance to the west bogged down. The Germans launched a strong counterattack. We set up three guns to fire to the front, but the fourth, as usual, we deployed in a camouflaged position off to one side, about 300 metres away from the rest of the battery. This gun was assigned to conduct flanking fire at the vulnerable side armour of any enemy tanks advancing toward us.

On 15 January, two German tanks crawled out of some nearby woods. We immediately knocked out one and the other crawled away back into the woods. A short time later, four panzers emerged and came straight at us, firing on the move. A line of German infantry was advancing behind them. Our infantry started to run away without a glance back. It seemed just like 1941 again. However, this Red Army infantry unit hadn't seen fighting before and primarily consisted of recently mobilized collective farmers from the liberated territories. The commander of this infantry regiment came running up to me: 'Dear man! Cover us, I beseech you, I beg you!' Almost crying, trying to be heard over the thunder of the guns, he kept pleading – 'Give us cover, while I rally the regiment! I'll nominate you for the "Red Banner"!'

From the right flank, three more German tanks appeared. A direct hit on the flanking gun sent it flipping into the air. The gun's crew was killed. We managed to knock out two more tanks, and the Germans fell back to their jumping-off positions.

I understood that they would attack again and ordered the battery to change positions. At dawn the next day, a large group of German tanks advanced down a parallel road. One of the tanks detached itself from the column. Not seeing the battery in its previous location, it moved on, straight toward our new positions. To do so, he had to cross a bridge. I decided to wait and to disable or destroy it on the bridge, in order to block the road to the other tanks. We in fact crippled it as it reached the middle of the bridge. It rolled forward a bit, shedding a track in the process. A short time later, a German prime mover appeared to tow the immobilized vehicle off the bridge. But we also knocked out the prime mover. Then all the tanks turned in our direction and opened fire at us. They plastered one gun position, killing the entire crew. A second gun was still operable, but the crew had been totally disabled.

I started to run over to this gun together with my orderly. There was a flash of yellowish-red flame directly in front of me and fragments whistled past me ... Jumping to my feet again, I rushed to the gun's position, but here there was a second explosion. I was tossed to one side. Fragments riddled my right hand, and fingers were hanging by their tendons. My orderly had taken a fragment in the belly and was on the ground, moaning.

Several soldiers of the operations platoon rushed over to us. I ordered them to render aid first to the orderly, because his wound was more severe. I tried to bandage myself. The driver of our Studebaker came running up, detached a piece of a board from a pile that was located nearby and laid my hand on the wood, fixing my fingers to the palms. He wrapped my hand to this self-made splint with a grease-soaked rag over the unchanged bandaging material. I left the battlefield, went to a medical-sanitary battalion, and then to a hospital. All the guns in the battery were knocked out, and all the members of the gun crews were killed or wounded. That's the way combat was ...

In February 1944 I received a letter from my mother, and in it I found a 'note' written by the regiment commander, which said that I had been fighting well, that I'd been recommended for two Orders of the Red Banner, and so forth. They had sewn my fingers back to my palms, but they didn't flex or move. I also couldn't flex my wrist; all the bones in my hand had been shattered and deformed.

Upon my discharge from the hospital, I beseeched the doctors not to invalid me out of the army; I spun some story that I couldn't live without the army. They took pity on me and assigned me to the second category of invalids and sent me to a reserve artillery regiment in my native city of Smolensk, where I assumed command of a training battery.

I arrived there and reported to the colonel that commanded the regiment. He rejoiced and said that it was no use crying over spilled milk, and that it was good that an officer with a lot of combat experience would be serving under him. But I asked him to release me for the acting army, and return me to my own guys. The response? 'About face! You are present for duty!'

I then went to the deputy political commander, showed him a letter from my regiment, and said that I, as a Communist, couldn't stay in the rear while the war was going on; that I wanted to defend the Motherland, that the Germans had slaughtered my family and I was obliged to take revenge.

The commissar lost his temper: 'And does this mean that in the rear I'm not making a contribution to the war effort?! Do you think that because you are a hero and wear an Order that here you'll be showing us where each man is to serve?!' But he had a talk with the colonel.

The next morning, the regiment commander summoned me and said:

> Listen, battery commander. I respect your desire to return to the front. But what will you, an invalid, be doing there? Fine, go – but be aware that we never saw you here in Smolensk, and we won't give you any sort of papers. Take care of yourself.

In May 1944 I found my regiment. No one stopped me on my way to the front and nobody checked my papers. The old officers of the regiment rejoiced over my return to active duty. They decided to 'cheer me up' as well. They told me, 'Go to headquarters. Go admire your new Order.' Then they informed me that a message had arrived at the headquarters about presenting me with the Order of the Red Banner for my last battle, but that the chief of staff Major Bykov had rewritten the award list and had inserted his own name in place of mine. So they were suggesting that I go and take a look at my Order that was decorating someone else's tunic. In the war, this happened often: some men would risk their lives, but others would receive the Orders. But to seek justice in the army isn't worth the effort.

I had no wish to serve next to a swine like Bykov. I asked if our regiment commander Cherniak had remained silent, having found out about chief of staff's 'stunt'. They answered that Cherniak had left at the end of February to assume command of the 640th Destroyer Anti-tank Artillery Regiment, which was located 20 kilometres from our current position. I said goodbye to the guys, then dropped by to visit my old battery. However, only three men of the executive staff remained of my old battery. At that moment, I had no assignment and I was 'free as a bird'.

I went in search of the 640th Anti-tank Artillery Regiment. Once I found it, I dropped by Cherniak's bunker to see him. At first he couldn't believe that I had returned. He embraced me and declared that we would serve together until the final victory, and that he would personally deal with all the bureaucratic paperwork connected with my assignment to the regiment. He placed a battery under my command. There was still one more joyful meeting. In this regiment, my old neighbour in Smolensk Ruvim Iakovlevich Dolin was serving as the chief of intelligence. He had been the city chess champion, and before the war we had played a lot of chess together. Ruvim was two years older than me and had graduated from the Smolensk Artillery School back in 1941.

Soon there was an incident that I still have difficulty explaining – I abandoned my guns and retreated without orders. What doesn't happen in war? Sometimes I considered myself battle-seasoned, fully familiar with the smell of gun powder, that I wouldn't duck at every passing bullet, that I had gone through fire and brimstone, and that I was now a hardened veteran, a key player. There you have it, and it all amounted to nothing. But it happens that the devil can snare even men such as that. For no apparent reason, your heart sinks into your boots; you can become anxious inside, and it becomes difficult to suppress your fear.

It happened near Zolochev. My battery had been ordered to support the infantry that was attacking L'vov. Having dug-in on the northwestern outskirts of Zolochev, we repelled an attack by German infantry and armoured half-tracks. Either this was a diversionary manoeuvre by the Germans, or they were attempting to find some way to bypass our unit and had unexpectedly bumped into us, but we repulsed their attack. Then suddenly it became quiet. After the thunder of combat, the sudden silence that fell over the battlefield seemed deafening, even though our ears were still ringing. A little later we caught the sounds of a battle going on somewhere in the distance. But on our sector, the silence at first alarmed us, but later lulled us.

I sent out scouts to clarify the situation. Having returned a short time later, the scouts reported that they'd seen neither any Germans, nor the infantry that we were supposed to be supporting with our fire. The infantry had vamoosed and hadn't let us know about it! The Germans might show up at any minute. I not only became unsettled, I'll even say it directly – I was scared. Experienced front-line soldiers are always uneasy over silence at the front. When combat is going on, everything is clear: the enemy is there and you are here. But when it is quiet ... what sort of intrigue is hiding behind it? Where will the attack fall, and in what strength? Our anti-tank guns were quite vulnerable, and even doubly so without infantry protection. If the Germans appear on the flanks or from the rear, you won't have time to turn the guns around or dig out the trail spades before the entire crew is killed! There was a reason why we were called 'condemned men'.

So, there was this silence. There was no enemy out in front of us. Our trucks, without which we could not move the guns, were far to the rear, under cover. But we still had dozens of boxes of ammunition with us. No communications – the cable had been severed. The radio operators, together with their radios, had been blown to pieces the evening before by a direct shell hit. I had no orders. The entire responsibility for the battery, for the men, was on my shoulders, and at that moment I felt strangely uneasy. I was alone ... You might think that I was getting cold feet at that moment. I looked at my men in the battery and I pitied the guys ... How many of my comrades, how many of my soldiers had I already lost over two years of war! Almost all the soldiers in the battery were still 19-year-old lads. And now, it didn't just smell of encirclement, it seemed more simply the case that they'd soon fall upon us and destroy us, and in the regimental roster they'd write – 'Missing in action'.

I made a decision. I ordered the dial sights and breech mechanisms to be removed from the guns and buried, for the boxes of ammunition to be hidden in a nearby barn, and for the guns to be abandoned in a ravine and concealed by branches! My order was carried out.

We managed to catch up with our own, which had fallen back 5 kilometres, and I reported to the regiment commander about what had just happened. He shot me a look that sent chills down my spine.

'You abandoned your guns! You want to go in front of a tribunal?! March back to the front with the infantry and don't come back without your equipment!'

I took the men of my battery and we headed back to join the infantry in the trenches. I was thinking that I'd had it from the shame, aggravation and malice I'd brought down upon myself. Well, that was OK with me. I was guilty. But how were the men of my battery guilty that I, their commander, was marked down as a deserter? So we crouched together with the infantry in the trenches and for two days we repelled German attacks. It wasn't easy to fire a rifle with only one functioning hand, but I quickly adapted to it. I prayed to God that I'd be killed; my conscience had started to torment me. I had indeed abandoned the guns, not my men, but nevertheless ... Two days later the Germans began to retreat, abandoning their own equipment. I set off back to the place where I'd left the guns like I'd been scalded. I couldn't believe my eyes – my precious guns were still there, none the worse for it. In joy I started kissing the guns. We dug up the breech mechanisms and dial sights, cleaned them, retrieved the ammunition cases from the barn, and went on the attack together with the infantry, now with our guns.

My soldiers understood why I'd made the decision regarding the guns and knew that I had risked my honour and head. All the soldiers came up to me and the Party organizer said, 'Comrade Captain. Thank you, so that if we survive this war we can tell our children about you.'

Years later I understood what kind of Man the regiment commander was. Man, capitalized. He had seen me before in battles and knew that I wasn't a coward. He had drunk from the bitter cup of war, had seen much, and knew that a man wasn't made of iron and his nerves weren't made of steel. A man can falter and buckle because of fatigue, overstress, and the constant expectation of death. But at the slightest provocation we would put him in front of a firing squad before the entire formation, as an example and lesson to others. We should have instead sought to inspire his self-confidence, and helped him straighten himself back up.

So many men were thoughtlessly and needlessly killed. Without adequate weapons or with no weapons at all, the untrained and totally green troops were hurled into the slaughterhouse of war, thrown under the tracks of German tanks, if only to plug a hole, or so that these tank tracks would go into a skid on the crushed human bodies and find no traction in their blood. The high commanders paid for their own faults and stupidity, for their own negligence, with the lives of others. To this day I think with gratitude of Lieutenant Colonel Cherniak. He could have simply had me shot in front of the formation, or in order not to dirty his own hands, he could have submitted my slaughter to the Special Department and the tribunal.

But during a battle, I never saw men in my destroyer anti-tank artillery regiments abandon their guns or flee from fire. I saw men go insane. I also saw men whose hair turned grey in an instant from horror. We once came under a bombing attack, and four of us jumped into a trench. Fragments tore off the legs and head of the officer lying on top of the pile. When the bombing ended we, soaked in another man's blood, clambered out of the trench, and saw that the hair on the head of one lieutenant of the operations platoon had turned entirely grey. But we had no readily apparent cowardice in the batteries; everyone one knew what was expected of us and we were ready to do our duty. The artillerymen and anti-tank crews were fated to look death in the face every day and every hour and to not yield to it.

I remember well how the destroyer anti-tank artillery units were organized for combat – and the tactics we used in battle against German tanks. If we were committed to a direction that was vulnerable to tanks as a full regiment, then the regiment commander chose where to place the batteries. All the batteries but one were pushed forward to fire over open sights, often out in front of the infantry's positions. One battery would remain in reserve in a defiladed position. We could effectively knock out tanks only at ranges out to 500 metres. Two of the batteries would take positions on the flanks in order to hit the side armour of the German tanks.

However, as a general rule the regiment was parcelled out and each battery operated independently. We would arrive in our assigned sector of defence at night; I would choose the firing positions for each gun; foxholes, slit trenches, gun pits and bunkers for the ammunition would be dug; and alternate positions would be set up, communications lines would be laid, and everything would be camouflaged. For the soldiers this was the hardest work. In the winter we would work up a sweat chopping at the frozen soil. In the spring and autumn we would have to set up positions amid the muck and clay. Digging in is one of the most hated recollections of any artilleryman. We didn't bother to set up dummy positions; this was an accepted tactic only when with the full regiment. By dawn, the battery was already dug-in, the vehicles had been driven to the rear, and a fierce battle was waiting for us, a battle not for life, but to the death.

In certain regiments, it was a practice to leave only three men in the firing positions: the commander, the gunner and the loader. The rest of the crew waited in trenches for when it would be necessary to replace comrades that had fallen. This was done to avoid excessive losses, but in my opinion, there was little sense in this practice. In an open firing position there was no refuge, neither in the trench or in a foxhole, nor around the gun. We had a tradition in the 640th Destroyer Anti-tank Artillery Regiment that the Komsomol organizer and the regiment's deputy political leader, as well as the majority of staff officers, would come to the batteries during a battle, bring up shells, replace the wounded and dead among the crews, and take prone positions in front of the guns with the machine guns. Whether this was good or bad, I don't know, but it was an act of self-sacrifice and characterized the fighting spirit of the anti-tank artillerymen. Only a few men would remain at the regiment's observation post, those genuinely necessary to organize the battle and to coordinate the batteries in action.

The guns were deployed at a distance of 30–50 metres from each other, so it would be possible to give voice commands and also as a means to enable dense blocking fire on a certain sector. The fourth, flank gun would set up about 300 metres from the battery's main positions. A telephone cable extended from each gun, and each crew had an assigned phone operator with a field phone.

The ammunition cases were positioned according to the following scheme: close to the gun on the left – armour piercing; to the right – armour-piercing discarding sabot and canister shells. High-explosive shells were kept about 20 metres behind the guns, but when necessary they were dragged to a closer point. All the shells were cleaned of factory grease beforehand. Even in the winter, no one ever repainted our guns, for example, in a white colour. My scouts occupied machine-gun positions in front of the guns; we didn't particularly rely upon the infantry at hand. In reserve, in each battery there were anti-personnel and anti-tank mines. If there were no infantry positions in front of us, over the night the scouts would emplace mines in front of each gun. If it was necessary to change positions during a fight, the guns were manhandled to the new position; the Studebaker trucks were never driven up to the battlefield.

Anti-tank rifles were only used in destroyer anti-tank artillery brigades; they had a separate company of anti-tank rifles.

We meticulously prepared for combat. Without exaggeration, they placed our lives on the map. One can picturesquely compare the destroyer anti-tank artillery regiments to gladiators, but when the armoured bodies of German tanks are moving toward you, belching death, here there is no association with Ancient Rome.

Several times a position selected at night, in the darkness, proved to be a bad one, but there was no time to change it and one had to accept combat in the position you found yourself. The battery commander would choose the target, and he would also give the order to open fire. If the battery commander was killed, then the platoon commander or gun commander would fight independently. The destroyer anti-tank artillery regiment's tasks were diverse. Of course our main assignment was to combat tanks. But often we were used to support our attacking troops with our fire, or were positioned next to the regimental artillery in order to solidify the defence. Allow me to refuse to discuss the question of the effectiveness of the guns when combating infantry or tanks; I don't want to assess whether the ZIS-3 or ZIS-2 was better, or the firepower of various artillery systems. We'll leave these nuances to armourers and specialists. I'm a practical man and I'm not cut out for academic debates and computations. Incidentally, at the front we sought to avoid talking about this subject. You fought with what you were given.

A bit on the subject of the German tanks: prior to 1944 we fought primarily against Pz-III and Pz-IV tanks. A heavy tank would advance in front, and behind it the medium and light tanks would form a wedge. But later, in 1944, things became much more complicated. I participated in several battles where the Germans made massed use of Tigers and Panthers, which I will tell you was an unpleasant 'treat'. The Germans were smart and sensible fighters; they didn't hurl their panzer units to their total destruction in head-on attacks, as was our style. They fought in battalions. Now the Germans would usually launch medium tanks in front that would fire on the move, without stopping, while Tigers or self-propelled guns would be stationary behind them. They waited until we would open fire and disclose our positions. A bit more on their equipment: At a range of 1 kilometre, we in fact could do no harm to a heavy tank, while their self-propelled guns or heavy tanks would simply and calmly shoot us up. One had to contrive some way to outlast such nightmares as the Ferdinand or Marder self-propelled guns. You watch through binoculars as a Tiger begins to get you in its crosshairs, and your heart sinks into your boots. The German tankers were superbly trained, especially in gunnery. Thus our preliminary calculation in the destroyer anti-tank artillery regiments reduced to 1 to 1; each of our guns, prior to its destruction, should knock-out one

German tank. Everything that followed depended on dumb luck, providence, serendipity and the artillery crew's level of training. Well, of course the number of German tanks attacking the battery was very important. Once the battery held out in combat against thirty (!) German tanks. We lost a lot of guys then, but the Germans did not pass! There was another incident; just four German tanks came at us and a duel began. We overlooked a flame-throwing tank that moved in behind us, approaching from the rear through ravines. I still don't understand why the German delayed in squirting us with flames; he was just 50 metres away from us. To our great fortune, the German tank bogged down in a deep crater, which seemingly toppled it onto one side, and two of my scouts blew it up with grenades, earning Orders of Glory for this feat.

The Germans rarely used infantry in panzer attacks; it was only in the movies that you see dense German lines advancing behind the tanks, spraying everything in front of them with submachine guns fired from the hip. What can you kill with a submachine gun at 300 metres? The German infantry would hug the earth and wait for when the tanks would break into the battery's positions, and only then, at a run, would they advance. Armoured halftracks often supported the tanks. Once, my gun crew was all disabled, so I manned the gun alone and destroyed three halftracks. As for the classic assault by infantry dismounting from tanks, this was purely a Red Army tactic. I extremely rarely saw any German infantry mounted on armour during an attack. This meant almost certain death. My younger brother Arkadii, who fought as the commander of a company of tank-riding submachine gunners, was wounded several times and managed to earn two Orders, until he was discharged from the army for disability after his latest severe wound. He told me after the war what losses the tank-riding companies suffered. It is difficult to relate, but they were worse than any penal company. The Germans, however, conserved both their men and equipment; this is a fact, and that is simply that. The notion that 'human blood is water' was ours alone.

In combat it is difficult to anticipate where the tank will go. Much depends upon the skill of the driver, and moreover we didn't know all the folds in the terrain out in front of us. The most favourable moment to catch a German tank in your sights was when he stopped in order to fire a series of shots from a brief halt. It was important to allow the tank to approach closely, as we said, to within 'pistol-shot range' – then there was a chance to survive. Tigers had to be hammered from several guns simultaneously at a range of 100–150 metres.

My last battle against attacking German tanks was at the beginning of March 1945. They collided with three regiments of destroyer anti-tank artillery deployed side-by-side, so they were unlucky, while we came out of this fight with small losses. By April 1945 we were transferred to Czechoslovakia. There, the Germans were digging their Tigers into the ground. My battery bumped into two such dug-in tanks in the mountains. We were pressing infantry of a Russian Liberation Army division, 'Vlasovites', toward sheer cliffs, and we were hollering at them, 'Komsomol-paratroopers, this is your final jump!' We appeared in time to deploy our guns and lent the infantry a hand. Together with the infantry troops, we advanced, manhandling our guns forward with their help, and ran smack into these 'Tiger pillboxes', dug into the earth on a hilltop. We were saved from certain death by a forward air controller who was attached to the regiment and who was with my battery at this moment. He called for Il-2 ground-assault aircraft, and they swept our path clear. Otherwise, I wouldn't be speaking with you now.

Well, altogether my battery in the 640th Destroyer Anti-tank Artillery Regiment destroyed 15 German tanks and self-propelled guns between May 1944 and March 1945. That wasn't a bad performance indicator.

The losses in the destroyer anti-tank artillery regiments were quite heavy, but many more men were killed while serving in the infantry. My comrade served in a rifle division, in which after the Kerch landing not more than thirty-seven men remained in the infantry regiments, not including the staff officers. In our destroyer anti-tank artillery regiment, we faced a similar situation four times, where all the remaining guns were merged into one battery, but we continued to carry out our assignment until the last man and gun. Just a few of the battery's veterans survived the combat journey from Tarnopol' to the Elbe River, and I can remember their last names: Sergeant Major Lisitsa, Sergeants and Privates Ivanov, Tkachuk, Iskanderov, Borisov, Avdeev, Nesterenko, Lebedev and Ziberov. I remember my gun platoon commanders Repin and Ulanov, but they arrived in the battery already after we had crossed the Polish–German border. But in general, it was considered the rarest thing to survive three combats with tanks in the destroyer anti-tank artillery regiment. We understood this, and we sought to sell our lives as dearly as possible, and we managed to destroy German tanks.

I now no longer recall that the artillerymen carried any good luck charms. As in the infantry as well, it was considered taboo to remove any objects from our own dead. Even when someone took the boots off of a corpse, it was believed that he was testing fate. A classic superstition was our belief that '13' was an unlucky number.

As regards presentiments, if a man suddenly closed up, walked around gloomily and didn't converse with anyone – it was a sure sign that he'd soon be killed. Or on the contrary, if someone suddenly starts laughing without any real reason, that was another 'alarm bell'. Many sensed their approaching death. You can't escape fate, much less in a destroyer anti-tank artillery regiment.

The issue of German prisoners and the German population is a complex one. We didn't take German tankers alive. If you looked at the treads of a German tank, you'd see the flesh of your comrades on it and everything coated with Russian blood. We shot the tankers right away as they were abandoning their burning tanks, not allowing them to escape or to raise their hands and surrender. The Germans incidentally did the same thing. But no artilleryman ever touched infantry prisoners. Their life was in the infantry's hands, and their treatment was up to them.

With respect to the local population, I don't recall that someone among the soldiers of my battery robbed a German or raped a German woman. My guys had a conscience. On the other hand, I consider it excessive to idealize or shed tears over the subject of the 'poor' German civilians. Here's a simple example. In May 1945, we were not far from Prague. Next to us was a howitzer-artillery brigade of the Supreme Command Reserve. If I remember accurately, it was the 98th Brigade. I had a talk with a Jewish lieutenant from this brigade, and he informed me that three weeks prior, the 3rd Battalion of this brigade had been totally wiped out. A large group of retreating Germans had suddenly fallen on the battalion's positions, emerging from some woods, and our men didn't even have time to defend themselves. A crowd of civilians were moving with the Germans, among which were many armed adolescents and women. And they pitilessly finished off and shot our wounded soldiers from their rifles and lady's Brownings. The only survivors were one female phone clerk, who received ten (!) bullet wounds, and one of the battalion scouts, who managed to crawl into the woods and from there witnessed this entire terrible and nightmarish scene. I don't think it necessary to add anything else.

The battle for the Sandomir bridgehead was my hardest fight. My battery was the first to cross the Vistula together with the infantry, in the vicinity of the village Purku-Gorn. Our crossing went smoothly for us; the battery lost only three soldiers wounded. We quickly threw up defensive positions and were immediately attacked by German infantry. We repulsed this attack and advanced another couple of kilometres, expanding the bridgehead. A short time later we heard the sound of engines. From out of some woods, two tanks cautiously crawled out onto a hilltop. They were moving slowly, lumbering across the uneven ground. I gave an order not to fire. I immediately realized that this was a reconnaissance probe. Having moseyed around a bit at a discrete distance from our camouflaged battery, these armoured 'boxes' retired. A short time later, a Tiger appeared, and confident of its own invulnerability, it advanced directly toward the battery. As soon as it exposed its side armour to the detached gun positioned on the flank, we dropped our camouflage from the guns and opened fire, and the Tiger was knocked out. Immediately another tank emerged from the woods, and accelerating, it overran the position of the flank gun and began to spin in place, grinding everything into the dirt with its tracks: the gun, the crew and the boxes of ammunition. At the same moment, engines started up in the woods on the hill; the Germans were preparing to attack. My intuition didn't fail me. Thirty tanks moved out and lumbered toward the battery. I understood that with my three remaining guns, I couldn't resist such an attack, and that this would be my last battle. In the best case we would only knock out several tanks, before they swept us away with fire and we'd be crushed beneath the tracks of this iron wave. The German fire intensified and our communications line was severed in multiple places by shell fragments. In addition, as always, for some arbitrary but constant set of circumstances, fragments from the very first German shells smashed the radio. We needed help and right away.

The German panzers halted 700 metres away from us and for some reason marked time there. My one chance had appeared. I sent a scout back to the riverbank with a written message, not even knowing whether he would manage to reach regiment headquarters in time. The main thing was that he not be killed on the way. The crews were frozen at their guns, ready to open fire. Eight tanks led by a Tiger resumed their advance toward the battery. We let them close to within 300 metres and opened fire. The Tiger got the jump on us by a second and the crew of the No. 1 gun was knocked out by a direct hit. Captain Ruvim Dolin, who was located with the battery, rushed to the unmanned gun and alone opened fire at an approaching tank. He put it out of action with his first shot. However, firing at a second tank, he missed and was immediately blanketed by the return shot. His exploit didn't ease the battery's situation.

Our infantry abandoned their trenches and in a word, skedaddled. German tank fire quickly destroyed the battery's remaining guns. One German tank came at my trench, where I was located with a signalman, and overran us, covering us with dirt. Fortunately for us, men of the battery quickly dug us out. I heard the hum of approaching motors in the sky; our Il-2s were approaching. The aircraft circled in behind the German tanks and bombed both them and our position simultaneously. The German attack was broken up. Thus the battery was saved from complete destruction. We lost twelve men killed and eleven wounded, and three guns were destroyed. The battery destroyed five German tanks. As later became clear, the scout I had sent had reached his objective, and the regiment commander had requested air support from higher command. We held this position for several more days. The remnants of a rifle battalion, twenty-five men, drifted into our positions and took up a defence 2 kilometres south of us.

We buried our dead on the battlefield. Two of them, Panichev and Endrikhin, were my good friends ... We had to fall back to find other friendly units. I sent out a scout team, and having returned, they reported that they had found four guns, two of which were disabled. There were no crews, but the position had ammunition. We didn't have our Studebakers, so we had to haul the guns back ourselves, as well as our wounded. We had just exited a village when we bumped into Germans that were attempting to encircle us. At a frantic pace, our fatigue seeming to have evaporated, we deployed the guns and set up an all-round defence. We barely managed to beat back their attack.

In the twilight hours, when we were slipping away from the Germans, we again came under fire. I yelled at the soldiers to get down. From the sound of the automatic firing, I realized that our own guys were firing at us. I tied a piece of bandaging to some stick and raised it over my head as if we were surrendering. The firing stopped. An officer walked out to us with a German machine pistol in his hands.

'Who's there?' he shouted, looking at us suspiciously.

'Friendlies, coming out of battle.'

'Documents?!'

Having checked our documents, he added, 'We thought that the Germans were pressing us again. We've just repulsed two attacks.'

Over the radio that the infantry had with them, I got in touch with my regiment. They sent Studabakers to retrieve us. Having loaded the wounded and shells onto them, we hitched up our remaining gun and the two we had stumbled upon, and soon we were back with the regiment. Cherniak greeted me with tears in his eyes.

He said, 'I had already written you off. We reported to army headquarters that one battery was fighting in a village. But when you fell silent, we decided that was it; your number had come up. We sent an order for you to retreat, but I guess the messenger didn't reach you.' We came out with forty-eight men.

For Sandomir I received the Order of Aleksandr Nevsky, and I don't hold any grudges toward anyone because I didn't receive the Hero title. Back then, many of the men put in for the highest distinction received a 'Star' instead of the Order.

On the matter of anti-Semitism in the army, to my great fortune I never encountered it. In our group of thirty men, yesterday's school graduates, who went into the army in June 1941, there were twelve Jews, and I was the only one to survive the war. Of the Russian guys in that same group, only Zhenia Mukhin and Vasia Alekseev, who served in the howitzer artillery, survived. Perhaps someone else made it through the war intact, but simply didn't return to Smolensk after the war and didn't let it be known. In the 45-mm anti-tank battery, in addition to me, there was one other Jew, a gun commander, and he was severely wounded in October 1942. In the destroyer anti-tank artillery regiment, at one time three of the five batteries were commanded by Jews. One soon was killed, and another, Grisha, was wounded in the legs and left the regiment. I've kept his photograph that he sent from the hospital as a keepsake.

I don't recall conflicts over nationality in my battery either. My orderly was from Dagestan, and the bravest scout, one of my three soldiers who each had two Orders of Glory, was a Bashkir – Galiman Iskanderov. Two of the gun layers were Kazakhs. But of course the majority of our soldiers were Slavs. So no one antagonized anyone else over an ethnical characteristic. We fought, and we didn't go into checklists and prejudices.

Chapter 11

One of the Very Few
Aleksandr Vasil'evich Rogachev

I was born into a working family on 21 March 1923 in the city of Efremov, which at the time was in Moscow Oblast, but since 1938, in Tula Oblast. I had an older brother Vladimir who was born in 1920, and a younger brother who was born in 1925. Both went through the war. My older brother was a mechanic in a bomber regiment, while my younger brother was a scout. Other mothers were envious: in our family three sons and a father went off to war and they all returned from it. However, my brothers passed away early, so I'm living out the final days for my entire family.

On the evening of 21 June, our School No. 1, in which I studied, was having its graduation ceremony, in which we were to receive our diplomas. I was the leader of a string band and I played the mandolin, balalaika and the guitar. My small orchestra of eight gave a good performance that evening. Our mood was happy, but the teachers and some of the invited parents seemed not to share our joy. Many of those who were present that evening felt trapped. The teachers were standing around with blank faces, lost in thought. Plainly they sensed that war was coming. My older brother Vladimir, who was called up for the army in 1939 from the second year of his study at the Moscow Hydro-meteorological Institute, wrote about this in his letters. He was serving as an aviation mechanic in a fighter regiment that was based right on the border close to Brest. Some of the statements in his letters were blacked out by censors, but I recall a letter from him that arrived in the first few days of June, in which he wrote: 'Mama and Papa, don't hope for a meeting soon. War, in which we will have to take part, is approaching.' My parents, particularly my mother, of course, were distressed.

At 11:00 p.m. that evening I was already home and had gone to bed. But on the morning of 22 June, announcements came that war had started. On 24 June, I and other guys of the school went to the enlistment centre. There was pandemonium there! A huge crowd! Young men older than us had been called up. Women were accompanying them. Accordions were playing, and there were songs and tears. We somehow fought our way through to the sentry, and he told us, 'Guys, don't meddle, keep working, wait your turn. For now they're calling up older ages.' We returned empty-handed, but soon joined an armed battalion that was helping maintain order in the city. At the end of July, I received my draft notice.

When I had gone through the preliminary review commission in February 1941, I had been assigned to the Navy. I was proud of this! I really wanted to become a sailor! I was a good swimmer, I'd grown up next to a river, I skated and skied, and engaged in sports, but when I received the draft notice and reported to the enlistment centre, there they informed me, 'No, dear fellow, the Navy doesn't need anyone right now. The infantry needs men.' Well, fine.

A detachment of conscripts formed up in the first days of August, which was headed by a lieutenant and Order wearer, who'd been wounded in the war with Finland. He was to lead us to a reserve rifle regiment, where we were to receive training and then join the ranks of the acting army. Only the lieutenant knew the location of this regiment and the route to it. So we moved out on foot from Efremov somewhere in the middle of August. We marched through Tula, Moscow and Riazan' Oblasts; to put it briefly, this reserve rifle regiment was located in Ioshkar-Ola, the capital city of the Mari ASSR [Autonomous Soviet Socialist Republic]. We covered this entire distance on foot! We marched 25–30 kilometres a day. We spent the nights in settlements and villages. Sometimes we were issued rations, but for the most part we were fed by residents of the places where we stopped. En route the detachment grew as draftees born in 1922 and 1923 joined our ranks. Yet it is characteristic that despite all the difficulties and hardship of this labourious trek, none of the detachment ran away. Everyone arrived at the destination!

We were quartered outside the city in the workshops of a ceramics factory. Our training began. Of course, the rations were meagre and the conditions were Spartan. We built two-level wooden bunk beds in the workshops where bricks were fired. We were still in our civilian clothing and footwear. But the training we received wasn't bad. We went over tactics, the theory of gunnery, and target-range practice. They were preparing junior lieutenants, company commanders and soldiers out of us. We were told, 'Your main training will be at the front. Here we're just prepping you for it.' I recall how he was always commanding us: 'Let's go, guys, be more cheerful, young men!' But our mood wasn't important: cities were being surrendered and the armies were retreating. Among ourselves we would say, 'Well, is it that the old guys don't know how to fight and can't hold back the Germans?! We'll get there and show them!'

Our training came to an end in the first days of November. In the middle of the month, we received a good-quality kit: flannel underclothing, a quilted jacket, a great coat, a camouflage cloak, a ski cap and felt boots. There were no helmets. Our 47th Separate Rifle Brigade formed up in Ioshkar-Ola and we loaded onto trains. We were told that the brigade would join the 1st Shock Army and would be defending Moscow. Somewhere around the 15th, the train pulled into Likhobory Station. On foot we marched along the Dmitrov highway in the direction of Iakhroma–Dmitrov. The march was difficult; we spent the nights in forests under the fir trees and campfires were prohibited. We would march 5 kilometres, a halt would be called for 10 minutes, and everyone would drop and immediately fall asleep. The command, 'Get up!' – and we'd struggle back to our feet. The winter kit was heavy, and we also had our rucksack and weapon. I was the No. 1 of a DP light machine-gun team. So I carried the machine gun, while my partner lugged two boxes that held four drums of ammunition each. We were sturdy guys, young – we marched 40 kilometres a day. We had bloody blisters on our feet. They would burst, dry up, and then you'd pull off your foot wraps to check them ... that's how we marched.

We deployed along the Moscow–Volga canal and took up a defence there. Then we launched a counteroffensive to liberate some villages. I no longer recall their names, of course. Of the larger towns and cities, I remember Solnechnogorsk, Klin and Shakhovskaia. There was very hard fighting for Klin. I recall entering Tchaikovsky's home and museum. The fascists had turned everything upside down in it. We gathered sheets of musical compositions ...

The fighting in the Moscow suburbs was very hard. There was deep snow and bone-chilling frosts. We would attack a village – as a rule it was on an elevation – after a weak preparatory artillery barrage. The platoon commander would give the order, 'To the right, one by one, move by bounds; move out!' What bounds?! There is snow! So we moved out. Bullets are whistling. You'd advance 6 metres, fall, find some more or less satisfactory cover, and start shooting. You'd wait for the remaining men to come up. They're closing ranks, but it is still 500 metres to the German held village. While we advanced 200 metres, the platoon would dwindle to fifteen or twenty men. An unsuccessful attack – what is to be done? The commander decides to fall back. We retreat under fire. When you look at these losses, there was no place on the field free of corpses; they lay there like bundles, with only narrow intervals between them, and you'd think: 'Can such a battle last for long? Why have so many men fallen for this accursed village, and we can't take it? Will we take it or not?'

We'd sit there, everyone begrimed with gunpowder, and we'd look at each other with the same thought: 'Let them kill us; if only a leg or arm isn't torn off. They can kill us all.' In the evening, march companies would arrive, either of old guys or young lads. They would all ask, 'What's it like here, guys?' We'd reply, 'Why ask? We'll make another attack and you'll find out what it's like.' The new replacement might be 35 or 40 years old, while we were all just 18 or 19, but they'd look at us respectfully. We'd make two or three attacks in a day, and none of this batch of replacements would remain. In the evening a new march company would arrive and replacements would again flesh out the platoon to its authorized strength. Meanwhile, we, the bones of the platoon, kept fighting. There was more or less a core group of approximately ten men, and from it perhaps one or two men would get killed or wounded, so the composition of this group changed every day. I will talk later about my last battle, in which I was wounded. In this same battle, the deputy platoon commander Senior Sergeant Medvedchenko was wounded in the leg. In the medical-sanitary battalion they rolled me away and the nurse said, 'Here are the platoon's last veterans – deputy platoon commander Medvedchenko and machine-gunner Rogachev.'

In 1941 we heard that there were cases of self-inflicted wounds in neighbouring battalions, but in ours I don't recall such a case. In a destroyer anti-tank artillery regiment or battery, this was strictly forbidden. Never!!! I recall the regiment commander dwelling on this point in front of a batch of replacements: 'We are a destroyer anti-tank regiment. We combat against tanks and have little chance of surviving intact. Whoever has weak nerves or thinks it better to fight in a different place – step forward, nothing will happen. We'll post you to different regiments.' No one stepped forward.

Our meals only very rarely made it up to us at the front. Either we were isolated, or we were lying under heavy fire and it was impossible to reach us. The soldiers would crawl back with a Thermos while we would break off an attack. Somewhere, somehow there would be a lull, and at this moment, perhaps once a day, but sometimes not even then (that's why we carried a dry ration of biscuits and sugar), the guys with the Thermos would come crawling in to our position: 'Soldiers, come eat!' In the Thermos would be split-pea soup with meat, but you couldn't stick your spoon in it – it would be frozen, and there would be no campfire to melt it and warm it up. We went around hungry. On the Northwestern Front, all we had were three biscuits and five lumps of sugar a day! We'd hack up fallen horses with a sapper's spade. We'd build a tiny fire and make a horseflesh stew – it was like rubber. That was nothing, we'd still chew it.

But you know, we didn't have a sharp appetite and we didn't feel the cold, because we were under constant stress and frazzled both physically and mentally. Thoughts of food would arise only when coming out of a battle, but they also only added to our fatigue and the feeling of emptiness inside. That's how much we suffered for our sense of mortal danger. True, with time our sense of fear subsided, but it seemingly left a void inside and only hatred alone would remain. We wanted to break through, to kill, to liberate, and only then it seemed there would be some relief. But here we fought and fought . . . and accomplished nothing. Even so, the thought of the uselessness of these terrible casualties never entered our heads. Yet in 1944, when we began to recall 1941, we'd think: 'Lord, how were we fighting there?! For what purpose did we suffer such losses? How inexperienced we all were!'

When however we conducted a successful attack, it seemed kind of easy. It seemed our comrades had not been killed in vain; this time we showed them. The enemy is lying over there dead. Or else we'd assault a village, fighting our way into it. We'd take it, but it was like there would be no dead Germans in it. You'd find perhaps 30 or 40 of them, but our dead would be around 700. Our soldiers and officers often asked, 'What is this? We take casualties, but it seems the Germans don't.' It was said that they always removed their dead and buried them.

The Germans fought very skillfully. They had a hardened, professional army with combat experience. The Germans had an excellent feel for the terrain and sited their positions carefully. Well, and their MG-34 machine gun was a terrifying weapon in a class by itself. One of our companies would try to attack, and they would have a squad with one machine gun that would stop it cold. The incoming fire was heavy, like a torrent. We'd take casualties and keep attacking and attacking, but until we destroyed them, we'd make no headway. In case of necessity, the Germans had vehicles at the ready. The garrison would load into them and head to the next village about 3 to 10 kilometres away. There it would stop and dig in again. In the winter the Germans never fought in an open field; they had bunkers and trenches, while we'd grab a bit of sleep in the woods before again going on the attack across the naked, snow–covered ground. That's how it went from village to village, always on foot ...

Yes, the MG-34 had a rapid rate of fire and was very accurate. It had a two-man crew. Usually they would choose a position very skilfully and camouflage it well. If I fired and they spotted me, I'd have immediately to change positions; you couldn't stay for very long in any one place. We were also young and inexperienced.

The enemy would go on the attack. In order to take aim at one and hit him required 4 or 5 seconds. While you took aim, you held your breath to steady the rifle. While doing so, he would cover a certain amount of ground. If he was coming toward you, you had to aim at his legs in order to hit him in the chest. If he was running away from you, then it was just the opposite. If you aimed at his head first, then over the 5 seconds before you fired, he would recede and the bullet would miss high. These are the ABCs of marksmanship.

If you're attacking, every 5 or 6 seconds you had to drop, and upon hitting the ground, it was necessary to roll to the right or to the left two or three times, and take cover behind a corpse or any sort of fold in the ground. When you rose again to attack, that German would be aiming at the place where he saw you drop, while you had shifted 1.5 to 2 metres. While he moved his rifle, you had another 5 or 6 seconds. But we didn't know all this; we were young. If you weren't killed right away, then with time of course such a method of advance would suggest itself to you, and you would figure out what you needed to do to survive. You quickly became experienced.

On 20 January 1942, we were withdrawn into some woods near the city of Klin. Our 1st Shock Army transferred to the Northwestern Front. At the end of January, we moved in trucks approximately 200 kilometres along the Leningrad highway, before disembarking and moving toward the front at night on foot. Our army was supposed to cooperate with the encirclement of the Germans' Demiansk grouping. Fighting went on day and night. We had few tanks and aircraft and little artillery. The German Luftwaffe dominated the skies. Primarily 45-mm guns accompanied us. We would ask, 'Why aren't you firing?' In response, we heard, 'We only have three shells per gun each day.' When we went on the attack, they'd pop off a couple of shots and that was it. There was no strong fire support. There'd be a brief mortar or artillery barrage, and then we'd rise to the attack. We always moved along forest roads. A tractor would tow a plow made of logs to clear the roads. Walls of snow about a metre and a half high were formed on both sides of the road. We would move along the road, under fire of course. Bullets buzzed through the air. We would assemble in some populated place. We'd resupply. Then we'd resume our advance. All the time we stuck to the forests. We never marched along good roads.

From the end of January to the end of February, we advanced as far as Ramushevo and we isolated the Demiansk grouping. Afterward we were switched to Staraia Russa and we were ordered to take it by 23 February, Red Army Day. We repeatedly attacked between 23 and 27 February, at times making three or four attacks a day, and then another one at night. The casualties were very heavy. I subsequently experienced very few battles as bloody as those on the Northwestern Front.

On 27 February, I was wounded in a night attack. That day we had gone on the attack – unsuccessfully. A second attack – and again heavy losses and we fell back to the jumping-off line. We drove back a German attack. Then we launched two more attacks, all without results. I went into these attacks robotically, thinking about nothing, but at midnight we were woken up for another attack and I felt apprehensive. I wasn't thinking about death, but I didn't feel right; I sensed that something would happen to me.

Immediately before the surge to the first German trench, I was firing a machine gun. Mortar shells began dropping around me. Two rounds exploded on either side of me and I realized that they had me bracketed. At the moment when I attempted to shift my position, there was another explosion. I only saw the flash before feeling such a strong blow to my side, it was as if someone behind me had struck me with a gun butt or a club. I lost consciousness. When I woke up, I was looking up into the starry night sky ... and it was so quiet ... only scattered fire was going on. I was lying right in front of a German position. We had gone on the attack just after midnight; around 0300, a lightly wounded Red Army soldier came crawling past me. I softly called to him. He crawled over. He said, 'Brother, are you alive?' I replied, 'I'm alive. Help me, friend.' He retrieved a towel from my haversack and wrapped it around the wound over my camouflage cloak. I was losing a lot of blood – the mortar fragment, as was determined later, had broken three of my ribs before embedding itself in the lower lung lobe.

He whispered, 'Hang on.' I wrapped my arms around his neck and we started crawling. We crawled for some distance. But there were so many dead bodies on this field that it was difficult to crawl. I told him, 'Listen, why are we tormenting ourselves by crawling? Get me on my feet.'

'They'll kill us.'

'They won't kill anything. We'll make better progress on our feet.'

He hoisted me up. I couldn't straighten up because of the tremendous pain. We set off. He was older, somehow skittish. He'd immediately drop prone at the sound of firing. I said, 'Quit falling, we won't be able to get back up. Those bullets that you hear have already flown past you. We struggled forward another 500 metres to the Lovat' River. I don't know how we made it down the steep bank – I kept losing consciousness. On the riverbank the medic approached, gave me an injection and took a look: 'O-o-o, from the 1st Battalion, 1st Company – Rogachev, the last veteran. Hardly anyone is left ...'

They laid me on a sled and an Alsatian sheep dog pulled me across a snow-covered field to Lower Ramushevo. There they put me in the back of a truck and took me to a hospital. In the hospital they attempted to extract the shell fragment, but were unable to do so. I was sent on to a front hospital. To reach it at first we travelled through the woods over a plank road in a ZIS-5 high-sided truck. They loaded us, the wounded, covered us with warm blankets, placed chemical heating pads on our legs, and set off. The bumpy road rattled us terribly. Each jolt in the side caused terrible pain, yet we had to drive 50 to 60 kilometres to reach Akulovo Station. Guys were moaning and screaming ... We arrived at the station at night. They laid us in a row on stretchers next to the railroad embankment. When they conducted the operation, they cut off all my uniform, and before sending me on they dressed me in some combat blouse. A captain came by with a flashlight, determining who was to go where. Our train had two passenger cars equipped with suspended net beds for the officers and four heated cattle cars for the sergeants and privates. When she came up to me, I was in a mental fog, and when she asked me a question, I didn't hear anything or understand anything. She illuminated me with the flashlight, and the combat blouse that I was wearing had a little black cube on the collar. Obviously, the shirt was from some junior lieutenant. She said, 'Place him in an officer's car.' Indeed, they placed me like an officer in the passenger car on an upper berth.

We pulled out of the station in the morning and within an hour to an hour and a half, Messerschmidt fighters dived on the train. They damaged the steam engine, killed or wounded the mechanic, and bombed the last two cars of the train, in which there were wounded men, doctors and nurses. The casualties were heavy. Then we had to wait until a new steam engine arrived to replace the damaged one.

I was taken to Iaroslavl' and spent a month in the hospital there. The doctors tried again to conduct an operation, but nothing came of their attempts – I kept suppurating and bleeding. I was gradually losing my strength, so they, in order to make sure that they didn't take any blame, sent me further to the rear, to Novosibirsk. I was assigned to the city hospital at No. 3 Red Prospect, which lay opposite the Party regional committee building. I stayed in this hospital until 15 August 1942. At first I lay in a common ward, in which there were approximately ten patients, but then when I had a setback and stopped eating, they transferred me to a tiny, separate room to die. Qualified surgeons from the Burdenko hospital were coming to this hospital to perform complex operations. So just then some surgeon arrived. He began to make his rounds. He stopped in my room and asked, 'Who's this here?'

'A hopeless case.'

'Show me his records.'

After examining them, he said, 'Well, get him to the operating room.' I recall the operating table, but I woke up and found myself in my tiny room again. The doctor had removed the lower portion of the left lung that contained the fragment. When I came around back to consciousness, I saw a plate holding cream of wheat on the table beside my bed. I was hungry, so I took a spoon and slowly started to eat. A senior nurse came in, saw me, and exclaimed, 'Lord, he's eating the cream of wheat. That means he'll live.' She went running to the doctor. A week later I was transferred back to the common ward. There they rejoiced: 'A-a-a, Sashka has come back from the dead!' Although I rather quickly turned the corner, I started to develop osteomyelitis and my wound continued to suppurate.

What was the mood among the patients? The older soldiers dreamed of being declared as invalids and going home, or at least being assigned to some purely administrative post; anything other than being sent back to the front. But the young artillerymen, tankers and infantrymen – all were ready to return to their units. Their desire was one and the same – to finish off the enemy. Such a feeling was held by everyone after what they'd done to us since 1941.

We wanted to pay them back, take our revenge, drive them from our territory and finish the war on the foe's turf. Well, of course there might have been someone who in fact thought that we might lose the war and that the losses might even grow, but he didn't say this aloud. In the hospital, just as in every unit, there were appropriate agencies that tracked the mood and might summon you to ask, 'Don't you think you should keep your mouth shut?'

By an order, the recovering patients were sent to a rest home in the city of Berdsk. There we regained our strength, and I began to play volleyball and to swim in the river. At the end of August I found myself standing in front of a commission. Three men were sitting there: the director of the hospital, the deputy political leader, and someone else. They asked, 'Rogachev, how's it going?'

'I'm fine.'

'Where do you want to go?'

'To the front.'

'Your wound still hasn't closed. Show us.'

I showed them. The wound was covered by a crust, and puss was again oozing from my ribs.

'We'll hope that it will heal. Maybe we should send you somewhere else than the front? What is your education?'

'Middle. Ten years of schooling.'

'Maybe you're exaggerating?' Many would have added to themselves perhaps that I was lying in order to get a better assignment.

'No. I've kept a copy of my diploma.'

'Give it to us; let us take a look.'

I retrieved it. The paper was filthy, covered with yellowed blood spots. When I departed for the front, I took this sheet along, I don't know why. I stuck it in the back pocket of my trousers in a bundle with some other documents, so it had passed through the entire war along with me. I don't know how it remained intact.

They checked it: Algebra – excellent; Trigonometry – excellent; Literature and Russian – excellent. I had only one '3'; the rest were '4s' and '5s'. They talked to each other for a moment, before announcing, 'OK, Rogachev, Team 65.'

I went out into the corridor. Other recovering patients were coming out. Some had been given 'Team 70', some 'Team 71'. Meanwhile I sat there and waited for someone else who would come out with 'Team 65'. No one did. The other guys were being grouped and getting their orders, while I just sat and sat. Soon there were just a few people left. I began to get worried and asked, 'Is someone else "Team 65"?' No one. Then someone came out and handed me instructions to go to Tomsk, to Nikitin Street, Building 23.

I gathered my things. But there was nothing in particular to gather: the worn-out front-line uniform I was wearing, my little tobacco pouch, a little tobacco and a small rucksack. I arrived in Tomsk early in the morning. I decided to look around the city first. I went to the university. I admired the Tom' River. Then I came out onto Lenin Street. The city was full of people going about their daily lives. I could see people selling sodas. Suddenly from behind me I heard, 'Comrade Soldier!' A patrol was standing there, an officer and two soldiers. 'What are you doing here? Your documents, now.' They inspected them. 'Why are you walking here? Nikitin Street is that way.' There was nothing I could do, so I had to go. I found the street and approached a high stone palisade, beyond which I could see guns, 152-mm howitzers and older ones from 1937, plus a beautiful white building. On the parade ground, soldiers were going through close-order drills. I wanted to go to the front, but here I faced more training and additional close-order drilling. This I didn't want, but what could I do? I lingered a bit in front of the gates.

A sentry asked, 'Why are you here, soldier?'

'I've been sent' – and I showed him my papers.

'What are you afraid of? Come in.'

That's how I wound up in the 1st Tomsk Artillery School. It was an accelerated ten-month course to create 152-mm and 122-mm howitzer platoon commanders. They placed me in quarantine, and then began intensive training through 13.5 hours of daily arduous lessons and drills. But I longed for the front. At one point a group came by to select men for the paratroops. Back in Efremov I had gone to the flying club, but I didn't finish its lessons, while the group chose only those who had completed them and had made jumps with a parachute. A lot of guys went to the screening; everyone said they had made jumps, but the panel didn't take our word for it – they chose only those who had documents that confirmed they were experienced parachutists. There was a longing to return to the front, to continue to fight and to win. But I had to train – close-order drills, theory, practice, gunnery.

On 20 April at the graduation exam, I commanded a live-firing exercise – I calculated the data and directed the firing. We graded out at the top. I acquired the rank of lieutenant, while those who had passed with a 'Good' mark or a 'Satisfactory' were made junior lieutenants. Five days later we were posted to the Red Army's Commander of Artillery in the city of Kolomna, Moscow Oblast. We were given a monetary bonus – 700 rubles, which we spent literally over the course of a week.

We arrived in Kolomna. We again were placed behind a high palisade in barracks with wooden bunks. The food was bad. Some kind of gruel . . . thin, so that guys didn't linger, but longed for the front. Every day representatives of units would arrive and select recruits from our reserve pool. Those needed by some unit who agreed to go departed. Representatives often came from the destroyer anti-tank artillery regiments. The older guys, the front-line officers now in the reserve, sought every possible way to avoid serving in these units. They were accustomed to being with the howitzers 1.5 to 2 kilometres behind the front-lines. But to wind up in an anti-tank regiment, God forbid with 45-mm anti-tank guns! . . . Although it was hard sitting in the rear, they wouldn't go: 'We're not prepared.' However, such a semi-famished existence had lit a fire under us, six young guys from the Tomsk school, so we decided, 'Enough sitting around here in the reserve, let's go, guys, and join the destroyer anti-tank artillery regiment.'

We were taken by truck to Korobcheevo, 7 kilometres away from Kolomna. There, the 1513th Destroyer Anti-tank Artillery Regiment was forming up. Actually, several such anti-tank artillery regiments were then forming in the environs of Kolomna. Major Vasilii Konstantinovich Zyl', who subsequently became a Hero of the Soviet Union, was the acting commander of our regiment. The regiment received its equipment – 45-mm Model 1942 anti-tank guns – and we began training.

In March 1943, the Urals Volunteer Tank Corps was forming in the Urals. According to its TO&E, each tank brigade in this corps was to have a destroyer anti-tank artillery regiment. However, the 62nd Tank Brigade in Cheliabinsk didn't have one. The corps commander Lieutenant General Georgii Semenovich Rodin came to visit us near Kolomna. We were raised on a combat alert. We were led out onto a field and given an order – to hit an embrasure at a range of 800 metres. With our third shell we hit it. Our battery graded out as 'Excellent', as did the other four batteries. Based on these results, our regiment joined the 30th Urals Volunteer Tank Corps.

Now let me talk about the '45' for a bit. In the regiment there were five batteries, each with four guns. They were towed by American Willys jeeps, to which first the trailer was hitched, and then the gun to the trailer. The Willys was a marvellous machine – mobile, powerful and with a low profile. You could drive it right up to the firing position. The gun itself was a very good one. Its sight had a $4\times$ scope. It fired very accurately, like a rifle. At 500 metres it was almost impossible to miss an embrasure. If the aim was accurate, the shell would fly true with a flat trajectory. Of course, in combat much depends on the gunner. He had to have strong nerves. There would be explosions around him, bullets would be whistling past, a comrade next to him would be wounded and fall on the gun trails, and he had to lay the gun coolly. The platoon commander would be located 1.5 metres to the right of the gun during a battle, the gun commander – to the left. I would give a command, and the gun commander would repeat it: 'To the left of landmark such and such. Sight, such and such. Shell, such and such. Fire!' But when you fire, you hear your shot; it is deafening, especially the armour-piercing rounds. In fact it isn't frightening to you – you can no longer hear the enemy fire; only watch as someone falls wounded or dead. Then you become so absorbed in the battle: you make corrections, give commands, fire again, and you forget that the other side is firing back at you. You're thinking only about hitting the target.

During a battle, we never had it so that only the gunner and loader were at the gun – there, all the crew is needed and everyone works. The gun crew consisted of six men. I've already mentioned that the gun commander stood to the left of the gun. The position for the No. 1 man – the gunner – was to the left of the gun's breech. The breech operator, the crew's No. 2, stood to the right of the gun. The loader, the No. 3 of the crew, stood behind the gun layer. Behind him were the No. 4 and No. 5 men, the trail handlers who stood side by side. The crew had no machine gun. The personnel were armed with submachine guns, both ours and German. I myself carried a PPSh, a TT and a German Walther. There were always a lot of weapons.

In a standard ammunition load, we had ten armour-piercing discarding sabot shells, ten canister shells, and thirty high-explosive and armour piercing shells. We knew no limits on our ammunition in 1943 or later. The velocity of the high-explosive shell was 800 metres/second. It was clearly visible in the binoculars as it flew toward the target. The armour piercing shell's velocity was 1,200 metres/second, while the armour-piercing discarding sabot reached 1,300 metres/second. The latter could penetrate 90-mm of armour. We easily dealt with Pz-III tanks. Of course, the shell couldn't penetrate the frontal armour of heavy tanks, but nevertheless we still had the task to fire at it from the front facing. We fired at its side armour when it showed it to us, otherwise we'd aim at the tracks – a hit would break the track, the tank would pivot in place, which would then allow you to fire at its flank.

In the first place it is important just to hit a tank, which is difficult when it is moving. If your shell hit and penetrated, you considered it shocked or knocked out. Normally the crew wouldn't wait for a second shell and they'd leap out of the tank. What was important was that it stopped and ceased firing. When the tank stopped, it was now easy prey.

The high-explosive shell was quite effective against infantry. Of course, its explosive force was small; therefore we more often relied on the fragmentation setting. The crater left by such a shell was tiny – only 10 centimetres – but the fragmentation damage was quite large. Moreover we fired at the infantry at a very rapid rate. As soon as they raised their heads, a second shell would be on its way.

We did have occasion to fire canister. I will talk about this later. Here the gunner aims the gun through its barrel at the legs of the attacking infantry. The canister cuts down the attacking line of infantry like a scythe. It is terrible fire.

As the first wave is cut down, the second wave is already crawling away. Therefore we weren't given many of these shells – ten per gun.

When driving up to the firing position, we immediately tossed the ammunition cases from the Willys and unhitched the gun. I would indicate where to place the vehicle so that it wouldn't be too far from the firing position, but at the same time it would be sheltered by folds in the terrain or screened by vegetation. The drivers would drive them away and construct revetments. The battery's guns were placed at a distance no greater than 20–30 metres from each other. If you placed them farther apart, it became impossible to control them – commands were given by voice. Sometimes, like at Korsun-Shevchenkosky, the guns stood at a distance of just 5 or 6 metres from each other.

As soon as we arrived, we checked the aim point. For this the gun's muzzle had four notches, vertical and horizontal. Through these notches we would extend threads and use them to line up the barrel at some cross-shaped target no nearer than 500 metres from the gun. Then we would align the sight with this target. If there was time, we would always without fail grease the wheel bearings, because if you forgot, a wheel might jam. We rigorously adhered to this. Otherwise, the gun required no special care. We'd grease the breech mechanism, but never dismantle it, because this was a complicated procedure. Sometimes the artillery mechanic would take away guns with worn-out barrels and bring back new ones. That was all.

So, we arrived at a firing position. I as the battery commander (I became a battery commander at the end of July 1943) would choose a position for the guns. This was a holy cause. The lives of my subordinates and their opinion of me as a commander depended upon how I selected positions. Of course, the fact that I had passed through the infantry in 1941 helped me quite a bit. The men of the battery would say, 'Our battery commander has come over from the infantry!' Before the gun would take its firing position, I would order, 'Gun commander, follow me.' He would creep behind me by about 5 metres, and my orderly would be on my right. I myself would crawl out, choose a position, and say to the gun commander, for example to Chichigin, 'Put your gun right here.' When I myself personally crawled around and pointed out to each where to deploy his gun, then the gun commander would say with confidence, 'Our battery commander has selected the firing position, now everything depends upon us.'

I was considered lucky and the soldiers greatly respected me. At the same time, in the regiment I was known as the *Shtrafnik*– a man who is serving in a penal battalion or company. All the batteries and personnel would be knocked out, so they would then form a single battery from the remnants of the five and I would be appointed as its commander. The remaining battery commanders now got something like a rest, while I continued to fight. Later, when the

Germans destroyed all my guns, only then would the entire regiment be with-drawn into the reserve for re-forming. My peers had already rested up, while I would get only a week before the equipment arrived.

Once we chose a position, we would dig an emplacement for the gun, but it often happened that we didn't have time to do this. Then with the sappers' spades we would dig channels the width of the gun's wheels, so that the gun would rest directly on its lower shield. We camouflaged the guns. We concealed the positions as far as possible with whatever we could find.

On the attack, when supporting an attack the gun was always loaded with armour-piercing shells with the trigger locked. The forward shield would be removed in order to reduce the height of the gun. In that way the gun's height was lowered to just over 50 centimetres. We'd stop, dig the wheels in, and the gun would settle even lower. We'd quickly cut several branches of a bush or maybe stalks of corn, if in or around corn fields. Everything was done to ensure the tanker didn't see you prior to your first shot. You'd let the tank approach to within 400, 300 or 250 metres and open fire – we couldn't hit it out to a kilometre, or even 500 metres. If we were supporting infantry, we'd manhandle the gun forward, keeping it faced toward the enemy. The command would be, 'The gun with the barrel forward, march!' The crew would grab the gun trail from the left and the right and start rolling it – on wheels it moved quickly. The gun would already be loaded with an armour-piercing round, in order to fire immediately at a tank or a machine gun. Even if you don't hit it, when a fireball goes flying right past you, your hands start shaking. At first we'd give the machine gun an armour-piercing shell, and then we'd set the range on the high-explosive shell and quickly blanket the target.

How did we aim at tanks? The Model 1942 gun had a direct fire range of 800 metres. We usually opened fire at around 400 metres. If the tank was moving laterally to you, you'd look in the binoculars, approximately determine its speed and calculate the lead. You'd command the gunner, 'Aim at the base of the turret, aiming offset one tank.' If I guessed the speed wrongly, the shell would fly in front of or behind the tank. Then you'd make a correction and fire again. At Kursk there were a lot of tanks, and they came straight at us. We primarily fired at the tracks, to make the tank pivot. While the tankers tried to figure out where the fire was coming from, in order to turn the turret, we give it a second shell in the flank; but normally they didn't wait and they'd leap out of the immobilized tank.

We remained at Kolomna until the middle of June 1943. Over this time we were given new uniforms, and all the officers received Finnish puukko knives with a decorated handle, while the soldiers received ones with black handles.[1] We also had a motorized rifle brigade, in which the men wore bulletproof vests. It was heavy – it weighed around 12 kilograms.

In the middle of June an order was announced that made our regiment part of the 4th Tank Army. Under our own power we drove to Naro-Fominsk, and from there on to the town of Kozel'sk. We arrived in Kozel'sk on 23 July. Just a few days later, we entered the fighting as part of the Briansk Front. What can I say? It was hot. The temperature rose to 25–27° C. It was arduous. You understand, if a man gets killed, his corpse is already reeking within 2 hours. Such a stench, and then they'd bring up a meal – you couldn't force down any food, so we drank water. There were constant attacks. There was a lot of aircraft overhead, both ours and those of the Germans. Air battles were going on constantly in the sky. We became so enraged by the constant air attacks that I deployed our guns on a hill and fired armour-piercing shells at them. My commander later let me have it: 'Look, you're not an anti-aircraft gunner; don't waste your shells firing at aeroplanes.'

On 7 August 1943, I happened to take part in a ferocious battle. I was ordered to support an attack by a tank company and infantry toward the village of Zuevskaia. I appeared before the commander of the tank company and reported that I was at his disposal. During battles the regiment headquarters often assigned separate batteries to infantry or tank companies and in essence turned over the command of us – we'd have no communications with it. The senior lieutenant tank commander told me:

> The infantry will start out now, and I'll advance behind it by around 50–100 metres, with a 20–40 metre interval between the tanks. You advance not more than 50–80 metres behind my tanks. You have a better field of vision, so your job is to silence anti-tank guns and tanks.

I returned to my platoon commanders, explained our assignment, and ordered the guns to be loaded and hitched to the jeeps.

The attack on the village began around noon after a short artillery preparation. The infantry moved out, and behind it the tanks. We were moving across a field of tall, ripe grain. Allowing our tanks to approach to within 300–400 metres, the Germans opened up with heavy fire. Several of the tanks burst into flames. We unhitched the guns approximately 300 metres from the outskirts of the village and returned fire. The infantry at first had become pinned down, but then came running back. The tanks began manoeuvring and were gradually drifting to our left, and we remained alone out in the open. We managed to dig little trenches for the wheels and threw off the gun shield. The guns practically sank into the rye. I ordered the commander of the 2nd Platoon to concentrate his fire on a mortar battery that was dropping a lot of shells around us, while I directed the fire of the No. 1 and No. 2 guns at tanks and anti-tank guns. The rye caught fire from the shell explosions. The smoke hindered our aim, but it partially screened us from the Germans. Then another tank started burning about 20 metres to my right. The Germans launched a counterattack with tank support, but all I was thinking about was the 100 shells inside that burning tank. Which way would it jump from the explosion and where would the turret land? I was continuing to fire, but I was keeping my right eye on the burning tank, waiting for it to explode. When the onboard ammunition did ignite, the turret was blown off, but thank God it didn't land on the gun. Gunfire, smoke and flames ... Oh, it was terrible!

We let the German infantry approach to within 50 or 60 metres and opened fire with canister. Of course, we also supplemented it with submachine-gun fire. They went rolling back to the village. That's when our infantry went back on the attack with the support of the remaining four tanks and seized the village. In this battle the battery destroyed two medium tanks, three assault guns, four mortars and around two platoons of infantry. In the process we lost two guns together with their crews, and one more gun was damaged. Only the No. 1 gun and crew, with which I was positioned, took no losses. Two of the Willys drivers were killed when their jeeps were destroyed. We lay there enfeebled by the heat and this combat near the gun.

Suddenly I felt clapping on my shoulder, and I opened my eyes. The regiment commander was standing there: 'You're alive?! Rogachev! Drink up!' From somewhere there appeared a bottle of water. I and the No. 1 gunner Mikhailichenko pounced on it together. I don't recall how much water we guzzled down ... For this battle I was decorated with the Order of the Red Star.

How many in all did I have to my credit? I wasn't counting, but over the entire war my battery destroyed more than twenty tanks and armoured halftracks.

The guys from the Urals were heroic men. They advanced, regardless of anything. There was a lot of courage and bravery, but little combat experience, so the losses the corps took were quite large. Of those five guys from the reserve that together with me took command of anti-tank gun platoons in the 30th Urals Volunteer Tank Corps' anti-tank artillery regiment, none of them survived the war.

In August 1943, the 4th Tank Army was withdrawn for rest and refitting. Before this, however, there was an episode I still recall. The Germans had fallen back behind the Nugr' River. We moved forward and began to dig in, taking positions along a scarcely perceptible road that was marked on the map. We were digging emplacements in the rye about 5 metres from the edge of the field. Everyone was digging, from the battery commander down to the gun trail handlers. The Willys drivers were also digging protective shelters. Beyond the tall rye nothing was visible to us, so we fired a shot with an armour-piercing shell and the stalks of grain fell down – we could fire high-explosive shells.

Suddenly we saw a Willys driving past us directly towards the Germans. It stopped and a major jumped out: 'Hey, soldiers, who's your commander?' We were all sunburned, the platoon commanders were hurrying the soldiers and swearing; it looked like the Germans were about to launch a counterattack, because we could see infantry gathering and an armoured halftrack had come up.

Senior Sergeant Chichikhin, a Vologda *bogatyr'* [an epic hero of Russian folk legends] irritably replied, 'What are you shouting? Who do you need?'

'You speak like that to an officer?! Who is your commander?'

'Lieutenant Rogachev.'

'Bring him here!'

'Comrade Battery Commander, some major over there is calling for you.'

'What sort of major? Does he have artillery or infantry shoulder straps?' I replied.

The major was now shouting, 'Come here immediately!'

So I ran over to the road, sweating profusely in the heat, my shoulder belt, map case and binoculars swinging: 'Battery commander Lieutenant Rogachev!'

'Which regiment?'

'The 1513th Destroyer.'

'What are you doing?'

'Setting up a firing position. The Germans are preparing to attack.'

'Who's in front of you?'

'Nobody.'

'What do you mean, nobody? Where's Rodin's headquarters?'

'You missed a turn. About 1.5 kilometres back down the road, you had to turn right.'

'Really?'

'Really.'

'Well, climb into the jeep.'

He turned the Willys around and we drove back about 500 metres toward the rear, where several vehicles were waiting for him. Some men in camouflaged jumpsuits without any signs of rank were sitting in them. I walked up to them and saw Front commander Zhukov sitting in one of them. Zhukov asked, 'Who are you?'

'Lieutenant Rogachev, commander of the 1513th Destroyer Regiment's 3rd Battery.'

'What are you doing?'

'Setting up firing positions.'

'Where's the headquarters of the 30th Urals Corps?'

'You missed a turn.'

He scowled at them: 'Come on, let's go.' Addressing me, he warned, 'Serve well, don't let them pass through you.'

'We'll stand to our death!'

They rushed off, while I rejoined my battery. Soon a messenger arrived on a motorcycle with an order to assemble in some area – we were withdrawn for reforming.

When Zhukov fell into disgrace after the war and it was being said about him that he was at times bad, and that he didn't spare his men, around New Year 1972 I wrote him a congratulatory postcard. I wished him good health and wrote that we, his former officers, appreciated him and would always remember him. I mentioned the incident back in August 1943. I asked him for an autographed copy of his memoirs.

Soon I was summoned and they handed me a signed copy. Back then, many generals unsuccessfully sought autographs, but I got one ...

You must remember – war doesn't happen without losses, and he was given orders that were impossible to carry out without the loss of a certain regiment or division. So I always admired Zhukov.

During our rest and refitting, we began to revive a little. A batch of replacements arrived – new crews and new guns. The regiment received the Guards honourific title, and it was re-designated as the 357th Guards Destroyer Anti-tank Artillery Regiment.

Approximately in the beginning of October 1943, the officers were gathered and informed that the regiment was going to be re-formed into a destroyer anti-tank artillery regiment that would be equipped with SU-76s. Its officers thus had to go through three months of additional training. We were told that those officers who wanted to be re-trained should give their agreement, while the rest would be assigned to the reserve of the Red Army's Artillery Commander-in-Chief. I gave it a little thought, talked with the other guys who had survived thus far, and decided that I wouldn't fight in these self-propelled guns. We had seen with our own eyes what this SU-76 was worth back in the Battle of Kursk. Its ZIS-3 gun was ineffective, its armour was thin, and it had no top armour to protect the crew from mortar fire. They easily burned ... so they were nicknamed 'Gor'ky's candles.' With the 45-mm on the ground, you can find a place to hide, but if a SU-76 was hit, you had no chance to get out of it alive.

At the end of November 1943 I was removed from my post and sent to Moscow into the pool of reserve cadres. I was thinking that I'd get an assignment to a battery of 152-mm guns, or at least to an SU-152 self-propelled gun battery. I had been trained on this weapon. But that didn't happen! It turns out that when the destroyer anti-tank artillery regiments were being formed, an order was issued that established a salary for us one and a half times the regular salary for an anti-tank crew member, awarded us cash bonuses for each destroyed enemy tank (500 rubles for the gun commander, 300 rubles for the gunner, and so forth), but also prohibited the use of destroyer anti-tank artillerymen in other types of artillery. Even after being discharged from hospitals, they were to be returned only to destroyer anti-tank artillery units, and nowhere else. We didn't know about this latter article of the order. I was given an assignment to report to the 5th Mechanized Corps' artillery commander, and there I was again placed in command of a destroyer anti-tank artillery battery of 45-mm guns in the 2nd Mechanized Brigade's 1st Motorized Rifle Battalion. The difference between the destroyer anti-tank artillery regiment and a destroyer anti-tank artillery battery of a motorized rifle brigade existed not in terms of the functions it carried out, but in terms of its subordination. The destroyer anti-tank artillery regiment was subordinate to the corps' artillery commander. He gave the orders, while the regiment commander allocated the batteries in order to carry out the orders. Here the battery was directly subordinate to the motorized rifle battalion commander, who attached the battery to one company or another. But this officer wasn't an artilleryman! He both protects and awards his own kind, while you must clear the road for them and you can't even think about withdrawing.

The brigade also had a battalion of 76-mm guns, but it had no vacancies. True, they promised to transfer me into it if a posting became available, but this never happened.

The guns and crews arrived. I remember a lot of Georgians – feisty guys. Gun commander Kakabadze, gunner Barbakadze, loader Saradze. There were also a lot of Slavs. We'd spend the evening together after our training was done for the day. I'd order, 'Sing a song!' First there'd be a Georgian song, then a Belorussian, then a Ukrainian. It was international.

At first the replacements feared the 45-mm gun, the 'Farewell, Motherland'. I told them, 'What are you afraid of? The 45 – that's still artillery and not the infantry!'

Around New Year we were urgently loaded aboard trains and we went to the Ukraine. We unloaded in the vicinity of Fastov-Kazatin, and from there conducted a night march of approximately 30 kilometres on foot to the town of Skvir. There we boarded trucks and travelled to Belaia Tserkov'.

At the beginning of January 1944 we were informed that the corps was joining the 6th Tank Army, which was then in the process of forming. Together with it we took part in the Korsun-Shevchenkovsky operation. We began the offensive from the large village of Tynovka. However, I quickly developed personal problems with the rifle battalion commander Ivan Rykov. Before the war, he had been a major of police in Saratov, but he'd been called up and somehow found himself appointed to the position of battalion commander, even though he didn't have the requisite training. He was somewhat cowardly and he always located his headquarters at least 1 to 1.5 kilometres behind the front line. The communications men didn't have enough cable! He also knew only one order: 'Battery, forward!!!' He issued directions without knowing the situation. I was always telling him, 'Why are you directing me where to position the guns?! On the spot I can see better than you. Do you want me to get killed in battle? I won't be any use to you then.' He'd reply, 'How dare you contradict me?!' We'd go back and forth like that.

So at Tynovka we went on the offensive. In front of us, there was hill that had piles of hay on it, under which the Germans had created machine-gun nests. It was about 1.5 kilometres to their positions, but my scouts spotted them. We also detected a platoon of 75-mm guns, and before the start of the artillery preparation, we had opened fire on them, forcing the crews to scatter. I told the battalion commander that he shouldn't hurl our infantry at the hill; machine guns would mow them down. But he refused to listen to me and gave the order, 'Battalion, forward!' The German machine gunners allowed them to approach to within 50–100 metres and then shot them down at point-blank range. The battalion lost almost 400 men killed and wounded. We took the hill. We walked past them – the young and the older guys, now lying dead on the ground.

I was boiling with anger inside. I turned the air blue at his address. He found out that I, a battery commander, considered him guilty for the needless death of men. Neither I nor any of the other battery men were decorated for this operation. He tore up twelve commendation lists! When the fighting subsided, an officer from the corps' Special Department drove up to see me:

'Aleksandr Vasil'evich, I want to speak a bit with you. Were you in the battle?'

'I was.'

'And what's your opinion?'

'My opinion was what it was, and it hasn't changed. No one can change it. The battalion was senselessly thrown right into machine guns.'

'Who's guilty?'

'The battalion commander!'

We had already reached the Prut River, when an order arrived to form up the battalion's personnel to witness a session of a military tribunal. We lined up in a field between some buildings. There was a table covered with broadcloth. They came out and announced, 'For such a case, an investigation has been conducted and this and that has been established. We've been informed about how he conducted himself, how he abused alcohol, and how he brought a battalion to its destruction' and so on. They ripped off his shoulder straps and Orders, which he had pinned on his own uniform just three or four days ago. The sentence: 'Battalion commander Major Rykov is to be cashiered and sentenced to the highest measure of punishment – execution by firing squad.' We were dumbfounded. Well, he of course spoke up: 'Give me the possibility to redeem myself; I'll make amends for my guilt in combat with my blood.' The tribunal went into one of the buildings for a conference. They then came back out and announced, 'The tribunal has decided to demote Major Rykov to private, strip him of his decorations, and replace the highest measure of punishment with three months in a penal battalion.' They appointed a sensible battalion commander to replace Rykov.

Well, let's return to Tynovka. On the first day we nevertheless managed to advance around 12 kilometres. The next few days also went well. The corps created a forward detachment consisting of the 233rd Tank Brigade, the self-propelled artillery regiment, the 1st Motorized Rifle Battalion and my destroyer anti-tank artillery battery, all under the command of the 6th Tank Corps' deputy commander Major General Mikhail Ivanovich Savel'ev. This detachment was to go forward and reach Zvenigorodka and link-up with a tank corps there, thus closing a ring around the Germans' Korsun-Shevchenkovsky grouping. We went on the offensive through the German rear areas. Having successfully fulfilled our mission, we were instructed to hold the inner ring of encirclement. The fighting was very hard. Lysianka, Dushakivka, Buzhanka, Bosivka – I've never forgotten these villages ...

I especially recall the village of Malyi Vinograd. We took it on 10 or 11 February. Through it ran the road to Dushakivka and Buzhanka, and there was a bridge there across the Gniloi Tikich River. The command directed the forward detachment's main forces toward the village of Bosivka, which was located about 5 kilometres away, while I was ordered to halt and take up a defensive position. In addition to my battery, there were about fifty to sixty men from the remnants of some rifle division, two tanks and two 122-mm howitzers. We took positions around the outskirts of the village. We camouflaged the guns on the top of a hill that was covered with apple trees. Just below us was a building and the road running to the bridge across the river, beyond which were the Germans. To the left of my position was a mound, which blocked the view of my guns' positions from the opposite side of the bank. Prior to this there had been fighting in these places; plainly our guys had been retreating and they had abandoned a lot of guns and equipment, including a pile of boxes of shells for the 45-mm gun. We lugged five or six cases to each gun position. We also gathered up several machine guns and an anti-tank rifle. We were armed to the teeth.

The Germans didn't make us wait long. When they were crossing the bridge, we blew it up. The banks of the river were marshy and the tanks couldn't make it across. We knocked out one that got bogged down. They launched a salvo of rockets at us from their six-barrelled rocket launchers, but the shells exploded some distance away from the battery. They hadn't been able to detect our positions accurately. They attempted to cross at a different point along the river and enter the town along our bank, but they had to skirt around a hill that covered our left, after which they came under fire from our tanks and my guns. I remember that the German infantry approached quite closely. Our infantry couldn't hold out and started to run. And you know, when they're running, but you can't run because you have no right to abandon a gun, you begin to laugh in spite of your inclination: 'Look how they're running! Look! Go on! Go on! Don't be slow! Quicker to the rear!' So we mocked them: 'Why are you running? Why are you abandoning us and taking to your heels?' Then when the Germans appeared on a rise about 250 metres away, I ordered, 'Armour-piercing!' When fired, the gun's report is ringing and powerful, and when the flaming, fiercely howling slug perhaps flies past you, it seems that it is coming right for you. It is terrifying ... That's how we held out in this position for seven days.

I didn't have any religion and my attitude didn't change during the war. You see, we were raised as atheists. Until the fifth grade, my mother took me to church for Easter. She would say, 'Everything is holy there; kiss the knuckle.' I approached, kissing the partition. Later, when I became a Young Pioneer member, I became a non-believer. At the front it didn't even come into my head to resort to an appeal for God's protection; for example, during a barrage or an air raid, I never prayed for help. Although we in fact were being bombed, and we went around at a whisker's width from death ten to fifteen times a day, no one prayed. Indeed, I didn't even know any prayers. Maybe someone of an older generation, but we younger soldiers – no.

I wasn't superstitious either. I've already talked about how I didn't feel well at Staraia Russa before I was wounded there. I didn't have any other premonitions. But gradually I developed an acute sense of danger. For example, after one battle I said to a platoon commander, 'Let's go wash up in the stream.' He replied, 'Let's go.' I walked rather quickly and he was trailing me. We were walking across a forest clearing: there was grass and some fallen birch trees lying around. I looked, and an alarm bell went off in my head: 'Why are birch trees lying like that in a clearing?' The closer we approached these birch trees, my legs began to move more slowly, as if they had lead in them. At some moment I raised a foot and something held me back from completing my step. At the toe of my suspended foot, I saw a trip wire. I glanced to the left – there it was, a booby trap that looked like a champagne bottle with its neck sheared off. I stood like a stork and waited. One ... two ... three ... There was no explosion. I carefully lowered my foot. Then I looked it over. The Germans had apparently set it several days before, and since the morning dew had been heavy, the ring had become a bit rusty. When I gently pulled on it, the cotter pin didn't budge and there was no explosion.

The platoon leader asked, 'Battery commander, why have you stopped.'

I replied, 'Valia, come here.'

He approached more closely and glanced: 'Oh, a booby trap! Get back!'

'Back where? Give me a branch.'

We had some cord. When I was tying it around the trip wire, my hands were shaking a little. We backed away and I gave it a jerk and there was an explosion.

Later I was summoned to headquarters and the chief of staff Guards Major Zyl' upbraided me: 'What are you, a sapper?! Just who do you think you are? You're a battery commander! You should have immediately sent for sappers!' Well, back in the specialist school, we had gone over demolition techniques, so I decided to make use of the knowledge I had gained.

The most frightening was when the infantry abandoned you. They run, and you're left all alone, and you have no contact with other elements. You are feverishly trying to figure out what you should do next, how to act. Here now all hope is on your own experience – run like everyone else, or stay where you are. Some soldiers grumbled, 'Our commander, he sees how tough we are. He doesn't want to flee.' Later they understood that you can't abandon a gun. If we left behind a gun, that meant an execution by firing squad for the battery commander and platoon commander. It happened that you'd abandon a gun, but the commanders would order you to go back and get it. But where could you find it? If located, it might be partially smashed, or partially dismantled by those who did remain in order to obtain spare parts. I remember once mortar men running away in retreat, and they had tossed their mortars into a stream; later they came back and dived into the icy water to retrieve them. We all laughed.

Then we resumed the offensive. The spring muddy season was so bad that we couldn't keep up with our own infantry in our Willys jeeps. There was a sea in every low-lying area. We would get the guns across them by hitching them to tanks, while we would stand on the gun trails. We dragged the Willys jeeps across the same way. As a result, the infantry took seats on the tanks and Studebakers, while we were ordered to stop until the roads dried out.

In April we set off to catch up with our own. We crossed the Prut and took up a defence in the area between the Prut and Jijia [Zhizhia] Rivers. We set up firing positions in a corn field on the outskirts of some little village not far from the banks of the Jijia River. In front and to the left of our positions, 150 metres away, there was a hill, on top of which stood a monastery, which was occupied by Germans. The battery had been attached to the penal battalion. I was summoned by a lieutenant colonel, the commander of this battalion:

> Look, a road runs across that hill. It is the only axis that tanks can take. Your task is to hold this road at any cost and don't let them pass. Otherwise they'll crush us. Until tanks appear, I advise you not to fire from your main positions. If you want to strike the Germans, do so from alternate positions.

We attempted to dig in deeply, but just 70 centimetres below the ground, water began to fill our positions. The heat was terrible, the humidity, a cloud of mosquitoes, and as I just mentioned, it was only 150 metres to the Germans in the monastery. So you spend all day lying in your little pit, on the lookout for targets. You're also constantly smoking in order to keep the mosquitoes away (we were given a pack of Suvorov tobacco every day; we rolled it into cigarettes). Meanwhile the Germans on this hill were walking about, running from one place to another, and firing their machine guns. The men of the penal battalion had fallen into the habit of going around and shaking peach trees. The Germans would chase them away with shellfire. I remember one guy came running up to me: 'Listen, Battery Commander, help me! There's a machine gun firing over there!'

We set up alternate, covered firing positions for our guns about 50 metres to our right among some buildings. At night we moved our guns into them. As soon as it became light, we opened fire at already disclosed targets. Once the Germans realized that they had a battery right under their nose, we ceased fire and returned at a run to our main positions. They hit the alternate position with a mortar barrage. The guns are covered, so only a direct hit might destroy one. The mortar fire ceased and I sent scouts back to the alternate position to find out how the guns were. They came back: 'All in order, Battery Commander. The guns are intact.' That night, we brought them back to the main position. The battalion commander said, 'You know, Rogachev, enough with your pranks. The Germans are getting angry. You hold the road.'

There my soldiers began to develop night-blindness. I had to send them back to the rear at night, where they'd be given vitamins. Everything was normal for me, perhaps because we were given the officer's supplementary rations. In the evening, when it grew dark, they'd bring dinner in Thermoses, but no one had much appetite. You'd drink a bottle of wine and nibble on something. There were American canned ham slices. You'd eat a couple of slices and only sip a bit of vodka. For the fighting in this bridgehead, I was awarded the Order of the Red Star.

Before the next offensive, we were withdrawn into the reserve to receive replacements. On 20 August 1944, as part of the 6th Tank Army we entered a breakthrough. Iasi [Iassy, Jassy], Barlad, Bacau, Berzunti, Foksani, Urziceni, Bucharest. The local population at first greeted us cautiously, smiling servilely. We responded with our kindliness. They were surprised; after all, they had heard propaganda that the Russians were coming and they'd be pillaging, raping and murdering as they came. But we had an order when crossing the border with Romania not to offend the civilian population and not to plunder. Then they started bringing us tomatoes, corn – we endured their *mamaliga* [cornmeal porridge] – eat up! Jugs full of wine. In contrast, our relations with the Hungarians were poor. The Hungarians are very treacherous and vindictive. They had fought ferociously until the end, until we reached their territory. But when we pressed them back to the border, they began to surrender.

In Bucharest, King Michael greeted us from a balcony. For that reason we had been ordered to discard the captured German duds we were wearing, because our own uniforms were quickly becoming threadbare, and to wear only our own combat tunics. We stopped in Bucharest. City life was going on as if in peacetime – shops were open, restaurants. We were given Romanian leu. The exchange rate at the time was 1 ruble per 100 leu. I was being paid a monthly salary of something around 2,000 rubles. For this amount of money you could buy a villa. However, little money ever reached our hands. A chunk of it was turned over to the Defence Fund, another portion went to mandatory bond subscriptions, and I was sending another portion of my salary back home to my mother. So with the money I had left, I bought myself a wristwatch. Some of the guys painted the town red. Our command, sensing that the Russian soul was on the loose in a peaceful setting, God forbid, ordered us to leave Bucharest and advance in the direction of Hungary.

That was when a battle occurred that I can call my own most unsuccessful combat. We were attacking a Romanian village. The infantry was pinned down by the fire of a machine gun that was positioned on the upper floor of a two-story building that stood around 250–300 metres closer to our positions than the other buildings. A gravel road ran in front of this building, and our infantry was taking cover from the fire in the roadside ditches. I was ordered by the battalion commander to move up my gun and to destroy this machine gun with direct fire. Before rolling out the gun, my orderly, the mortar battery commander Senior Lieutenant Sergei Verkholashin (he always stuck close to me, believing that I was lucky and that he wouldn't be killed next to me) and I moved toward the road in dashes. Of course, we couldn't go a bit to the left, where there was a cornfield and we could find concealment among the stalks. No, we started running across an open field with scraggly grass and sparse, scrawny bushes. We hadn't managed to reach the roadside ditch, when the machine gun concentrated its fire on us. We dropped. There were little fountains of dust right in front of us. We were lying there and waiting, realizing that at any moment we'd be killed or wounded. Sergei was lying on my left, and a bullet struck him in the eye. He started to scream.

I sent back my orderly with an order for the No. 1 and No. 2 guns to move up to me. When the guys began rolling up the already loaded guns, the machine gunner killed one and wounded two of the No. 1 crew. At this moment I was already making a dash for the ditch, and from there I began to issue commands. With our third shell, we struck the window from which the machine gun was firing. The firing ceased, and behind the building, Germans started running toward the village across a field – a barren field. These two guns opened fire at them, while I ordered the remaining guns to be brought up. Shells were exploding, Germans were running and falling ... I don't know how many of them we killed there.

I didn't have to run to that ditch – I held up the moving up of the first two guns, Sergei had been wounded, and there were casualties in the crew. In general, I had screwed up.

In 1943 we normally buried the dead. We made transfers from a map that indicated the place of burial and who was buried there. We buried them in their uniforms. After the grave was covered, we'd erect a tablet to mark the gravesite. We adhered to this procedure rather strictly. Well, in 1941, it all depended. We discarded our identification medallions designed to identify us if we were killed. We were supposed to write all of our information on it, but there was a widely held superstition that if you filled it out and wore it, you'd be killed (probably because they were called death medallions). It often happened that a corpse would be found without any documents or identification tag – they'd be buried, while someone would be sent a notice: missing-in-action.

I remember we were moving through the Transylvanian Alps. Their peaks rose to 2,000–2,500 metres. The road, about 6 metres wide, crept around precipices every 100–150 metres. The Luftwaffe kept working us over. Although we had anti-aircraft guns in the column, we suffered large losses from the air attacks. Nevertheless, we broke through the thin German defences and advanced in the direction of Turda. Near this city I was wounded in street fighting. I was searching for targets through my binoculars, and a rifleman or a sniper fired from a rooftop and hit me in the right thigh. Fortunately, it missed the bone and a month later I was reporting for duty.

Then there was the fight for Budapest. We moved behind the infantry, which had been formed into assault groups, helping them with our fire. I was ordered to move to join some rifle company. It was advancing, but then a messenger arrived from the commander: 'Battery commander, a machine gun is firing over there.' I went running up to the battalion commander. Together we looked to see how to deal with this machine gun, how to move the guns into position, and who I should assign to fire. Street fighting is the most terrible combat. You don't know where the fire will be coming from. Here the German was firing from the second or third floor. We wouldn't place our guns in the middle of the street. On the contrary, for example, we'd set up in a store shop window. We'd smash the glass and roll the gun into the store. We'd be firing at the opposite side of the street. We would fire a couple of high-explosive rounds 'with a nose cap' on the detonator, so that the shell would explode inside the building, and then just for its psychological effect, we would give the spot an armour-piercing round. The fire would cease, but the Germans knew all the passage-ways. We would wait for him, but he'd appear in a completely different place and unexpectedly open fire.

In the last days of March 1945, we crossed the Austrian border in the vicinity of the city of Keszeg, after which our corps broke through the woods in the direction of Wiener Neustadt. We entered the city on Easter Day. The Germans were completely unready for the appearance of our units. Only the Vlasovites offered resistance. In a word, we hated them worse than the Germans. They could not count on any mercy in fighting, where a soldier is simultaneously the judge, prosecutor, and executioner. If that was the case – that was it. Some would emerge and come running with their hands up in the air, but from our position we would greet them with fire. If one *was* taken prisoner, he'd be led away somewhere … In this city, I personally killed seven men in combat with my submachine gun. We were rolling the gun, and they had dug into a cellar and were firing back. I and two other guys entered the building. We broke into the cellar and picked them off there.

I fought against Germans, Hungarians and Romanians. If I compare them as adversaries, the strongest, of course were the Germans. In second place, for their cruelty and stubbornness in battle, I would select the Hungarians. All the rest were weak, and the Romanians were in general … *mamalizhniki* [a mocking reference to the national dish of Romania, *mamaliga*]. When in 1944 they came over to our side, they would be sent forward first. We would stand in readiness. We watched as they launched their attack. Then the Hungarians and Germans would counterattack – and the Romanians would turn tail and run. We already knew that now we'd be given the command to charge. They'd run away while we were now attacking. In addition, we never left a Romanian in a security outpost overnight.

Having seized the city of Wiener Neustadt, we moved on Vienna. We broke into the outskirts of Vienna and became tied up in street fighting. Our battalion commander was Ivan Timofeevich Goncharov, who was only 20 years old. He was always saying, 'Don't straggle! Artillerymen, follow me! Onward and onward!' Our vehicles couldn't negotiate the narrow back alleys. The infantry would slip through via courtyards and front gardens, while we had to drive down the streets. But there, such a fire would open up from the windows that you dared not even lift your nose. We lagged behind. But the battalion carried out its mission and seized the Central Railway Station. For this, Goncharov was deemed worthy of the title Hero of the Soviet Union. Subsequently, he was killed right before my eyes. After Vienna, we were attacking some mountain village. After the artillery preparation and an attack by light bombers, we broke into its outskirts. The infantry was pinned down. A sniper was firing at us from a church, and panzers appeared from behind some homes. We deployed our guns behind some wine vaults and opened fire at the sources of incoming fire, and then at the German tanks as well. At this time, Goncharov with his battalion headquarters was running between one piece of cover and another a bit behind my battery – he was a brave man. Literally within just 3 metres of me, the sniper killed him.

After Vienna we moved to liberate Czechoslovakia. On the night of 2 May, I was severely wounded in a night fight for the city of Vishkov. We were repelling a counterattack. I was standing with binoculars and directing the fire. A sniper fired from a nearby building, and plainly, he wanted to hit me in the head, but he struck my arm. The bullet smashed a bone. I thought the wound was insignificant, but it proved to be quite serious. I was sent first to an army hospital in Vienna, and then to Budapest. There the doctors performed several operations in the effort to save my arm. An infection set in that almost reached my shoulder. The doctors told me that if it progressed any further, they'd have to amputate my arm, but thank God, this didn't happen. I remained in the hospital until the middle of August 1945. That month, I was invalided out of the army, assigned to the 3rd Category of invalidity for six months with a subsequent re-examination of my case, and then I was sent to Moscow.

I decided to enroll in the Moscow Highway Institute. Two times I went to see the rector about admission, because the entrance exams had already been given. I persuaded him and as an exception, I was accepted on the condition of taking the exams. It was difficult to study, especially because the returning veterans, though still young, were still quite a bit older than the other students. I was 22 years old when the war ended. I'd been awarded the rank of senior lieutenant in March 1945, but prior to my discharge from the hospital I wasn't aware of this. We really weren't interested in this, nor in the honours and decorations. We didn't fight for medals, but instead to defeat the foe. When we were firing at the Germans we didn't see them as individuals but as the enemy. Let's say a machine gun is firing at you from a location. We hit it, and it falls silent. Advancing, we dropped by to look at the result. There they are, lying there dead, and the machine gun is smashed. Our work! We had a sense of satisfaction. We hadn't fired in vain.

I had perhaps a bad habit about writing letters. The first letter home I wrote in September 1942, when I wound up in the specialist school. I believed when I was in combat, it was totally wrong to write home, because if you wrote a letter and sent it, a day later you might be killed or badly wounded. At home, they'd receive the letter saying that you were alive and well, fighting on the axis of N-city, but now you were no longer. I made a pact with myself that I would only write when I was coming out of battle. Thus I sent a letter home once every six months or so, not more. For my parents, of course, this was hard. I began to write more frequently, perhaps every month or so, only at the end of the war when things were going much better. There were no longer any particularly fierce battles, and indeed, a certain confidence had appeared that we were approaching the end of the war, fighting our way to victory. Did it become harder to fight near the end of the war? Of course, such thoughts started to visit like, 'It would be great to live to see the victory.' But this had no effect on my conduct – I didn't become more cautious, or more cowardly, anything like that. It was the same with the platoon commanders and gun commanders – each one was thinking that way, but kept their thoughts to themselves. Indeed, these thoughts didn't manifest themselves in any way, and everyone behaved as they always had. No one asked for any indulgences and begin to fight any worse.

But I did send a few packages home from the front. When we crossed the border, it was permitted to send 10 kilograms home. In Romania, of course there was no time for this, when we were advancing 50 kilometres a day. But when I was lying in the hospital in Budapest, we were given forints, or as we called them, pengi. I received 1,500 pengi. An individual mug of beer cost 3 or 4 pengi. I went around to the shops. I purchased material for a suit and sent it home. I had a leather coat sewn for myself for 300 or 400 pengi. I also had an accordion. The soldiers had given it to me when I'd been wounded. It was battery operated; they'd picked it up in Vienna. I didn't know how to play it, but later I learned how – I had an ear for music.

We were received with great joy and with open arms after the war. There was no detachment or indifference. At the same time, we didn't make any attempt to stand out or show off. Well, I had been fighting and fighting. I arrived home, and now I had to return to peaceful living. Oh, I quickly became so bored! I was so eager to begin my studies. Such an ambition was good; despite all the difficulties, there was always optimism and high spirits.

However, for example, at the front we didn't get sick. No cold, no sores, nothing bothered us. Some thought, 'If I could only get sick! Then I could loll around a bit in the medical-sanitation battalion while I recovered.' But we never contracted any illnesses. As soon as we arrived home from the front, however, then immediately we came down with all sorts of medical problems. Either a stomach ulcer would appear, or the formation of pus in a wounded lung ... In general, the health we had at the front was strongly disrupted.

But when you're lying in bed and can't fall asleep, you think back on combat episodes. I see distinctly each hill, each valley. Here's that forest fringe, the villages where guys were killed; here's where we moved out ... I recall the faces of soldiers with whom I spent these four years. They're standing there alive in front of me, although now almost sixty years have passed. But I don't want to go back. Such a thought never visits me. But I often ponder, 'Did I correctly choose the position in that battle and properly deploy the guns? Three of the men in a crew were killed. Perhaps if I had deployed the guns in a different place, then perhaps they wouldn't have been killed?' Such analysis continues to the present day. I feel morally responsible for each wounded, killed and lost soldier. And you think, 'Wasn't it your fault here?'

Note

1. The 30th Urals Volunteer Tank Corps was renowned in both the Wehrmacht and the Red Army for the black-handled 'Finnish' knives the men carried. This was actually the Russian-produced NR-40 knife, based on the Finnish puukko knife and manufactured in a factory in the Urals. In fact, a modified version of the Finnish knives had been popular in the world of Russian criminals and they were banned in the Soviet Union in the 1930s. The Winter War, however, had revealed that the Red Army soldiers lacked a good knife, so the Soviet Union began mass-producing the NR-40, a knife once popular among Russian criminals!